Women and Learning in English Writing, 1600-1900

Women and Learning in English Writing, 1600–1900

Deirdre Raftery

FOUR COURTS PRESS

Set in 10.5 on 12.5 Bembo by
Gough Typesetting Services for
FOUR COURTS PRESS LTD
Fumbally Lane, Dublin 8, Ireland
e-mail: info@ four-courts-press.ie
and in North America for
FOUR COURTS PRESS
c/o ISBS, 5804 N.E. Hassalo Street, Portland, OR 97213.

A catalogue record for this title
is available from the British Library.

Printed Great Britain
by the Martins Printing Group, Bodmin, Cornwall.

For my parents,
Coleman Raftery (*d*.1996) and Valerie Raftery

Contents

List of Illustrations

Preface

Completing this research has been greatly faclilitated by the support which I have received at Trinity College, Dublin. I would like to thank Trinity Trust, for making it possible to engage in research at Cambridge, Oxford and London, and for the award of the Luker-Cobbe Bursary which made possible a lengthy period of research at Girton College, Cambridge. I would also like to acknowledge the support of the Provost and Fellows of Trinity College, in granting me an award from the Grace Lawless Lee Fund, and express appreciation for the support and goodwill of my colleagues and students at the School of Education, Trinity College, and the Centre for Women's Studies, Trinity College.

A number of colleges and libraries have facilitated this research. I would like to thank the following: the staff of Trinity College Library, and in particular that of the Department of Early Printed Books; the Mistress and Fellows of Girton College, Cambridge; the Mistress and Fellows of Somerville College, Oxford; Kate Perry (Archivist), Girton College; Mary Clapinson (Keeper of Western Manuscripts), Bodleian Library, Oxford; F.W. Radcliffe, (Librarian), Cambridge University Library; William A. Moffat (Librarian), Huntington Library, California; and the Archivists at the National Library of Wales, the British Library, London and at Harvard.

I would also like to acknowledge the continued support and goodwill of Dr Maryann Valiulis (Centre for Women's Studies, Trinity College), Dr Helga Robinson-Hammerstein (Department of Modern History, Trinity College), and my colleague and friend Susan M. Parkes (School of Education, Trinity College) for her guidance and wisdom.

Finally I would like to thank Ciara Bagnall who willingly took on the task of proof-reading this typescript, Norah (Belle) Golden whose enthusiasm for this research matched my own, my husband Peter for his love and encouragement, and my parents to whom this work is dedicated.

Acknowledgements

The co-operation of a number of libraries in providing manuscript material and illustrations used in this book is gratefully acknowledged:

MS. Malone 17, MS. Ballard 43, fol.29 by kind permission of the Bodleian Library, University of Oxford.

MS Somerville Notebook, Dep. c. 356 by kind permission of Somerville College, Oxford.

Additional MS. 42511 by kind permission of the British Library, London.

The Davies Papers, The Bodichon Papers, and MS Lady Barbara Stephen by kind permission of the Mistress and Fellows of Girton College, Cambridge.

Title pages from *A Serious Proposal to the Ladies* (Mary Astell, 1696) and *Astronomical Dialogues Between a Gentleman and a Lady* (John Harris, 1719) by kind permission of the Board of Trinity College, Dublin.

Title pages form *Hic Mullier: or, The Man-Woman* (1620) and The *Scholehouse of women* (1541?) by kind permission of the Huntington Library, San Marino, California.

Title pages from *Sir Isaac Newton's Philosophy Explain'd for the Use of the Ladies* (Francesco Algarotti, 1739) and the *Polite Repository or Pocket Companion* (1807) by kind permission of the Bodleian Library Oxford.

The Girton Cricket Team and the Girton Fire Brigade by kind permission of the Mistress and Fellows of Girton College, Cambridge.

Introduction

Through a study of English writing published between 1600-1900, this book examines the ideological grounds on which higher education was opened to women in England. Over the last two decades, several important studies have focussed specifically on the development of female education in England in the late nineteenth century.[1] It has widely been regarded as a period of "unexpected revolution",[2] because it was marked by a number of important developments in formal education for girls and women. However, while the actual opening up of higher education to women might be viewed as a late nineteenth century "revolution," the ideological basis for this development could more accurately be described as a process of evolution. This ideological evolution took place in an on-going debate about women and education that dated back at least to the Renaissance, a debate which took place in print culture written by generations of writers. This book examines a large sample of this print culture, tracing the developments in the debate that eventually resulted in the opening of higher education to women. It illustrates that arguments in favour of the higher education of women date from Plato's *Republic*, and against it, from Aristotle's *Historia Animalium*. Vives, Thomas More, Milton, Defoe, Hannah More, and Mary Wollstonecraft, were a mere handful, albeit the better known, of the writers who addressed the question of the education of women. There were many more writers and thinkers who, like the Enlightenment scholar Anna van Schurman, engaged in the debate about "Whether a Maid may be a Scholar".[3]

The study embraces pamphlets, books, periodicals, essays, medical literature, propaganda literature printed for private circulation, and publications such as diaries and almanacs. As both image and reality were deemed important in shaping contemporary attitudes to women's education, it was decided to include reference to selected novels, drama, and verse. Most of the works examined were published between between 1650 and 1870, and many therefore reflect developments in the debate between the publication of Mary Astell's *A Serious Proposal to the Ladies for the Advancement of their True and Greatest Interest* (1694), and the publication of Emily Davies's *The Higher Education of Women* (1866). The choice of Astell and Davies as the key writers with whom to begin and end this study was based on research which indicates that Astell is the earliest known woman to have published a proposal for an establishment for the further education for women, while the work of

Emily Davies, in the founding of Girton College, Cambridge, marks the fruition of this idea.

The many categories of pwriting examined in this study suggest a sustained interest in the subject of female education in the period under review (see Appendix). A number of short discussions about education for women appeared in the late seventeenth century, such as Edward Chamberlayne's *An Academy or College: Wherein Young Ladies and Gentlemen May . . . be Duly instructed in the True Protestant Religion* (1671), and Clement Barksdale's *A Letter touching a Colledge of maids: or, A Virgin-Society* (1675), while Astell's *Proposal* (1694) offered a more developed discussion of the formal education of women. Women were also the subject of what are categorised as "attacks" and "defences": that is, published attacks on the female character, soul or intellect, and responses which appeared in defence of women. Attacks included *The Female War* (1697), while defences included Sarah Fyge's the *Female Advocate* (1686), and Judith Drake's *Essay in Defence of the Female Sex* (1683, 1696, 1697). In the eighteenth century, women and learning were treated in comic and satiric plays such as Thomas Wrights' The *Female Virtuosoes* (1721), and Thomas Horde's *The Female Pedant* (1782), and in verse they were praised in Duncombe's *The Feminead: or, Female Genius* (1757) and ridiculed in Pope's *Dunciad* (1733). Female learning was also praised in historical works such as Agrippa's *Female Pre-eminence* (1670), Thomas Heywood's *General History of Women* (1624, 1677), Richard Burton's *Female Excellency* (3rd edn., 1728), Amory's *Memoirs of Several Ladies of Great Britain,* (1755) and the *Biographium Faemineum* (1766).

The eighteenth century saw a proliferation in the number of text-books, almanacs, and books of instruction published for a female audience. The titles of such works often included a descriptive term such as 'monitor', 'preceptor', 'repository', 'stricture', 'closet', 'cabinet', or 'dispensatory'. The titles also suggested that the books were a form of indispensable guidance for ladies. Popular examples include the *Lady's Companion* (1740), the *Lady's Preceptor* (1790), the *Young Lady's Parental Monitor* (1790), the *Ladies' Dispensatory: or Every Woman her Own Physician* (1739, 1740, 1777), and *Strictures on Female Education* (1787). There were also addresses, essays, lectures and sermons for women, including *An Epistle to a Lady* (1753), *An Essay on the Education of Young Ladies* (1794), *Lectures on Female Education and Manners* (1793, 1794), *Female Tuition* (1784), and *Epistles for Ladies* (3rd edn., 1756). In addition to such books of guidance, there were text-books directed at young women. Titles include Demarville's *The Young Lady's Geography* (1765), and John Greig's *Teacher of Mathematics: the Young Lady's New Guide to Arithmetic* (3rd edn., 1803).

Another popular genre of writing in the eighteenth century was the conduct book. Among the best known conduct books examined in this study are

George Saville's *The Lady's New Year's Gift: or, Advice to a Daughter* (6th edn. 1699), James Fordyce's *The Character and Conduct of the Female Sex* (3rd edn., 1776), John Gregory's *A Father's Legacy to his Daughter* (1774) and Thomas Gisborne's *An Enquiry into the Duties of the Female Sex* (7th edn., 1806). Women published in increasing numbers in the eighteenth century, and this study includes an examination of Mary Wollstonecraft's *Thoughts on the Education of Daughters* (1788), Priscilla Wakefield's *Reflections on the Present Condition of the Female Sex; with Suggestions for its Improvement* (1798), and Hannah More's *Strictures on the Modern System of Female Education* (1799). By the mid-nineteenth century, with the growth of the popular periodical, the subject of women's education reached a wider audience. It was discussed in all the major periodicals of the time, and in a large number of less well-known magazines and journals. *Macmillan's, Blackwood's*, the *Contemporary Review*, the *Quarterly Review*, and a number of Christian magazines debated developments in female education with regularity.

It is may be assumed, as Lawrence Stone has elsewhere argued, that print sources which have survived and are available for examination are fairly representative of what has been lost. But, as Stone cautions, "no document can tell us more than what the author of the document thought,"[4] and thus much print culture may have reflected no more the interests and perspectives of individual authors. To reflect the norms of social and moral thought of the period under survey in this study, it was necessary to examine a large sample of work and to balance the study of literary representations of education with details of contemporary education based on studies of literacy, schooling and educational theories.

To compile the sample of print culture for this study, a number of catalogues and bibliographies were consulted. Works published in the form of books were located in the *Wing Short Title Catalogue of Books Published in England, Scotland Ireland and Wales, 1641-1700*, (2 Vols., 1948), the *Eighteenth Century Short Title Catalogue*, and the *Nineteenth Century Short Title Catalogue*. These catalogues included titles of fiction and non-fiction publications. Additional published catalogues and bibliographies consulted were the *Catalogue of Original and Early Editions of Some of the Poetical and Prose Works of English Writers* (1893), the *New Cambridge Bibliography of English Literature* (3 Vols., 1969-1974.), *Nineteenth Century Fiction: A Bibliographical Catalogue* (4 Vols., 1981-1985), and *Checklist of Women Writers, 1801-1900*, (1990). The search for relevant miscellanies and periodicals was undertaken through the standard bibliographies in this field, namely: *A Bibliography of English Poetical Miscellanies, 1521-1750, The Wellesley Index to Victorian periodicals, 1824-1900, The Waterloo Directory of Victorian Periodicals, 1824-1900*, and *Women and British Periodicals, 1832-1867*.

In addition, library catalogues were consulted at Trinity College, Dublin; Cambridge University Library; the Bodleian Library, Oxford; the National Library of Wales; the National Library, Dublin; Girton College Archives, Cambridge; the British Library, and the Schlesinger Library, Harvard. The library catalogues, particularly the CD ROM *British Library General Catalogue of Printed Books to 1975* (1992), made it possible to get some idea of the numbers of publications which treated of female education.

The subject of higher education for women was of greatest interest to men and women of the middle and upper middle ranks. Additionally, the majority of those who wrote about women's education were identified as either Evangelicals, Dissenters or High Church Anglicans, and all had received some measure of education. They were, therefore, usually either men who had participated in college education, or women whose fathers or brothers had participated in college education. The perspectives which authors brought to the subject of women's education often reflected social, religious and educational influences. Women themselves made their greatest contribution to the debate in the late nineteenth century, at a time when female literacy had improved and schooling for middle-class girls had become more widespread. While the focus of this study has been on printed sources, attention has also been paid to letters, diaries and personal documents which informed the understanding of the evolution of the idea of higher education for women. In particular, the papers of Emily Davies illuminated the examination of the eventual opening of university education to women, and illustrated that the success of the struggle for women's education was due to the ability of a few individuals to realise the ambitions of generations of earlier women.

The broad sample of writings examined in this study have allowed a number of conclusions to be drawn about the evolutionary process whereby women gained access to formal higher education. Firstly, and most significantly, throughout the period under examination, there was a perception that the nature of woman could be defined. The nature of woman was closely determined by her biology which destined her for marriage and motherhood. It was also defined by Church teaching, which used the authority of the Bible to establish woman's primary role as that of helpmeet to man. The synthetic view of woman which emerged suggested that education was not necessary for her to fulfil her destiny. From Renaissance thought, the debate about the education of women inherited a set of arguments, supported by classical and biblical *exempla*, that promoted the idea that a woman's education should equip her for nothing more than the duties of a virtuous wife and mother. The education of women was associated with the private sphere, while the education of men was associated with preparation for public life. Education was thus both determined and limited by gender. However, to the public eye gender could be determined by education. In defining the nature of woman, it was commonly thought that woman was "opposite" to man, and female was "opposite" to male. Because of this, it was neither necessary nor desirable that she should be educated as though she *was* man. From the Renaissance, it was suggested that women, in becoming learned, ceased to be women. This argument had a profound and lasting impact on the debate about the education of women.

Education was seen to compromise a woman's femininity, by making her "other" than woman. Reverting to the basic model of woman and man as polar opposites, writers argued that a woman who was learned, and therefore not feminine, was masculine. In reminding women that learning made them less attractive to men, eighteenth century conduct literature sent a similar message to women that learned women were not truly women. Particularly virulent attacks on intellectual women were penned by nineteenth century doctors and journalists who popularised the idea that education "unsexed" women. Popular novelists did not directly challenge this image of learned women; in fact they were seen to collude with the authors of conduct literature in presenting clever women as freakish or sexless, while feminine women secured happiness though marriage.

As a consequence of the supposition that education "unsexed" women, there emerged over some two hundred years a substantial *corpus* of print culture which limited female learning to training for the domestic sphere. Female education for the public sphere was seen to threaten social, religious and sexual mores. In particular, residential college education, which implied removing women from the domestic sphere, and placing them in a traditionally male environment, posed a threat not only to social order but to the nature of woman. University colleges for women became possible when Emily Davies, founder of Girton College, Cambridge, illustrated that intellectual women posed no threat to the social structures of family life, nor did they compromise their femininity.

Another concern which surfaced in writing, and which mitigated against the opening of higher education to women, was that communities of women threatened religious and social conventions. Between 1536 and 1539 all English nunneries had disappeared. It could therefore be argued, by those who opposed college education for women, that community life for women no longer served any particular purpose, other than to bring back popery. Indeed Astell's *Proposal* was seen to have foundered because of its "monastic overtones." From a social point of view, literary tradition held it that when women grouped together they spread malicious stories and caused trouble. From the Renaissance, groups of women were portrayed as vain gossips who conspired against men. Literature throughout the period under examination in this study illustrated an antipathy towards groups of women such as the eighteenth century Bluestocking *salonières* and the women of the nineteenth century organised women's movement. Such women challenged the con-

ventional social structure in which women were "relative creatures." As Nina
Auerbach (1978) has argued:

> As a recurrent literary image, a community of women is a rebuke to the
> conventional ideal of a solitary woman living for and through men,
> attaining citizenship in the community through masculine approval
> alone.[5]

For men, college life involved mutual approval, friendship, and shared
professional aspirations. Women, however, were not expected to aspire to
professional or public life. Additionally, it was not believed that they had the
same capacity for deep friendships as men, nor was it believed that their
mutual respect was of as much value as the approval of men. As Elizabeth
Nestor (1985) has pointed out, in "the mid-nineteenth century an extraordinary public debate raged over women's capacities for friendship and commu-
nal activity."[6] It arose out of the contemporary debate about the value of
forming Anglican sisterhoods, but it is here suggested that it had a direct and
serious impact on the founding of women's colleges. As a solution to the
mid-nineteenth century problem of "surplus women," noted in Chapter Four,
writers such as Anna Jameson in *Sisters of Charity* (1855) and Frances Power
Cobbe in "What Shall we do with Our Old Maids?"(1862) argued in favour of
the formation of Anglican sisterhoods, which would organise women's charitable work within a legitimate institutional framework. Had the acceptance
of Anglican sisterhoods become widespread, it is arguable that it would have
had a positive effect on the development of women's colleges. While
sisterhoods aimed at charitable work, and colleges aimed at academic work
and vocational preparation, both relied upon a public acceptance of the idea
of community life for women. When a number of scandals turned the public
against convent life for women, it is arguable that it had a deleterious effect
on the image of women's colleges.[7]

Just as Emily Davies proved that education did not "unsex" women, she
proved that community life for women was both viable and worthy. Ironi-
cally, she did this by imitating, as closely as decorum allowed, the male model
of college education. From the start, she did not allow that Girton College
would be perceived as a female seminary. She also insisted that Girton students would follow the courses studied at the Cambridge colleges for men,
and that they would sit the same examinations. Additionally, they were encouraged to form college societies and to participate fully in collegiate life. In
establishing Girton along the male model of college education, she endeavoured to disassociate it from any possible accusations of being an "inferior"
type of college.

It may therefore be concluded that the pioneering success of Girton

College was a result of the ability of Davies to recognise the grounds on which women had traditionally been denied education. She assured the public that Girton students would not compromise their femininity, and she demonstrated their suitability for academic work by insisting that they follow the male model of education. Her skill, it is argued, owed much to the fact that she could see clearly that these were her tasks. However, it would do a serious disservice to Davies to suggest that her contribution to the higher education of women was no more than a series of successful manoeuvres. While Davies knew what was needed in order to court public favour, she – like Mary Astell – also "courted Truth." She saw the pursuit of Truth as an intellectual exercise. Believing that the unimpeded pursuit of knowledge brought one closer to intellectual truths, she argued that women should have access to the univeristy system by which men pursued universal truths. One of the first Girtonians, Constance Maynard, regarded Girton as "the keep of all knowledge," a sentiment shared by many of the early students who supported Davies in her desire to establish a university college for women.

The mid-nineteenth century marked the opening of formal higher education to women with the founding of Queen's College, Bedford College and Girton College. The impact which these early colleges had was significant. They were discussed in a range of popular print sources and, without a doubt, the work of Emily Davies was central to the campaign to open the degrees of the University of London and of Cambridge University to women. It has been possible, therefore, to see this particularly fruitful period in the history of women's education as one of revolution, and that it marked sudden, or unexpected, change. This book essentially supports the view that this was indeed a time when great change occurred in the provision of education for women, but illustrates that the idea that women should be educated evolved from a long and complex history of debate.

In tracing this evolutionary process, this book examines writings which appeared between 1650 and 1870, and finds that the purpose of female education changed at different times. It was variously seen as promoting female virtue and piety, female reason and self-worth, and female independence and equality. However, those who promoted formal education for women were united in a belief that such education would equip women to develop the capacity of reasoned judgement. For some writers, the aim of educating women was to make them better wives and mothers. For others, the aim was to give women intellectual and social liberation. Significantly, both Mary Astell, who wrote the first formal proposal for an institution for the education of women, and Emily Davies, who pioneered the opening of formal higher education to women, shared the belief that these aims were not mutually exclusive. In the writings of Emily Davies there were resonances of decades of debate and rhetoric leading firmly back to Mary Astell, the woman whose ideas anticipated the pioneering work of Davies and who, like Davies, "courted Truth with a kind of Romantick Passion."

'Whether a Maid may be a Scholar': Defining the Female Intellectual Sphere

THE RENAISSANCE NOTION OF WOMAN

If . . . we are to employ the women in the same duties
as the men, we must given them the same instructions.

Plato, *Republic*, Book V.

In his *Republic*, Plato (427–348 BC) presented the earliest known argument for
the education of women equal to that of men. He argued that inadequate
education, and not a lack of innate ability, was responsible for the inferior
powers of reason popularly attributed to women. With little variation, this is
the salient argument of the corpus of writing in support of female education
for over two thousand years. It is possible that interest in the question of
female education was not maintained with consistent passion and commitment over this extraordinarily long period: between Plato and St Jerome
(340–420) there was no significant document presenting the argument for
female education; similarly, while the medieval nunneries afforded many
women with the opportunity to learn Latin and Greek, Kersey (1981) notes
'an absence of significant female educational classics between the time of
Jerome and the beginning of the Renaissance in the fourteenth century'.[1]
Between the seventh and fifteenth centuries, there were, however, seven
books of formal instruction for women written in England or by English
writers. These were *De Laudibus Virginitatis* (seventh century), *Exhortatio ad
Sacra Virgines* (1160), *Ancien Riwle* (c.1250), *Myroure of our Layde* (fifteenth
century), *Garmont of gud Ladeis* (c.1500), and a seventh untitled and anonymous work.[2] These works, advocating humility, chastity and obedience, indicate that there was a basic distrust of women in the Middle Ages. This was
based on an identification of women with the body and temptation, in opposition to man 'who was identified with spirituality and seen to be threatened
in his spiritual quest by women'.[3] These books anticipated the genre of advice or conduct books that flourished in the eighteenth century, and continued to be written well into the nineteenth century with little change in their
ideological basis.

During the Renaissance, conduct literature was favoured by Protestant religious reformers such as Thomas Becon (1512-67) and Miles Coverdale (1488-1569), who 'emphasised the importance of the inculcation of proper beliefs in children to secure their salvation'.[4] By stressing the importance of the role of the mother in the salvation of her children, these reformers stressed that women should have a knowledge of the Bible. Questions about the nature and educability of women were also addressed by Catholic humanist scholars of the circle of Sir Thomas More, Erasmus, Vives and Sir Thomas Elyot. They produced six important works treating of the question of female education,[5] largely at the behest of Catherine of Aragon who had brought Vives (1492-1540) to England to educate Princess Mary. These were *De Ratione Studii Puerilis and satellitium sive Symbola* (1523), *Office and duetie of an husband* (1529), Richard Hyrde's 'Dedicatory Letter' to *A Devoute Treatise upon the Pater Noster*, translated from Erasmus's Latin text (1523) in 1524, More's 'Letter to William Gonell' (1518?), Elyot's *The Defence of Good Women* (1545) and, arguably the most influential text, *The Instruction of a Christian Woman* published by Vives in 1523. In it Vives cautiously suggested a programme of work to occupy young women in caring and domestic roles. However, as it was usually women who raised children, Vives recommended that they should receive a classical education combined with domestic science. He feared, nonetheless, that learning might affect women's nature, making them outspoken and deceitful. In particular, he suspected that 'the subtyltie of lerning shulde be a norisshement for the malitiousness of [women's] nature'.[6]

Erasmus and Vives, belonging to the Renaissance milieu, reflected a sympathy to the cause of female education popular in Italy at that time. In England, it was Bacon's *The Advancement of Learning* (1605) which provided the impetus to the development of the 'science' of teaching, and with it the question of female education. Bacon suggested that 'God hath formed the minde of man as a mirrour or glass, capable of the Image of the universal world', a concept that would be seized upon by Mary Astell (1668-1731) in forging her philosophy of female education. Astell and others committed to reform in women's education used Bacon's premise to assert that, since there was no sex in souls, then the faculty of reason was not given exclusively to men.

Bacon's greatest interpreter was John Amos Comenius, who developed his own study of the theory of learning to include women in his major work, the *Magna Didactica* (1657). In it he wrote what appears to be the earliest formal acknowledgement of the equal intellectual capabilities of men and women, arguing that women 'are endowed with equal sharpness of mind and capacity for knowledge (often with more than the opposite sex) and they are able to attain the highest positions'.[7] However, he circumscribed the limits of female learning by adding that women should not 'be educated in such a way that their tendencey to suriosity shall be developed', and concluded that woman should be educated 'to promote the welfare of her husband and her family'.[8]

The beginning of the Renaissance in the fourteenth century, then, may be said to have marked the re-emergence in writing of the question of female education, and the structuring of arguments in support of, and in objection to, female education into a formal literary debate. From then until the late nineteenth century the arguments varied only slightly from century to century. That a conclusion should prove so elusive is an indication that the debate represented fundamental polarities of thought: one which supported, and one which questioned, the contemporary ideology of femininity. Two 'versions' of the spiritual, moral, physical and intellectual limits of Woman emerge in the literature examined in this study, and the Renaissance, with its love of type and stereotype, provided a wealth of commonplaces about the nature of Woman which may be traced in educational writings up to the last decades of the nineteenth century. These commonplaces were invariably rooted in the authority of classical literature and the Bible.

In the eighth century BC, Hessiod's mythic tale of Pandora, the first woman, told of how she brought countless troubles to the world by lifting the lid from the jar. From the Bible, while both testaments gave examples of wicked and virtuous women, the story of Eve is the reference most frequently cited by those who sought to surpress female learning. Her role in the expulsion from paradise was manipulated by writers from the Early Christian Era to the nineteenth century as proof that, like her mythic counterpart Pandora, she brought evil into the world and woman's consequent subjection to man was thus the word of God. Because Eve's words beguiled Adam, woman was debarred from teaching and preaching in public (I Tim 2: 11-12), and this argument was frequently cited by those who purported to see no point in educating women. Leonardo Bruni (1370-1444), the first humanist to write about the education of women, had similarly argued that 'rhetoric in all its forms – public discussion . . . and the like – lies absolutely outside the province of women', while Vives, in the *Instruction*, clearly established the justification for confining women's intellectual interests to study and not teaching:

> For Adam was the fyrst made: and after Eve, and Adam was not betrayed, the woman was betrayed in to the breche of the commandment. Ther for bycause a woman is a frayle thinge, and of weake discretion, and that may lightly be decyved, whiche thinge our fyrste mother Eve sheweth, whome the dyvell caught with a lyght argument. Therefore a woman shuld not teche, leste when she hath taken a false opinion and beleve of any thyng, she spred it in to the herars, by the authorite of maystershypp, and lyghtly bringe other in to the same errour, for the lerners commonly do after the teacher with good wyll.[9]

Bruni, Vives, Erasmus, More, and a number of authors of popular broadsides and pamphlets, gave the question of women's education unprecedented attention. However, unlike Plato, these authors did not allow that women should be given 'the same instruction' as men. This was because, unlike Plato in the *Republic*, they did not envisage a public role for women. What may seem to be a move towards redefining the notion of woman was, therefore, limited. Consequently, the historian Joan Kelly, in her essay, "Did Women Have a Renaissance?' (1977),[10] concluded that 'there was no renaissance for women – at least not during the Renaissance'. Her essay challenged scholars to re-evaluate the influence of the Renaissance milieu on the social and intellectual development of women. Shirley Nelson Kersey (1981) concluded that it was 'conducive to [their] educational advancement'[11] but subsequent research has questioned the extent to which this is accurate. M.E. Wiesner (1986) indicated that the humanists, although they allowed women some rational capacity, sharply restricted the development of that capacity.[12] Both Weisner and Kelly argued that changes in marriage laws, the demise of female guilds and the contraction of the female role in farming and commerce between the sixteenth and eighteenth centuries suggest that women experienced 'relative loss precisely in those periods of so-called progressive change'.[13] Simon Shepherd (1985), in his study of Renaissance pamphlets for women, concluded that despite the contemporary atmosphere of experimentation, questioning of classical authorities, and attacking of 'custom', women were 'left to the precepts of traditional wisdom'.[14] Janis Butler Holm (1987) equally exposed the 'myth of a feminist humanism', pointing out that the small sample of learned seventeenth-century women and the texts of writers such as More, Vives and Hyrde, have contributed to the erroneous image of a literary movement which encouraged women to enter the masculine worlds of Arts and Letters. She concluded that 'increasingly, as readers of humanist pedagogy scrutinize the proposed ends to which female learning was to be turned, they are finding that, for the most part, these purposes were quite different from those of male learning and remarkably consistent with the traditional expectations of women's lives'.[15]

As Shepherd has noted, the Renaissance was characterised by a spirit of enquiry: '. . . [the] world was newly observed, tested and experimented upon'.[16] This spirit of enquiry prevailed among the two groups of thinkers who showed interest in women: the humanists who 'were engaged in an examination of Christian writings and teachings and a rediscovery of classical writings . . . [and] the Reformers [who] were interested principally in a reappraisal of biblical materials'.[17] Yet in his study of scholasticism in European intellectual life, Ian Maclean (1980) concluded that 'there [was] less change in the notion of woman throughout the Renaissance than intellectual ferment and empirical enquiry of various kinds might [have] lead one to expect'.[18]

From early Greek thought, he argued, the Renaissance inherited but failed to jettison the notion of female as opposed to that of male. Renaissance scholars were also aware of a stock of commonplaces about women, the most extensive collection of which was André Tiraqueau's *De legibus connubialibus* (1513). This work, together with Castiglione's *Il libro del Cortegiano* (1528) contributed to the reproduction of 'synthetic views of woman which concord with the intellectual outlook of their day'.[19]

Maclean's study offers invaluable insight into the Renaissance use of classical and biblical *exempla* when debating the question of female education. That Renaissance scholars should have allowed women a measure of education was based on the widespread acceptance that woman was made in the image of God. The pauline interpretation of Genesis 1:26-7 (1 Cor 11:7) was clarified by Augustine, and his definition of image in *De trinitate,* which allowed woman three faculties of mind (passive intellect, active intellect and will), was referred to by nearly all Renaissance writers.[20] Renaissance doctors also salvaged details from ancient writings which they frequently fitted to their own schemes in order to comment conclusively on the physiology of woman:

> Woman rarely goes bald (that is 'burns up' her hair). . . . She takes longer to form in the womb . . . reaches puberty earlier, and ages more quickly because of the corrupting effect of her dominant humidity. Her physical shape . . . is also the result of colder humours, which do not possess sufficient energy to drive matter up towards the head . . . [hence the] less perfect mental faculties. . . .[21]

Women were also said to be more prone to illness due to the influence of the uterus, and the 'etymological association of hysteria with ὑστέρα (uterus)'[22] was well known and frequently cited as a reason why women had weaker powers of mind than men. The most celebrated of the *loci classici* cited by Renaissance scholars was Aristotle's *Historia animalium* IX.I [608a 21ff], which attributed characteristics to women that continued to influence writers on female rationality in the late seventeenth century. In it, Aristotle wrote that 'woman is . . . more querulous, more apt to scold and strike . . . more void of shame or self-respect, more false of speech, more deceptive.[23] Ian Maclean has also noted that in the Renaissance, women were 'associated with a privation of meditative powers (*contemplationis defectus*) which . . . [made] them, with rustics and the simple-minded, well suited to devoutness, but ill suited to intellectual life'.[24]

Despite the contemporary opinion that women were ill-suited to learning, many women learned to read and became serious scholars. They were living proof that women were suited to scholarship, and those who opposed female education had to find new grounds on which to denounce them. We consequently find that Renaissance authors who opposed the education of women increasingly began to argue that learned women were either without virtue or were masculine. For much of the Middle Ages, the ideal state for women, as articulated by the church, 'was that of *integritas,* total virginity, that is, uncorrupted sexual and spiritual purity'.[25] While Renaissance scholars argued that the advancement of piety and virtue justified the liberal education of women, the limits of such an education were defined by the absence of public roles for women. Equally, the advancement of female virtue would 'determine that any subjects which did not contribute to religious virtue had no place in a woman's program of study'.[26] Early humanist works addressing the question of female education assumed that girls would be educated at home, and that their education would be directed towards domestic life. In the most influential of these works, Vives recommended that young women read the moral philosophers, the Bible, the Church fathers, and Christian poets such as Prudentius and Ararus. Since women neither governed nor taught, they did not need history, grammar, or logic. He defined the goal of their education as 'the study of wisdome, which doth enstruct their maners and enfourme their lyving, and teacheth them the waye of good and holy lyfe'.[27] In women, therefore, wisdom was associated with sexual purity and the restrictions on women's lives prescribed by Vives were imposed in the name of chastity, the greatest female virtue. He associated learning with chastity in the *Instruction,* giving the example of the daughters of Sir Thomas More, 'whome theyr father, nat content only to have them good and very chast, wold also they shuld be well lerned, supposynge that by that meane they shuld be more truly and surely chast'.[28] In the *Office and Dutie of an Husband* Vives indicated that, next to chastity, silence was the greatest female virtue. The husband, as the wife's teacher, was advised to limit his wife's learning and to prescribe the boundaries of discourse available to her:

> Let not thy wife be overmuch eloquent, nor full of her short and quick arguments, nor have knowledge of all histories, nor understand many things, which are written. She pleaseth me not much that giveth herself to poetry, and observing the art and manner of the old eloquence, doth study to speak facundiously.[29]

The Catholic humanist theorists assumed that women could be virtuous, and were therefore worthy of education. They did, however, identify a limited function for this learning. This included the education of children within the home. In this respect, they were like the Protestant reformers whose interest in the redefinition of the roles of family members advanced the status of the mother within the home. By placing emphasis on the 'importance of the inculcation of proper beliefs in children to secure their salvation',[30] the Protestant reformers advanced a programme of studies to prepare women for their important role of motherhood. This programme, as Travitsky notes, 'was less intellectually rigorous than that of the humanists and stressed knowledge of the Bible and training in practical skills'.[31] The Protestant reformer Thomas Becon concluded that 'the vertuous education and bringinge up of the womankinde'[32] thus necessitated their schooling. While the humanists and the reformers 'joined religious enthusiasm and educational impulses into ideologies aimed at producing pious, learned women',[33] they did not promote the female pursuit of truth. From the *corpus* of Renaissance writing on female education, the formal debate inherited the association of female virtue with education. Though this is the first significant development in female ideology as expressed in educational writings, it illustrates an assumed limited female sphere. The virtue of the learned lady was related exclusively to piety and chastity. Intellectual virtue, whose end is truth, relates to speculative reason.[34] Research indicates that the association of intellectual virtue with women was an Enlightenment phenomenon.

If the Renaissance theorists contributed the stereotype of the virtuous learned lady to the debate, then Renaissance pamphleteers promoted the image of the *Hic Mulier*, or masculine woman. The Pamphlet Wars, in which the nature of women was hotly debated, comprised a series of attacks and defenses of women, published between 1542 and 1640 (approx.), some of which condemned women whose dress and appearance was considered unfeminine. The first of the pamphlets, *The Scholehouse of Women*, was a lengthy attack on women, written in rhyme royal, and, possibly due to its vulgar humour, it went through four editions between 1541 and 1572. Defenses of women which followed included *A Dialogue defensive for women against malicious detractors* (1542), by Robert Vaughan, and *The Praise and Dispraise of Women* (1568), by C. Pyrrye. A particularly vitriolic attack of women was John Knox's *The First Blast of the Trumpet Against the Monstrous Regiment of Women* (1558), in which he railed against the rule of Queen Mary, arguing that a female ruler is 'repugnant to nature; contumlie to God, a thing most contrarious to his revealed will and appeared ordinance; and finallie it is the subversion of good order, of all equitie and justice'.[35] The year 1589 saw the first woman enter the Pamphlet War when Jane Anger published the *Protection for Women*. It was quickly followed by Stephen Gosson's attack on female vanity, *Quipps for Upstart Newfangled Gentle-Women* (1595).[36] By the beginning of the next decade, and with the accession of James I to the throne, the attacks reflected specific dislikes concerning women's clothes, hair and pursuits.[37] In 1620, the misogynist King James ordered 'the church, the theatre, pamphleteers, ballad makers, and singers [to] join in vilifying as 'masculine' the women who rode in easy costume and armed themselves'.[38] Another lengthy 'Pamphlet War' ensued, which included three pamphlets dealing directly with King James's directive against the *Hic Mulier* (see fig.1).[39]

The period therefore saw the identification of atypical female behaviour with masculinity. Consequently, since the intellectual sphere had been exclusively the domain of men, learned Renaissance women were charged with being masculine and freakish. Hannay (1985) notes that 'Cassandra Fedele was called a 'miracle', a male soul in a female body', and Isolta Nogorola was praised for overcoming her own nature by seeking 'true virtue which is essentially male'.[40] The virtuous woman and the masculine woman, female stereotypes which gained currency in the Renaissance, were attractive because they were easily understood and identified, and they reinforced an ideology of femininity which limited the female sphere. However, like all stereotypes, they obscured perception of reality: the reality remained that many women wished to pursue learning and engage in a wider sphere. Publications which dealt with women's education, especially those by women, indicate continued negotiations with the ideology of femininity and suggest as much about the writers who participated as they do about the ideology itself. Many women writers complied with the ideology, and negotiated, piece-meal, for a widening of the intellectual sphere. Other women internalized and sought to fulfil the ideals embodied in the positive images of women in humanist and reforming essays, and in pamphlets. Equally, many more internalized the negative images of women as shrewish, vain, weak and stupid. The veracity of these Renaissance commonplaces about women was taken for granted by late seventeenth-century writers such as Mary Astell when they embarked upon writing educational tracts. They then went on to argue that, deprived of education, women could not possibly be expected to be otherwise. There is much evidence that women writers themselves accepted that chastity and piety were female virtues: they then argued that these virtues were more easily defended by women who read and understood their Bible.

The Renaissance, without a doubt, contributed much to the form and content of women's educational writings as seen in this study. But, despite the erudition, the rhetoric, the classical and Christian humanist opinions and *exempla*, and the comprehensive popular pamphlet debate about the nature and role of women, the debate about women's education was not concluded. Much had yet to be written by women themselves.

HIC MVLIER:

OR,

The Man-Woman:

Being a Medicine to cure the Coltish Disease of the Staggers in the Masculine-Feminines of our Times.

Exprest in a briefe Declamation.

Non omnes possumus omnes.

Mistris, will you be trim'd or truss'd?

Loncon printed for J.T. and are to be sold at Christ Church gate. 1620.

Fig. 1   Title page from *Hic Mulier: or, The Man-Woman*, 1620

WOMEN, LITERACY AND EDUCATION IN THE SEVENTEENTH CENTURY

While the first English printed books appeared in the fifteenth century, few women wrote for publication before 1640.[41] From about this time, however, they increasingly participated in public life and on several occasions in the 1640s and 1650s they joined together to present petitions in parliament, and a select number of them published their essays and letters. Patricia Crawford (1985) has documented the considerable increase in women's publications during the Civil Wars and Interregnum,[42] rooting this development in a compulsion felt by seventeenth-century women 'to bear witness to their own different reality'[43] and, in some cases, a desire to challenge existing ideas about their roles.

An examination of selected women's writing published in England between 1640 and 1700 reveals a sustained contemporary interest in the question of female education which Crawford and other historians interested in seventeenth-century publications have not explored.[44] These publications, however, are central to any endeavour to account for the increasing awareness of the need for reforms in female education. They include Bathsua Makin's *An Essay to Revive the Ancient Education of Gentlewomen in Religion, Arts and Tongues* (1673), Hannah Woolley's *The Gentlewoman's Companion* (1675), and Mary Astell's *A Serious Proposal to the Ladies for the Advancement of their True and Greatest Interest* (1694). To some degree, the titles of these pieces belie the contents: they are not revolutionary feminist tracts. These women sought to secure recognition from society that women could and ought to engage in learning, but they did not dispute contemporary beliefs that woman was man's helpmate and that her 'sphere' was the home. That they were interested, exclusively, in the education of women of the middle and upper ranks is evident from the titles of their work: they addressed 'ladies' and 'gentlewomen' and proposed schools and colleges catering for an intellectual rather than vocational education. Their curricula contrast with those of educationalists concerned with the Charity School movement and with the grammar schools.[45] While the former prepared girls for 'spinning of wool . . . sewing, knitting'[46] and to go into service, the latter offered a basic education in reading, writing and arithmetic. The grammar schools were built for the education of boys, and only a small number of middle-class girls would have attended, if the schoolmaster had been willing to conduct a class of 'petties'.[47]

The increasing interest in the question of the education of girls of the middle and upper ranks reflects concern at the paucity of provision.[48] But the problems facing the historian interested in the education of English girls after the Reformation are considerable, as both Simon (1966) and Cressy (1975) have noted, for the simple reason that little of it was formal, therefore documents and records are few. By the late seventeenth century, however, an alternative to home education for middle-class girls appeared: the boarding school. The earliest English boarding schools for girls were commercial ventures, and the majority of them were located in Hackney, Chelsea and Putney, although there are records of such schools in Manchester, Kent, Oxford, Leicester, Burchester and Exeter. Roger Thompson (1974) noted that Hackney was known as 'The Ladies University of the Female Arts'.[49] The first boarding schools for girls were not necessarily run by women: Josephine Kamm (1965) observed that Robert Perwick's school at Hackney flourished between 1643 and 1660, with one hundred girls enrolled at one time, while Dorothy Gardiner (1929) has indicated that men also ran successful dancing schools.[50] While they were often far from adequate, their existence marked the development of the concept of private schooling for girls, the refinement of which would concern many contemporary writers interested in the education of girls and women.

With the gradual but steady increase in educational provision for girls came an increase in female literacy and in the number of published women writers.[51] David Cressy's research indicates that levels of female literacy improved significantly between 1670 and 1720.[52] It was at precisely this time that a number of important publications written by women appeared, in which arguments for female education were articulated. It was also at this time that the influence of the French movement known as the *querelle des femmes* reached England, promoting the image of learned women and prompting English women to construct their own arguments for the eductaion of their sex.

THE 'WOMAN' QUESTION IN THE LATE SEVENTEENTH CENTURY

The late sixteenth and early seventeenth centuries marked the development in Europe of a wide-ranging dispute about women's nature and abilities, which greatly influenced the history of women's educational writings in England. It was known as the *querelle des femmes,* and it originated in seventeenth-century France. This movement originally concerned noble women, particularly a circle known as the *Précieuses* which formed a literary and social coterie at the Hôtel de Rambouillet, gathered together by the highly cultured Marquise de Rambouillet. It was here that women first came to associate with men in polite society on an equal footing, and both sexes benefited from their exchanges: women were recognised as the intellectual equals of men, and their society spread a love of refinement and of letters among men of rank. The *Précieuses* were not feminists: theirs was a self-centred movement with no altruistic propaganda and no great interest in the question of female education. They cultivated the art of conversation, and composed *bouts-rimes*, *madrigaux* and portraits, and their showy clitism soon brought them widespread ridicule.

Probably the greatest achievement of the salons of the *Précieuses* was the production of such women as Mlle de Scudery and Mme de Sevigné, 'women whose learning and literary talent reached a standard far higher than that which had hitherto been attained by members of their sex'.[53] Both women had a keen interest in the education of women and both wrote well on this, but by the middle of the seventeenth century the *Précieuse* was characterised by conceited affectation in both manner and content of conversation, and was looked upon with aversion and contempt. The sect developed easily into another cult of learned ladies known as *des femmes Savantes*. While both the *Précieuse* and the *Savante* shared a desire to be admired, the *Savante* excited admiration through a display of learning. The bookish *Savante* was equally a subject of ridicule in much of the popular literature of the day, thus while both the *Précieuse* and the *Savante* raised the ideal of the intellectual capabilities of women, and of their education, their extravagance produced a reaction in French society which prevented reform.

The emergence of the French female intellectual attracted the attention of serious writers and reformers such as Fenélon (*De l'education des filles*), Mme De Maintenon (founder of the Maison Saint Cyr) and François Poulain de la Barre. Poulain laid down the grounds for the argument in favour of female education, echoed by English writers throughout the seventeenth and eighteenth century, in *Egalité des deux Sexes* (1673), and in *De L'Education des Dames* (1674) he developed a curriculum for women in which Cartesian philosophy was prominent. Poulain argued that women's apparent inferiority to men was due to their defective education which kept women in a state of subjection. He examined what were commonly held to be the characteristic female frailties and defects, and concluded that either they were not peculiar to women, but were equally noticeable in men, or they were due to women's defective education. Richards (1914) suggested that while interest in women's education in France is traceable to the Hôtel de Rambouillet and the *Précieuses*, it was killed by the folly of those who had been its original cause, and serious writers, including Poulain, went unheeded as a consequence of the hostile reaction to female intellectuals which had set in by the middle of the century.[54] However, this movement influenced attitudes to female education in England.

Hostile attitudes to the education of women in France travelled to England via plays and literature, and a number of satirical works ridiculed learned women. Dorothy Gardiner has noted the impact of the plays of Molière 'on the problem of women's education'.[55] Additonally, translations of Fénelon's popular publication *De l'education des filles* (1687) influenced the publication of conservative works by Englishmen – clergymen, educators and moralists – appeared, promoting a mistrust of the 'woman question', and there also appeared publications by women such as Mary Astell, who were clearly aware of the growing debate in France about women and learning. A 'debate' about the education of women thus emerged in English print culture at a time when female literacy and female publishing were increasing, and when a formal debate about female reason had been initiated in French print culture.

The pamphlets, essays, letters, and advice books examined in this study indicate clearly that the synthetic view of woman, which emerged in the Renaissance and drew authority from classical and biblical *exempla*, remained intact until the late seventeenth century at which time this debate began in English print culture. The debate initiated a serious questioning of the premises on which this view of woman had been built. It would prove difficult to dispute the biblical evidence for the fallen, and thereby subservient, state of woman and significantly no women writers in this study questioned the ultimate superiority of man before the middle of the eighteenth century. Equally difficult to prove was that women could compete physically with men: the assumption of the physical inferiority and innate weakness of woman is not questioned in women's educational writings until the mid-nineteenth century, when pioneers of girls' high schools and colleges included gymnastics and physical education in the curriculum. What seemed ripe for dispute by the mid-seventeenth century was the premise that women had inferior intellects. Jaded arguments which 'proved' this were challenged by the publications of a number of women such as Hannah Woolley, Bathsua Makin, and Mary Astell.

While Mary Astell stands out as the female pioneer of women's education in seventeenth-century England, the influence of three other women must be acknowledged: the brilliant Dutch scholar Anna Maria van Schurman, Bathsua Makin, and Hannah Woolley. It would appear that the earliest record of a woman entering the debate over female education is van Schurman's *Disertatio, de Ingenii Muliebris ad Doctrinam, et Meliores Litteras Aptitudine*, first published in 1641, and translated to English as *The Learned Maid, or Whether a Maid may be a Scholar* in 1659. Anna Maria van Schurman (1607–78) was a Protestant woman, educated largely at home in her native Cologne. She is recorded as one of the first women to learn Oriental languages, and in addition to Persian and Arabic, was fluent in French, English and Italian, and wrote her scholarly works in flawless Latin. In her *Disertatio*, she began:

> Num foeminae Christianae conveniat
> studium Litteratum?
> Nos affirmativam tueri conabimur.[56]

Early in her thesis she defined her title further by explaining that by
'conveniat' she meant expedient and decent. While van Schurman argued
that it was indeed decent for a Christian woman to be a scholar, many of her
contemporaries and successors would seize upon the terms of this definition
and insist that it was not at all decent for a woman to study. Perhaps anticipating controversy, van Schurman qualified her position by saying that studies
should not distract a woman from household duties and prayer. However,
she stated confidently that learning would make women happier and more
virtuous, thus it would be to the glory of God.

Anna Maria van Schurman had clear ideas as to what subjects were suited
to female study, broadening the Renaissance curriculum to include grammar,
logic, rhetoric, physics, metaphysics, history and languages, and relegating
mathematics, poetry and art to the status of mere ornament or recreation.
Despite her forward-looking approach to the education of women, van
Schurman did not encourage them in the practice of Law, in military life or
in oratory at the church, court or university. Her thesis was based, simply, on
her deep-rooted belief that while learning was not necessary to women's
salvation, it increased their contemplation and understanding of the love of
God. Her influence in England was not only felt through translations of her
work, but also through the influence she had on the Englishwoman Bathsua
Makin with whom she corresponded.

Bathsua Makin had known Comenius through her brother, the linguist
and mathematician John Pell, who had been one of a group of progressive
men who brought Comenius to England in 1641 to address the question of
the place of science in education. Comenius believed that science should be
the foundation of the educational system, taught from infant-level upwards,
and available equally to male and female students. Bathsua Makin found that
his theories were compatible with her own interest in science and in female
education. Her entry into the debate on the latter subject came late in her
life, a life about which there are few records. Her brother's fame has ensured
that some basic details about Makin are known, but apart from some letters
and her crucial document outlining her ideas for the education of women,
nothing remains to help recreate the life of a woman who 'received nation-
wide recognition in her own day for her learning and scholarship'.[57] What is
known about Makin is that she shared her brother's facility for mathematics
and languages. Through him she was introduced to van Schurman who exercised a major influence on Makin's theories, and it is possible that Makin
visited Holland at some time. Because of her reputation as a scholar, Bathsua
Makin was employed by Charles I as tutor to the clever young Princess Elizabeth, in whom she fostered a love of languages and science. When the princess later went to live in Holland, she became an intimate friend of van
Schurman with whom she shared a love of anatomy. Despite Makin's fine

teaching, she did not receive a salary from the King, and when she petitioned the Council of State in 1655 for payments of arrears totalling £40 per year her request was denied. It is not known how or where she supported herself after the execution of Charles I: it is possible that she kept a private school in 1649, but definite records are lacking.[58] Mary Mahl and Helen Koon (1977) have noted from letters of John Pell at the British Library that Makin had one son, but there are few other references to his sister. It would seem that he sometimes found her a formidable woman, although she sustained an interest in his mathematical research (it was he who introduced the division sign used in algebra).

Makin is of significance here because of her publication of a pamphlet urging the improvement of the education of women, and outlining a school prospectus, entitled *An Essay to Revive the Ancient Education of Gentlewomen* (1673). It is documentary evidence of the development of the education debate in the late seventeenth century. To ensure that her *Essay* received an unprejudiced response, she attributed it to a 'gentleman', a custom quite common among seventeenth-century female writers. Dedicated to 'all ingenious and virtuous ladies, more especially to her Highness the Lady Mary, eldest daughter to his Royal Highness the Duke of York',[59] the 'gentleman' disengages himself from the contemporary debate on the role of women suggesting that it would be dangerous to attempt to contradict custom, yet in outlining the premises of the debate he exposes the beliefs which frustrated Makin:

> Custom, when it is inveterate, hath a mighty influence: it hath the force of Nature itself. The barbarous custom to breed women low is grown general amongst us and hath prevailed so far that it is verily believed (especially amongst a sort of debauched sots) that women are not endued with such reason as men, nor capable of improvement by education, as they are . . . these things are . . .verily believed by many who think themselves wise men; to contradict these is a bold attempt.[60]

However, the putative gentleman who writes that he does not 'plead for female preeminence . . . [as] God hath made man the head', soon abandons the traditional conservative argument that education should prepare women for motherhood and for the salvation of their souls. The *Essay* changes in tone as Makin supplants platitudes with genuine anger at the ignorance in which young women are brought up:

> Merely to teach gentlewomen to frisk and dance, to put on a whisk, to wear gay clothes, is not truly to adorn but to adulterate their bodies; yea (what is worse) to defile their souls . . . . Had God intended women

only as a finer sort of cattle, He would not have made them reasonable . . . .[61]

The influence of van Schurman is evident in Makin's prescribed course of study for women. She included grammar, rhetoric, logic, physics, mathematics and languages, and echoed van Schurman in arguing that music, painting and poetry are only of ornamental value. Her essay then took the form of a series of numbered points in which she explained the value of female education, concluding that the educated woman is more fulfilled, of greater use to her family and of greater service to the nation. She then posed a number of traditional objections, such as 'If we bring up our daughters to learning, no persons will adventure to marry them' and 'They will be proud and not obey their husbands', only to reply bluntly that female ignorance secured exploitation and not protection, and that a wise man should not want an ignorant wife. In addition, Makin broke new ground by suggesting something which her predecessors had not: that female education could help women to become financially independent.

Bathsua Makin's *Essay* acknowledged that only females of rank should pursue learning: in this she may have again been influenced by van Schurman, or she may have simply accepted the aristocratic imperatives of exclusiveness and rank. The prospectus for the school at Tottenham High Cross which followed the *Essay* was designed with the hope of attracting girls of the highest birth and rank in society. More conservative in tone, it allowed that girls should devote time to the standard accomplishments such as needlework, music and dancing, although it also included a demanding programme of scientific study. In fact, it is correct to say that Bathsua Makin devised the first scientific curriculum for girls, including in it astronomy, botany, mineralogy, geology, physics, geography, arithmetic and mathematics.

The publication of Makin's ideas was followed by a letter by Clement Barksdale (1609-87), the English schoolmaster responsible for the translation of van Schurman's widely popular *The Learned Maid*. His publication, *A Letter Concerning a Colledge of Maids; or a Virgin Society* (12 August 1675), contained the first proposal for a woman's college, to be modelled on the Halls of Commoners at Oxford. His college was to contain an extensive library, accommodate twenty ladies and their maids, and provide tuition in practical divinity and devotion, history, learned and modern languages, and lady-like accomplishments. The women could be removed at the discretion of their fathers, in order to marry. Nothing came of his plan, and he did not develop a rationale for female education in which their intellectual abilities were proven or their vocational abilities proposed. Perhaps it is for this reason his letter goes almost unnoticed by historians documenting the development of female education in England.

Makin's closest English contemporary was the teacher and writer Hannah Woolley. Woolley, born in 1623, was orphaned at the age of fourteen and turned immediately to teaching to earn her living. Little is known about her early life, except that at the age of fifteen she was mistress of her own little school, and she eventually married a Mr Woolley, master of the free school at Essex, with whom she had four sons. She was a widow by 1662, when she published her first book, *The Ladies Dictionary*, a type of early cookery book including experiments in candying and preserving fruit and flowers. Woolley continued to publish books for women in order to support her family, for although she married again, her second husband also died. It was not until 1675 that she abandoned the subject of domestic science, when she published *The Gentlewoman's Companion*, asserting that women were capable of intellectual pursuits and developing Makin's thesis to boldly state that she believed that female ignorance was the result of a male conspiracy, and briskly concluding: 'we are debarred from the knowledge of human learning lest our pregnant wits should rival the touring conceit of our insulting Lords and Masters'.[62] It is possible that Hannah Woolley died within the next year, for no further records of this industrious woman remain. Her last publication restated what her contemporary, Makin, had said and anticipated the writings of Mary Astell who inherited something of their beliefs and who pushed out the limits of the seventeenth-century ideology of femininity.

A SERIOUS PROPOSAL: MARY ASTELL AND EDUCATION FOR WOMEN

According to the baptismal book of the Church of St John's at Newcastle-on-Tyne, Mary Astell was born on 12 November 1666, to Mary and Peter Astell.[63] The couple had been married in 1665, and, in all, they had three children. Her education, received at home from an uncle, was sufficient to enable her to read widely and in the classical languages, although she was always humble about her intelligence. Her father, a businessman, died in 1678. After her mother died in 1684, Mary Astell left for London, and records indicate that she was living in Chelsea in 1712 where she paid fifteen shillings poor rate on a property in Robinson's Lane. She may well have been living in Chelsea as early as 1695, at which time she published *Letters Concerning the Love of God*, dedicated to her neighbour and friend, Lady Catherine Jones. Lady Catherine, daughter of the Earl of Ranelagh, who rented a considerably finer property at four pounds, introduced Mary Astell to a wide and influential circle of people. Records of Mary Astell's life in Chelsea indicate that she was a popular woman whose home may even have taken on the image of a salon.[64] Among Astell's aquaintances were the Dean Atterbury, Sir Hans

Sloane, Lady Anne Coventry, the Anglo-Saxon scholar Elizabeth Elstob, and
the 'Queen' of the Bluestockings, Lady Mary Wortley Montagu. Her illustrious circle of friends, and the influence which she obviously held over them,
testifies to the respect in which Astell was held in her own lifetime. She had
nothing to offer by way of connection or money, but her fame as a writer and
her wit and intelligence secured her quite a prominent position in society for
a single woman of no consequence. The best-known and most controversial
of her publications were *A Serious Proposal To the Ladies for the Advancement of
their True and Greatest Interest* (1694), (see fig. 2), Part II of the *Proposal* (1697),
her correspondence with John Norris, Rector of Bemerton, published as
Letters Concerning the Love of God (1694), and *Some reflections upon Marriage*
(1700). She then published a series of pamphlets between 1704 and 1705,
indicating her involvement in political and religious controversies of the time.
In *A Fair Way with the Dissenters and their Patrons* she attacked Defoe, she
opposed Shaftesbury in *Bart'lmy Fair or An Enquiry after Wit*, and she defended
the royalist party and the Established Church in *An Empirical Enquiry into the
Cause of the Rebellion and Civil War in the Kingdom*, and again in *Moderation
truly Stated*. Her contributions to such controversies are of little interest today, but her pproposal for the building of a college for women is a milestone
in the history of female education. *A Serious Proposal* was printed anonymously in 1694 as she feared she would be 'the Butt for all the Fops in Town'.
It was directed to women, and it sought first to convince them that the seventeenth-century theory of female incapacity was groundless. Conventional
arguments as to the vanity and frailty of women could be disputed if women
were prepared to value their minds and their souls:

> Your *Glass* will not do you half so much service as a serious reflection
> on your own Minds. . . . 'Twill not be near so advantageous to consult
> with your Dancing-master as with your own thoughts. . . . Let us learn
> to pride ourselves in something more excellent than the invention of a
> Fashion: And not entertain such a degrading thought of our own *worth*,
> as to imagine that our Souls were given us only for the service of our
> Bodies.[65]

Astell thus presented a new concept to women, that of self-worth. Using
Platonic imagery, she linked the attainment of self-worth to the pursuit of
knowledge and to spiritual well-being: 'Neither will any pleasure be denied
you, who are only desir'd not to catch at the Shadow and let the Substance
go'. Lest her readers should think that her *Proposal* was a criticism of women,
she aimed 'not to expose, but to rectify Failures',[66] arguing that blame for
women's inferior social position should be laid on the poor education they
received, adding: 'instead of inquiring why all Women are not wise and good,

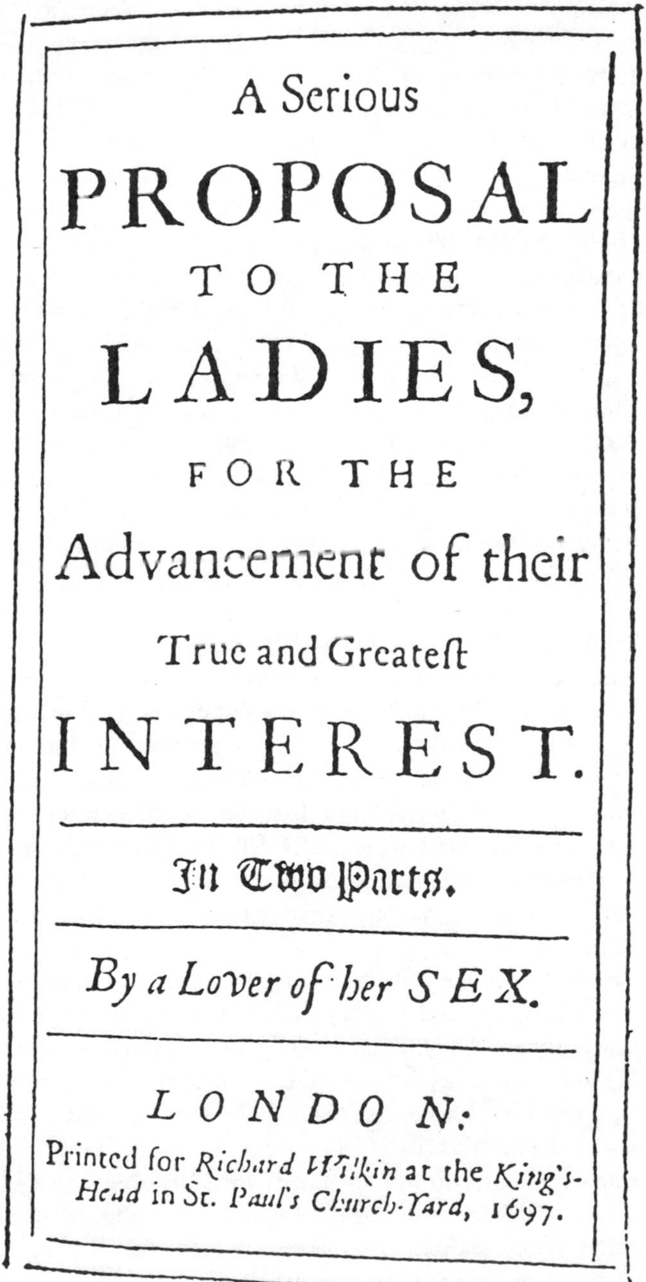

A Serious

PROPOSAL

TO THE

LADIES,

FOR THE

Advancement of their

True and Greateſt

INTEREST.

𝕴𝖓 𝕿𝖜𝖔 𝕻𝖆𝖗𝖙𝖘.

By a Lover of her *SEX*.

LONDON:

Printed for *Richard Wilkin* at the *King's-Head* in St. *Paul's Church-Yard,* 1697.

Fig. 2 Title page from *A Serious Proposal to the Ladies, for the Advancement of their True and Greatest Interest* [Mary Astell] 4th edn., 1697

we have reason to wonder that there are any so'.[67] Were women to be trained properly to judge and make choices, Astell argued, they would not grow up guilty of the 'Feminine Vices' of pride and vanity. What made the *Proposal* acceptable to seventeenth-century conservatives was the fact that Astell linked the cultivation of the female intellect with the greater glory of God, and argued that the 'desire to advance and perfect its Being, is planted by GOD in all Rational Natures'.[68] Astell then concluded the first half of the *Proposal* by positing that in ignorance lay the root of evil. The solution to the problem of female frailty and ignorance was, Astell suggested, that an institution be established for their education and spiritual development. She referred to this institution a 'Monastery', and a 'Seminary to stock the Kingdom with Pious Ladies'[69] and therein lay her downfall, for it was perceived by influential churchmen as an attempt to bring back popery. Strongest opposition to Astell's college for women came from Bishop Burnet, who prevented a prominent lady from contributing £10,000 to the plan.[70] The Preface to the *Proposal* suggests that the anonymous benefactor might have been Princess Anne, to whom Part II of the *Proposal* was dedicated in 1697. As Bishop Burnet was tutor to Princess Anne's son, it is possible that they discussed the matter.

Astell's defence of her position included repeated denials that the institution was monastic rather than academic, and as late as 1705 she made this point in *The Christian Religion*. However, she did not manage to revive interest in the *Proposal*, and turned her attention to her scientific interests and to the establishment of a charity school for girls in Chelsea. The school was established in 1729 for the education of daughters of the Pensioners of Chelsea Hospital, with the financial assistance of Astell's loyal friends, Lady Catherine Jones, Lady Elizabeth Hastings and Lady Ann Coventry. Two years later, Mary Astell died following an unsuccessful mastectomy performed in the crude conditions of the time.

Her death deeply saddened her very large circle of friends, some of whom managed to pass her ideas to the next generation of learned English women. Lady Ann Coventry and Lady Mary Wortley Montagu told anecdotes about her to the eighteenth-century 'Bluestocking' ladies, and Elizabeth Elstob recalled facts about her life for her first biographer, George Ballard. Such scant information was all that historians had to work with prior to the publication of Ruth Perry's impressive study, *The Celebrated Mary Astell* (1986).[71] While Mary Astell was well known in her later years, her works rapidly vanished from circulation. *Book Collector 10* (1961) attempted to trace all primary sources for Astell, noting that as early as 1740 her books were rare. Because there was a revival of interest in Astell around 1730, there were new editions of three of her works, one in Dublin and two in London. Astell thereafter slipped from public consciousness until the revival of interest in the 'woman question' following the publication of Maria Wollstonecraft's *A Vindication of the Rights of Woman* (1792). At that time a mild interest in Astell was re-awakened, for at least two writers disputed Wollstonecraft's title of champion of the women's cause, arguing that it was Astell who had defended the rights of women one hundred years earlier. In 1891 Karl D. Bulbring published a paper[72] contradicting an article in the *Westminster Review* (1891) which had stated that Wollstonecraft's *Vindication* was the first formal plea for equality of education and social position. This argument was again taken up in 1898, when an article appeared in the *Westminster Review* (1898), which concluded: 'Mary Astell must be regarded as the pioneer of the modern 'Woman's Rights' movement. The influence of her thoughts and her arguments may be clearly traced from her day to this'.[73]

Astell again vanished from print, until the revival of interest in the women's movement in this century. While her first biography was written by Florence Smith in 1915,[74] the significance of her thoughts and writing is only now recognised. Joan K. Kinnaird in the *Journal of British Studies* (1979) has debated Astell's 'conservative contribution to British feminism' acknowledging that while proto-feminism had its genesis in the Restoration period, Astell made no claims for the equality of women. Kinnaird ultimately concludes that in Astell and her contemporaries lie the *conservative* origins of the movement, promoting 'the dignity of women, educational reform and the ideal of companionate marriage'.[75] Most recently, Ruth Perry (1986) has gathered together Mary Astell's poetry, letters and writings, and has recreated the social history of the England in which Astell lived and wrote, to give a compelling picture of her life.

In assessing Astell's contribution to women's history, Ruth Perry has concluded that 'her most significant and lasting contribution to the history of ideas has been her feminism',[76] adding that she 'began the modern dialogue in print about the power relations between the sexes', she was 'the first thinker to question the benefits of marriage in the bourgeois era' and 'she was the first woman to live alone publicly without forfeiting her respectability'.[77] While it is important to note this list of 'firsts' attributed to Astell, it is equally important to analyse the achievements that she herself had sought rather than those we can attribute to her in hindsight. Her abiding interest was in female education and her best known tract was *A Serious Proposal*. For this reason she has been erroneously given a number of other 'firsts': in particular she is noted as 'the first writer who formally and decidedly advocated the rights and abilities of the fair sex',[78] 'the first author to suggest that women's schools should be comparable to existing men's schools'[79] and she is often referred to as the first writer to propose a college for women. Without returning to Plato for early references to the equal suitability of men and women for education, we have already noted that her advocation of the 'abilities of the fair sex' were superseded by Comenius, van Schurman, Makin, and Woolley and that Clement Barksdale was the first writer to formally propose a women's college and to suggest that it should be modelled on the system of male education.

There remains to decide the nature of Astell's contribution to the history of women's education. Mary Astell was the first Englishwoman to make a sustained proposal for an institution for the education of noble-women, and, as Perry has noted, the first English writer to fully articulate ideas that had been developing through the century and to relate them concretely to life *as she knew it*. Her *Proposal*, containing no plea for women's access to university or the professions, reflected the conservative seventeenth-century view-point that the family was the natural unit of society and she never challenged the right of the husband to rule the family. What was unique about Mary Astell was the way she argued with profound philosophical logic towards a 'proposal' of how to educate noble-women. She brought all the forces of her intellect to bear on her argument which buckled under the weight of a few ill-chosen words. Within the *Proposal* lie examples of her grasp of pedagogy, not seen in van Schurman, Makin, Woolley or Barksdale, suggesting that she may well have been the first Englishwoman to understand and write on the significance of early childhood education. She was also probably the first respectable woman writer in England, and, because of the popularity of her work, the first widely read female polemicist. But what is not in doubt is that it is in her work that can be found the genesis of the movement for the higher education for women in England.

2

Strictures and Vindications: Eighteenth-century Theories of Female Reason

PRESCRIBING THE LIMITS OF LEARNING: TEXTBOOKS, ADVICE BOOKS AND CONDUCT LITERATURE

While the seventeenth-century advocates of women's education associated learning with using one's free time responsibly, and with glorifying God, in the eighteenth century there emerged a secular ideology of female rationality which provided the *raison d'être* for female education. There were many influences on the emergence of such thought, quite apart from the arguments articulated by the women themselves. In particular, Lockean thought proved that the theological basis of the argument of women's inferiority was groundless, by stating that a wife's subordination to her husband was a matter of contract, the terms of which could be varied in different social conditions. Locke also argued that women should receive a similar education to men, and that political power should not be based on 'a divinely instituted patriarchal power traceable back to Adam'.[1]

In the eighteenth century, the unprecedented interest in the female condition and in female education was partly inspired by the philosophical shift towards rational thought. It was also partly due to changes in the economic and social structure of England which had brought home to women the limited roles that they might expect to fill. As Roy Porter (1982) has noted, the duties of the eighteenth-century lady were to obey her husband, bear and raise children, and run a household – all while maintaining a graceful and genteel image.[2] Increasingly in the eighteenth century, duties performed by the lady of the house were assumed by domestic staff, the presence of which in many middle-class homes denoted the rising aspirations of the merchant trading class at this time. However, as Janet Todd (1980) has noted, the improvement in standard of living for the middle classes in England resulted in women, who were a more moneyed and marginal than before, needing occupation and seeking education.[3]

These social changes directly influenced publishing for women. For example, in order to satisfy women's demands for entertainment and education, publishers turned out text books, advice books, conduct literature, magazines or 'miscellanies', and almanacs. While some of these publications were written purely as a form of light entertainment, others were designed to provide instruction on matters of conduct and social etiquette. A number of publications also appeared which were designed for female self-education, and provided informal instruction to women who were denied access to college education. Particularly popular were books which promoted women's scientific interests, such as Elizabeth Carter's translation of Francesco Algarotti's *Sir Isaac Newton's Philosophy explained for the Use of the Ladies* (1739), and Priscilla Wakefield's *An Introduction to Botany* (1760). There were also anthologies of writing compiled and sold as readers for women. Creswick's *The Female Reader* (1798), and volumes such as *Angelica's Ladies Library* (1790) and *The Young Lady's Parental Monitor* (1790) provided young women with moral lessons and conservative wisdoms.

Less serious in tone, though still of educational value, were the books of general instruction such as the *Female Instructor* (1815), and Anna Barbauld's *Female Speaker* (1811). The almanac or diary, and the 'miscellany' were also popular forms of publication for women, the former had some educational value, while the latter provided entertainment. Diaries and almanacs, such as *The Ladies Diary, or the Woman's Almanack* (1704), and *The Diarian Miscellany* (1775) contained some scientific information, while miscellanies, such as the *Female Spectator* (monthly, 1744-46) were a form of magazine for women containing stories, letters and recipes. Though essentially a form of light entertainment, the miscellanies provided general information for women, and occasionally carried serialised didactic fiction which carried a moral lesson to readers.

There was also a number of publications offering advice on domestic work or outlining programmes of education suited specifically to women. Such works, which may be categorised as advice books and conduct literature, sharply circumscribed the female sphere. However, the proliferation in publishing for women at this time marked a new awareness of the intellectual capacities of the female sex.

> George Eliot studied Chemistry . . . Samuel Taylor Coleridge's daughter, Sara, resorted to geology and botany to alleviate the distress of poor health . . . Maria Edgeworth . . . relished astronomy and confessed to a zany 'taste for mechanics'. . . . Lord Byron's daughter, Ada, Shelley's first wife, Harriet Westbrook, Mrs. Gaskell's daughter, Meta, and numerous other women all shared the same fascination and enthusiasm for the study of different branches of the science.[4]

This impressive list of amateur women scientists suggests that in the eighteenth-century women were allowed to enjoy this intellectual pursuit at a time when their formal education was minimal and their intellectual prowess barely acknowledged. By the end of the seventeenth century, there was a growing public tolerance for women with intellectual aspirations, as long as such women kept these aspirations in perspective. The *Athenian Mercury,* a popular journal which had recognised the female magazine market by including regular editions on female interests, indicated the tenor of the debate in 1691 in an edition devoted exclusively to answering 'several questions lately sent . . . by a young gentlewoman'. The inclusion of the word 'proper' in question six indicates the nature of the contemporary dilemma, while the reply, flippant and vulgar, reflects the widely held belief that there were limits to what an intellectual woman could reasonably hope to pursue:

Question Six: 'Whether it be proper for Women to be Learned?'

> Answer: 'All grant that they may have some Learning, but the question is of what sort, and to what Degree? Some indeed think they have *learn'd* enough, if they can distinguish between their *husband's breeches* and another man's: but those who have no more wit than this comes to, will be in danger of *distinguishing* yet further, or else not at all'.[5]

The sentiment of the reply, blaming women's ignorance on their own lack of interest in learning, is both a plagiarism and a distortion of a passage in Hannah Woolley's *The Gentlewomen's Companion* (1675) in which she wrote:

> The right Education of the Female Sex as it is in a manner everywhere neglected, so it ought to be generally lamented. Most of this deprav'd later Age think a Woman learned and wise enough, if she can distinguish her Husband's bed from another's. . . .[6]

Woolley quite obviously did not lay blame on women themselves. She continued by adding:

> I cannot but complain of, and must condemn the great negligence of Parents, in letting the fertile ground of their daughters lie fallow, yet send the barren Noodles of their sons to the University. . . .[7]

The *Athenian Mercury* continued its reply, delineating limits for female education. Reading and writing could be taught to females, but it did not recommend 'letting 'em meddle with the edge-tools of Philosophy, for these wise reasons: because forsooth it takes 'em off from their domestic affairs . . . because it generally fills 'em too full of themselves, and makes them apt to despise others'.[8]

In addition to giving women an inflated sense of their own importance, study could distract them from their domestic duties. The study of science withstood such arguments for it did not require that the student devote time to acquiring the classical languages, the hallmark and preserve of a gentleman, nor did women need to devote unbroken hours of work to this pursuit. As Phillips (1990) has illustrated, the trappings of the amateur scientist likened chemistry experiments to domestic and culinary work, and science did not have a sufficiently high status to warrant the exclusive attention of men. In addition, 'the student needed no more elaborate preparation than commitment, application and an independent mind'.[9]

Most influential educationalists of the day had promoted women's interest in science. Comenius, who had urged the use of the vernacular and the study of science in the curriculum, insisted on the intellectual equality of women, and encouraged them to undertake scientific studies. Phillips notes that he 'devised an impressive vindication for such studies . . . [and] made science palatable by linking a knowledge of science with an understanding of ethics'.[10] It was through the writings of Bathsua Makin that the theories of Comenius reached girls and women. Her curriculum design, included in her *Essay to Revive the Ancient Education of Gentlewomen* (1673), was emphatically scientific:

> To buy Wool and Flax, to die [*sic*] Scarlet and Purple, requires skill in Natural Philosophy. To consider a Field, the quantity and quality, requires a knowledge in Geometry. To plant a vineyard, requires understanding in Husbandry: She could not merchandize, without Knowledge in Aritmetick: she could not govern so great a Family well, without Knowledge of Politicks and Oeconomicks: She could not look well to the wayes of her Household, except she understood Physick and Chirurgery: She could not open her Mouth with Wisdom, and have in her Tongue the Law of Kindness unless she understand Grammar, Rhetorick and Logick.[11]

The Postscript to the *Essay* included that 'Gentlewomen may learn the Names, Natures, Values and Use of Herbs, Shrubs, Trees, Mineral-Juices, Metals, and Stones'[12] and lest anyone be in doubt of her ability to impart such knowledge she concluded the prospectus of her school thus:

> Those that think these Things Improbable or Impracticable, may have further account every Tuesday at Mr. Masons Coffe-House [*sic*] in Cornhill near the Royal Exchange: and Thursdayes [*sic*] at the Bolt and Turn in Fleet-street, between the hours of three and six in the Afternoons, by some Person whom Mris. Makin [*sic*] shall appoint.[13]

The closing decades of the seventeenth century saw a small but impressive number of published works arguing for the intellectual importance of scientific study. Bishop Thomas Spratt had published *The History of the Royal Society of London, for the Improving of Natural Knowledge* (1667) in which he argued that scientists were expanding human knowledge, and no less than six of the thirteen published works of Margaret Cavendish, Duchess of Newcastle, were on scientific topics. Initiatives were taken to cater for the increasing female interest in science in the eighteenth century. As Phillips (1990) has noted, instruments were specially made for them, public lectures were tailored to suit their educational level, and advertisements for microscopes, which were something of a status symbol for learned women, appeared in women's magazines.

Text books from this period also indicate the growing participation of women and girls in science. In 1688 Aphra Behn translated the hugely popular *Entretiens sur la pluralite des mondes* (1686) by Bernard le Bovier, Sieu de Fontenelle. It appeared as *The Theory or System of Several New Inhabited Worlds*, and was written in the format of a dialogue between pupil and teacher. This essentially Socratic device was popular among writers of text-books for women, and was used to great effect by John Harris, the science lecturer and teacher, in 1719. His textbook, *Astronomical Dialogues* (see fig. 3), indicates the popularity of the study of the globes which were, like the microscope and the mineral cabinet, to be found in the homes of learned ladies. Harris's text allows the young student to retain feminine charms, even though she has intellectual pretensions. It opens with her announcement that, as 'the Tea won't be ready this Hour', she would like to occupy the time with a lesson:

> Let me understand then, first the Difference between these two Globes, and why one hath the Cities, Countries, and Places of the Earth drawn on it, like a Map; and the other Circles and Stars. . . .[14]

The tutor, in his reply, indicates a growing contemporary belief that women might be of greater use to society if they had an education:

> I am glad, said I, Madam, by the warm manner of your Enquiry, to find that you are in earnest; and I have often wished that the same Curiosity and Love of Knowledge would inspire more of fair Sex, for it would mightily enlarge their Empire and Power over ours, by endowing them with more real and lasting Beauties, such as would improve with Time, and strengthen even in Age itself.[15]

A popular eighteenth-century device to attract female book-buyers was to dedicate the text to a lady. One such work was the popular *Astronomy*

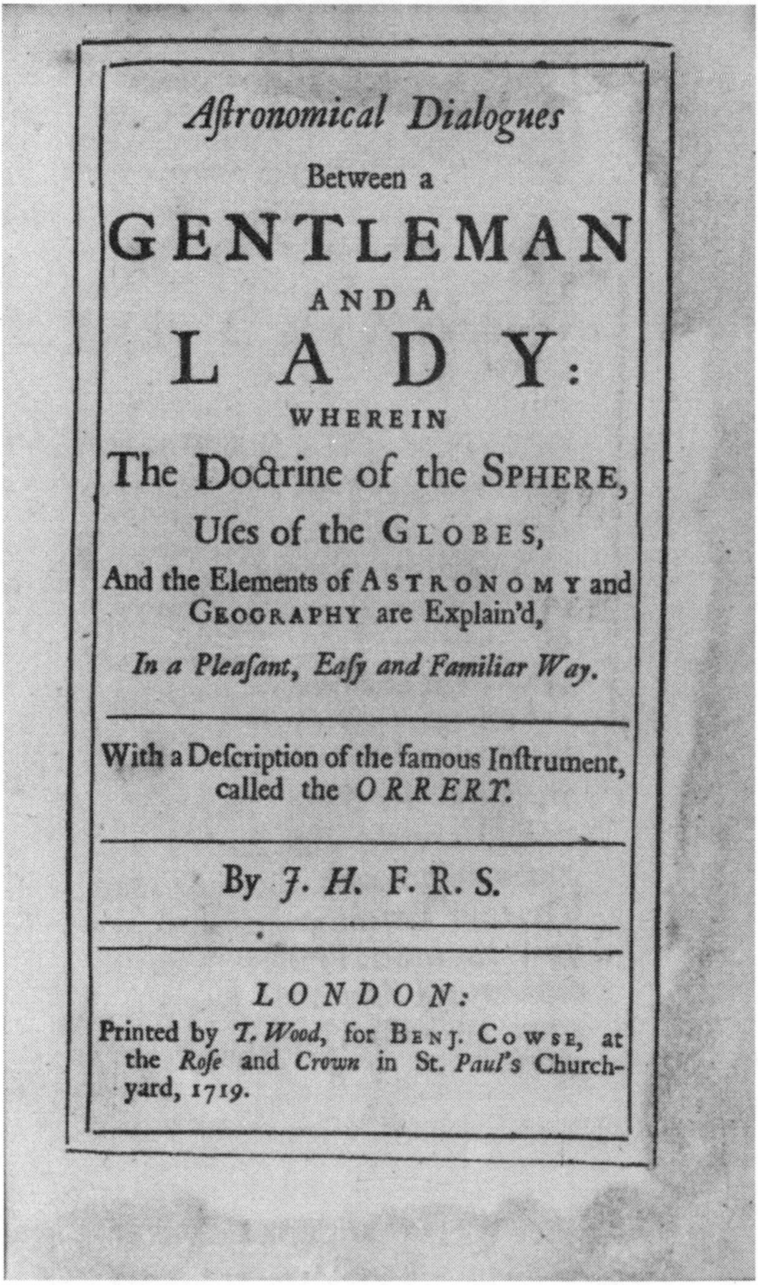

Aſtronomical Dialogues

Between a

GENTLEMAN

AND A

L A D Y:

WHEREIN

The Doƈtrine of the SPHERE,

Uſes of the GLOBES,

And the Elements of ASTRONOMY and
GEOGRAPHY are Explain'd,

In a Pleaſant, Eaſy and Familiar Way.

With a Deſcription of the famous Inſtrument,
called the *ORRERY.*

By *J. H.* F. R. S.

L O N D O N:

Printed by *T. Wood*, for BENJ. COWSE, at
the *Roſe* and *Crown* in St. *Paul's* Church-
yard, 1719.

Fig. 3 Title page from John Harris, *Astronomical Dialogues* (1719)

(1727), by Charles Leadbetter, dedicated to Catherine Edwin. Perhaps the most popular of all the texts, and one which rivalled that of Fontanelle, was *Il Newtonianism per le dame* (1737), by Francesco Algarotti. This text was translated into English by Elizabeth Carter (1717-1806) in 1739 (see fig. 4), and it established her as a leading eighteenth-century intellectual. Algarotti had come to England in 1736, and his letters of introduction from Voltaire included one to Lord Hervey who welcomed him into English society and introduced him to the author and celebrated hostess, Lady Mary Wortley Montagu (1689-1762). Both Lord Hervey and Lady Mary fell in love with the attractive Algarotti, and Montagu even left her husband to follow him to Europe, although her love was unrequited.

Examinations of the library of another celebrated hostess, Lady Elizabeth Vesey, have given some indication of the interests of eighteenth-century intellectual women. Intact until 1929, it contained several editions of Euclid, various geometry books and a large collection of scientific, historical and political works. The reputation of contemporary circles of female intellectuals was enhanced by the achievements of Elizabeth Carter, in *Sir Isaac Newton's Philosophy explained for the Use of the Ladies in Six Dialogues on Light and Colours* (1739), and in her formidable *Epictetus* (1758),[16] and on the educational writings of Hester Chapone (1727-1801) and Catherine Macaulay Graham (1731-91). That Carter's *Epictetus* was popular with women is indicated by the 280 female subscribers listed in the pages preceding the work. Among the hundreds who subscribed were the libraries of Cambridge (Trinity, Benet, Caius, Jesus, St John's), St John's College, Oxford, and Eton College Library which ordered two copies.

In the second half of the eighteenth century, and in the early decades of the nineteenth century, women increasingly produced their own scientific text books. Among the most popular were Priscilla Wakefield's *An Introduction to Botany* (1760), which reached its eleventh edition by 1841, Sarah Trimmer's *Easy Introduction to the Knowledge of Nature* (1782), Jane Marcet's *Conversations on Chemistry, intended more especially for the female Sex* (2 vols., 1805) which reached a sixteenth edition by 1853, and Mary Somerville's *On the Connexion of the Physical Sciences* (1834), which ran to ten editions over forty years and was translated into several languages. Somerville (1780-1872), born late in the eighteenth century, was a product of an era which had become enlightened in the suitability of scientific study for women. She was probably the earliest professional woman scientist and her publications resulted in her being labelled the 'Queen of Nineteenth Century Science', though her personal journal suggests that she did not believe it was possible for a woman to be truly creative in science.[17] Her contemporary, Maria Edgeworth (1768-1849), also pursued scientific studies. Her 'Harry and Lucy' stories published in 1801 as *Early Lessons*, were essentially elementary

Sir ISAAC NEWTON's

PHILOSOPHY

Explain'd

For the Ufe of the LADIES.

In SIX DIALOGUES

ON

LIGHT and COLOURS.

From the *Italian* of Sig. *Algarotti.*

VOLUME I.

Quæ legat ipfa Lycoris. VIRG. Ec. x.

LONDON:

Printed for E. CAVE, at St. *John's-Gate,*
MDCCXXXIX.

Fig 4 Title page of Sir Isaac Newton's *Philosophy Explain'd for the Use of the Ladies* (1739) by Francesco Algarotti

science books. Edgeworth at this time also produced her major work, *Practical Education* (1801) which supported scientific study for girls.

Such was the development of women's interest in science that publishers devised ladies' diaries which reflected this interest. The most popular of these was the *Lady's Diary or the Woman's Almanack . . . Containing many delightful and Entertaining particulars peculiarly adapted for the Use and Diversion of the Fair-Sex* (1704) designed by the schoolmaster, John Tipper. It was a pocket-sized book containing a wealth of scientific information and an almanac. While the earliest editions also contained domestic tips and romantic fiction, he heeded the requests of women who complained of this, and by 1709 the diary contained only scientific and mathematical information.

The type of information contained in diaries and almanacs varied from publication to publication, but typically they listed historical or scientific facts and included a place for jotting notes. For example, the *Polite Repository or Pocket Companion* (see fig. 5),which appeared between 1790-1808, could be used as a diary and contained a double page for each month. It also contained a 'repository' for notes and accounts, a list of the Kings, Queens, Admirals, Baronets and Members of Parliament, and a set of illustrations by John Peltro, after watercolours supplied for the almanac by the famous landscape gardener Humphrey Repton. It thus brought images of English architecture to those who had little opportunity to travel.

Popular miscellanies, like almanacs and diaries, also provided a crude form of education for women, though they were principally published as light entertainment. They are mentioned here, however, because their popularity indicated growth in female literacy. Popular miscellanies were published as periodicals, and contained a variety of material including essays, letters, recipes, stories, and riddles. Those directed at a female audience included the *Female Spectator* (1744-46), the *Female Preceptor* (1813-14), the *Ladies Magazine or, Polite Companion for the Fair Sex* (1759-63) (see fig. 6), *Lady's Monthly Museum, or Polite Repository of Amusement and Instruction* (1798-1806), the *Lady's Museum* (1760-61), and the *Lady's New and Elegant Pocket Magazine, or Polite and Entertaining Companion for the Fair Sex* (1795-96). Of these, the *Female Spectator*, the *Ladies Preceptor*, and *Lady's Monthly Museum* made occasional contributions to the debate about female education.

The *Female Spectator*, a major single-essay serial periodical, was written by the novelist and dramatist Eliza Haywood (1693-1756). It carried a leading essay in each edition, and sometimes developed the essay theme in several successive editions. In its first number, which appeared in April 1744, Haywood declared that the *Spectator* aimed 'to reform the faulty and give an innocent amusement to those who [were] not so'.[18] It was not a radical publication, however, and, like the *The Female Preceptor,* reinforced the contemporary ideology of femininity. For example, *The Female Preceptor* carried a

PEACOCK'S

POLITE REPOSITORY,
OR
Pocket Companion;

Containing

An ALMANACK,
The Births Marriages, &c. *of the*

SOVEREIGN PRINCES of EUROPE,

Lists of both HOUSES of PARLIAMENT.

Officers of State   Navy and Army

The **Baronets** of **England**

And various other articles of

USEFUL INFORMATION.

Ornamented with Elegant Engravings.

and ruled Pages for Occurrences Cash. Account &c &c.

To be continued Annually.

London.

Printed for W. PEACOCK & SONS. Salisbury Square.
FLEET STREET.

Fig. 5 Title page from *The Polite Repository, or Pocket Companion* (1807)

THE
NEW LADY'S MAGAZINE;
Or, POLITE *and* ENTERTAINING
COMPANION FOR THE FAIR SEX:
Entirely Devoted to their Use and Amusement.

A WORK far Superior to every other PUBLICATION of the KIND hitherto
PUBLISHED, OR now PUBLISHING.

CONTAINING

More in Quantity, and a much greater Variety of New, Original, and select Pieces (in Prose and Verse) on very curious, useful and entertaining subject—together with a greater and more elegant Variety of Copper-plates, than are to be found in any other Work of the Kind whatever.—And including, among an infinite Variety of other useful and interesting Particulars, Essays, Letters, Dissertations, Treatises, and curious Productions, relating to

History,	Happiness,	Sentiments,	Affluence,	Virtue,
Geography,	Manners,	Accomplishments,	Voyages,	The Stage,
Music, .	Literature,	Honour,	Travels,	Dress.
Amusement,	Biography,	Improvement,	Medicine,	Education,
Politeness,	Criticism,	Instruction,	Prudence,	Conduct,
Cookery,	Translations,	Entertainment,	Fashion,	The Married State,
Confectionary,	Talk,	Gardening,	Philosophy,	Prosperity,
Friendship,	Wit,	Œconomy,	Morality,	Poetry, &c. &c.

And many other Miscellaneous Subjects of Knowledge and Pleasure, which will render this New Lady's Magazine a most agreeable Companion (far preferable to any other Work of the Kind) to Female Readers, of every Age, Rank, and Condition in Life.

TOGETHER WITH

A faithful Register and Journal of the whole Transactions of the Times, Foreign and Domestic : Births, Marriages, Deaths, Promotions, Preferments, &c. and a Critical and Impartial Review of such new Books and Publications as are offered to the Ladies either for their Improvement or Entertainment.

The Whole Published under the immediate Inspection of

THE REV. MR. CHARLES STANHOPE,
Of QUEEN'S-SQUARE, GREAT ORMOND-STREET.

BY THE KING's ROYAL LICENCE AND PROTECTION,
AND
INSCRIBED TO THE PRINCESS ROYAL OF ENGLAND.

VOL. I.

EMBELLISHED with the greatest Variety of elegant, superb, and numerous Copper-Plates, Portraits, Patterns, Songs set to Music, and other EMBELLISHMENTS which will be worth of themselves alone above four TIMES the Price of the whole Work.

LONDON:

Printed, by Royal Authority, for ALEX. HOGG, at the KING's ARMS, No. 16, Paternoster-Row, and sold by all Booksellers, Stationers, and Newscarriers, in Town and Country.

[To be Published Monthly, Price only 6d.]

Fig. 6 Title page from *The New Lady's Magazine; Or, Polite and Entertaining Companion for the Fair Sex* [1764]

series of essays titled 'On the Female Mind', the essence of which was indicated in the opening essay:

> Instances, without doubt, may be adduced, where talents truly masculine, and of superior masculine excellence, have been bestowed on the softer sex; but they are so rare, that the union is not to be looked for.[19]

The genteel tone of these opinion forming periodicals made them suitable reading material for girls. The *Lady's Monthly Museum*, for example, was received in numerous boarding schools and academies for girls.[20] Also popular were books of general instruction or advice. They offered young women tips on domestic work such as cookery, preserving, and the making of medicines. Some were specific, while others were superficial and broad. The *Ladies Dispensatory: or Every Woman her Own Physician* (1739) contained information on surgery, while the *Ladies Complete Pocket-Book* (1760) offered general advice. Some advice books suggested suitable programmes of education for young women. Lady Pennington's popular advice book, *An Unfortunate Mother's Advice to her Absent Daughters* (4th edn., 1768) proposed that young women should be 'well acquainted with . . . English . . . Italian . . . arithmetic, history, geography and music',[21] while the Marchioness de Lambert, in *Advice of a Mother to her Daughter* (1790) recommended the study of Greek and Roman history, and the plays of Cicero and Pliny for a 'taste for virtue'.[22] Mary Wray's the *Ladies Library* (1714) proposed that women should study grammar, and arithmetic, and they should also read Greek and Roman history in translation. Wray, recognising that women were disadvantaged by their ignorance of the classical languages, argued that she did not 'see the Necessity of a Woman's learning the ancient tongues'[23] when they could progress more rapidly at history in the vernacular. She went on to argue that women should despise the 'affected piece of Pedantry in men of certain Learned professions' which had created a 'custom' of considering Greek and Latin to be 'venerable'.[24] She thus presented an early argument for a special curriculum for women, based on their needs and on expediency, rather than on a desire to imitate the curriculum of men. Wray was definitely familiar with Mary Astell's *Proposal* (1694). The penultimate chapter of Wray's work, titled 'Ignorance', contained a passage lifted verbatim from the *Proposal*, in which it was argued that it was 'from ignorance, from want of Understanding' that women 'quit the Substance for the Shadow'.[25]

Wray took the Lockean position that private education, under the supervision of a parent or instructor at home, was superior to boarding school education, and argued that 'the common education of young Gentlewomen at Boarding-Schools [was] . . . useless, and indeed pernicious'.[26] It was a position shared by Clara Reeve (1729-1807) in her book of advice on female education, *Plans of Education* (1792). Written late in the eighteenth century, it included a sharp commentary on the growing popularity of boarding schools, and was obviously directed to parents, rather than girls themselves:

> In every town, village, and even hamlet, there are persons found who take upon them the great and important charge of female education: and over their doors are seen in letters of gold,

> '*A Boarding School for Young Ladies*'

> Adventurers of all kinds have found resources in this profession . . . . What must we think of the negligence and credulity of such parents as intrust their most precious treasures, their children . . . to the care of the unknown. . . .[27]

Such schools offered a superficial education in the 'external accomplishments'[28] at the expense of a good basic education. Reeve and many of her contemporaries, including Mary Wollstonecraft and Maria Edgeworth, were critical of such schools which produced girls 'full of pride, vanity, and self-consequence'.[29] Maria Edgeworth, in *A Practical Education*, argued that 'the market [was] . . . over-stocked' with accomplished ladies, and challenged her readers with the following question:

> Out of the prodigious number of young women who learn music and drawing, for instance, how many are there, who, after they have become mistresses of their own amusements, continue to practise these accomplishments for the pure pleasure of acquisition? [They] will prefer the more indolent pleasure of hearing the best music that can be heard at concerts.[30]

The merits of boarding school education were also debated by the Revd John Bennet in *Strictures on Female Education* (1787). He used the male model of boarding school education against which to measure female education, and concluded that boarding schools were not necessary for girls. Boarding schools for boys established 'confidence' and fostered 'early lasting friendships . . . which frequently lead the way to worldly honour and advancement'.[31] As Bennet considered that confidence in women was 'an horrid bore', and as they did not need a network of friendships in order to prosper in public life, he concluded that young women should be educated quietly at home. Bennet shared the position articulated by Rousseau in *Émile* (1762) that the woman's education was 'for the man':

The qualities which every man of real taste and sense wishes, particularly, to find in a woman, are innocence, simplicity, and domestick worth. . . . Boarding schools wholly counteract these dispositions . . . . Like hot beds, they give a forwardness to fruits, but deprive them of their natural healthiness. . . .[32]

Conduct literature, like the books of advice examined above, guided their readers away from the kind of frivolity induced by superficial education, and reinforced the importance of education for marriage. Conduct books are here distinguished from advice books because they focussed specifically on female behaviour rather than the female intellect. While advice books often proposed a scheme of education, conduct literature attempted either to correct faulty behaviour, or to prescribe appropriate behaviour, and conduct books invariably linked appropriate female behaviour to an understanding of female duty. They thus took, as a starting point, the premise that young women were in need of correction. The *Female Guardian* (1784) carried the sub-title 'Designed to Correct some of the Foibles incident to Girls and supply them with Innocent Amusement for their Hours of Leisure'.[33] The *Female Monitor* (1800) which carried the subtitle 'The Whole Duty of Women', taught its readers to avoid curiosity, affectation, and vanity, and, echoing Rousseau, to cultivate the 'arts of endearment'.[34]

Thomas Gisborne, in *An Enquiry into the Duties of the Female Sex* (1797), called upon women to 'consider the real and deeply interesting effect which the conduct of their sex [had] upon society'.[35] He listed the contribution of women 'to the welfare of mankind' as follows:

In contributing daily and hourly to the comfort of husbands, of parents, of brothers and sisters. . . .

In forming and improving the general manners, disposition and conduct of the other sex. . . .

In modelling the human mind during the early stages of its growth. . . .[36]

Throughout the work, the influence of Rousseau is evident. For Gisborne, woman's life, like that of Sophie in *Émile*, was relative to that of the man, thus female education was to be planned around woman's domestic role. Woman, he argued, was, by nature, physically weaker and more delicate and modest than man. Like Rousseau, Gisborne argued that these distinctions between men and women formed the basis of the argument for the different education of men and women. The education of women and girls emerges, in Gisborne's work, as an education in conduct:

> The primary end of [female] education is to train up the pupil in the
> knowledge and application of . . . principles of conduct. . . .[37]

The principles of conduct appropriate to young women were laid down
in a number of popular contemporary conduct books. The most widely read
conduct books of the eighteenth century were Dr James Fordyce's *Sermons to
Young Women* (1765), Dr John Gregory's *A Father's Legacy to His Daughters*
(1774), and *Advice to a Daughter*, by George Saville, Marquis of Halifax,
which first appeared in 1688, and was reprinted at least fourteen times
throughout the eighteenth century. Halifax, an aristocrat and a Whig, saw
marriage as an establishment 'upon which the order of humane Society doth
so much depend' and argued that there was no place in the natural order for
female education other than education in submission:

> You must lay it down for a foundation in general, that there is *Inequality*
> in the *Sexes*, and that for the better oeconomy of the World, the Men,
> who were to be the lawgivers, had the larger share of reason bestow'd
> upon them; by which means your Sex is better prepar'd for the *Compli-
> ance* that is necessary for the better performance of those *Duties* which
> seem to be most properly assigned to it.[38]

For Halifax, the subjection 'demanded of members of the state by a just ruler,
[was] extended, by a . . . patriarchal analogy, to women within marriage'.[39]
For Gregory and Fordyce, writing later, the object of female education was
still social stability, but their new language of sensibility masked actual power
relations by offering women, as Vivien Jones (1990) has pointed out, 'the
promise of romantic attachment and personal choice'.[40]

By and large, eighteenth century conduct literature advised women that
happiness could be secured only by subverting the desire to be educated, or,
at very least, by hiding one's education. As Gregory cautioned in *A Father's
Legacy to his Daughters* (1774):

> Be even cautious in displaying your good sense. It will be thought you
> assume a superiority over the rest of the company. But if you have any
> learning, keep it a profound secret, especially from the men, who gen-
> erally look, with a jealous and malignant eye on a woman of great parts,
> and a cultivated understanding.[41]

Advice which limited the development of the social and intellectual female
was not exclusively the reserve of men. Hannah More wrote that 'girls should
be taught to give up their opinions betimes, and not pertinaciously to carry
on a dispute, even if they should know themselves to be in the right',[42] while

Lady Pennington's *An Unfortunate Mother's Advice to her Absent Daughters* (4th edn., 1768) advised:

> A sensible woman will soon be convinced, that all the learning her utmost application can make her mistress of, will be from the difference of education, in many points, inferior to that of a schoolboy: this reflection will keep her always humble, and will be an effective check to that loquacity which renders some women such insupportable companions.[43]

The fact that popular conduct literature counselled women to hide their erudition suggests that learned women were more visible by the end of the eighteenth century. It also suggests that erudition was viewed, at least by some men and women, as unfeminine and that it drew into question a woman's chances of finding a husband. On the other hand, the last decades of the eighteenth century saw an increase not only in scientific works by and for women, but a serious interest in the question of female education. Arguably the esteem in which some women scientists and novelists were held, and their relative success in these fields, had contributed to increased confidence among women. In addition, women began to equate education with civil liberty. The century had opened with the words of Astell, Makin and Woolley on the lips of learned English women. By the end of the century the complexities implied by the struggle for their intellectual emancipation had been articulated most clearly by Mary Wollstonecraft and Hannah More.

VINDICATIONS: MARY WOLLSTONECRAFT AND THE FEMALE MIND

Both Mary Wollstonecraft and Hannah More were writing during a period of great social and political upheaval. It is therefore important to examine the background to their writing, not only to sketch out a backdrop to their lives but to see the extent to which these two women differed in their interpretation of the times in which they lived. One of the most powerful influences on contemporary England was the French Revolution. English radicals began to question the power of the aristocracy, and they challenged traditionalists such as Edmund Burke. This period of great change brought with it an air of optimism, reflected in the works of the Romantic poets. But, as Miriam Brody (1992) has argued, the intellectual core of English radicalism in the late eighteenth century had its roots in four decades of agitation: it was 'as old as Locke's *Second Treatise* (1689) and as recent as Rousseau's *Social Contract* (1762)'.[44] It is small wonder that these two writers had such a powerful influence on the more radical of the two writers examined in this chapter: Mary

Wollstonecraft. Locke had argued that the consent of the individual was a prerequisite for the legal authority of a government, and this could be withdrawn as freely as it had been given. As such, the Constitution could be changed by the individuals in the community if they reasoned that the power invested in the authorities had been abused. This ability to reason intelligently was cultivated by education, and the connection between civil liberty and education was obvious to Wollstonecraft when she argued firstly for the rights of man, and later for the rights of woman.

Supporters of the *status quo,* including Edmund Burke, emphasized the infallibility of the governmental system and the hierarchical order within society, arguing that respect for rank and privilege was a necessity if the country was to flourish. The Constitution guaranteed that the balance of power would be passed on to successive generations of English gentlemen, and, in return, the nobility would protect the Crown and the people. In Parliament, Lords and Commons were autonomous, thus a crucial question was *who* should reform parliament, rather than how it should be reformed. For Burke, who had no faith in the rationality of the people, Parliament needed only the approval of the Houses; it was above change and should be protected from the threats of radicals and dissenters. By the second half of the eighteenth century, 'it was estimated that 144 powerful individuals could in fact return a majority in the House'.[45] The House of Lords, comprised of Lords who inherited their seats, together with the House of Commons, which represented a tiny fraction of the English population, sat with little representation of England's dissenting population who were proscribed by the Test and Corporation Acts 'from holding any Crown appointment, or belonging to any municipal borough, or holding Oxford or Cambridge University degrees'.[46] In addition, since 1678 no town had received borough rights or rights of representation. The new industrial centres of Leeds, Manchester and Birmingham were disenfranchised. In such a climate, the dissenting communities of Presbyterians, Baptists and Independents sent, from their prestigious Dissenting Academies, repeated petitions to Parliament, and in the 1790s the reform movement had gained widespread popular support. Thomas Paine's the *Rights of Man* had, by 1793, sold approximately 200,000 copies (a significant figure when compared to the 30,000 copies of Burke's *Reflections* which had sold), and the meetings of popular democratic movements such as the London Corresponding Society sometimes attracted over 100,000 people. As tensions mounted, its leaders, Thomas Hardy, John Horne Tooke, and John Thelwall were indicted as traitors in 1794, and Pitt repressed free speech with the Treasonable Practices Act. Additionally, the Seditious Meetings Act, and suspension of Habeas Corpus in 1798 served to dampen the spirit of reform. Against this backdrop of demands for freedom and human rights, it is hardly surprising to find that a number of educated women should make a formal bid for civil rights for their sex. Mary Wollstonecraft took it upon herself to make the most sustained and radical argument for female emancipation, having seen that those articulating the contemporary demand for the 'rights of man' did not automatically extend those rights to women, and she laid the demand for female education as the cornerstone of the establishment of the equality of the sexes.

While best remembered for her *Vindication of the Rights of Woman* (1792), Mary Wollstonecraft published nine works during her lifetime, and a further two publications went into print after her death.[47] Their titles suggest a diversity of interests over some ten years, yet most of her books were educational. She wrote both to educate and to discuss education, and in so doing she exposed fundamental weaknesses in contemporary thought concerning the education of girls. This would lead her to debate the position of women in society with an unprecedented passion and logic, and would earn her, in her own lifetime, the much-quoted title of 'hyena in petticoats'.[48] A century later, her life would be re-appraised and a study of her works would testify to her threefold gift: 'the practical skill of the educator, the zeal of the reformer, and the thoughtfulness of the philosopher'.[49] Because she lived in an era which supported the image and the education of woman as presented by Rousseau in the fifth chapter of *Émile,* it is pertinent to examine her life to see the extent to which it complied with this image. From this can be ascertained the extent which her personal experiences influenced her rationalist philosophy of female education. Such an examination leads one to the conclusion that her childhood experiences of family life may well have jaundiced her opinion of marital happiness and family unity, while her subsequent experiences as a governess and teacher doubtless directed the course of her early educational writings.[50]

Wollstonecraft, the second of seven children, was born in 1759, in Epping Forest near London. Although eager to rise in the world as a gentleman farmer, her father had not the industry of her grandfather who had generated the family wealth out of his weaving business and he moved his growing family from farm to farm in England and Wales, never settling in any one place for any length of time, and gradually dissipating his wealth. His frequent ill-humour, and her mother's obvious preference for her eldest son, caused Mary to seek comfort and companionship in her friendships, the closest of which was with Fanny Blood whom she met when she was sixteen. It was with Fanny that she would eventually open a school in 1784, although she first sought independence and paid employment by working as a companion to a wealthy widow in Bath. She returned home after a short time to nurse her dying mother, became the sole supporter of her father, and eventually financed the education of her brothers and sisters. With her sisters and Fanny Blood, she established a school in 1784, choosing Newington Green, the

centre of an intellectual Dissenting community, as the location. Her neighbours at Newington Green included the elderly Dr Richard Price, a parliamentary reform activist, with whom she formed a lasting friendship. His
influence on her thought is obvious: he espoused the primacy of reason arguing that 'Sense sees only the outside of things; reason acquaints itself with
their natures . . . knowledge implies an *active* , vital energy of the mind exerted about intellectual objects, whereby they are understood, and satisfacto-
rily comprehended.'[51] Wollstonecraft developed her argument for female
education on precisely this premise, arguing that the contemporary syllabus
of 'novels, music, poetry and gallantry, all tend to make women the creatures
of sensation'.[52] In her *Vindication of the Rights of Woman* she quoted Thomas
Day's *Sandford and Merton*:

> If women are in general feeble both in body and mind, it arises less
> from nature than from education. We encourage a vicious indolence
> and inactivity, which we falsely call delicacy; instead of hardening their
> minds by the severer principles of reason and philosophy, we breed
> them to useless arts, which terminate in vanity and sensuality.[53]

Price, in his *Review*, describes the 'surprising sagacity and inexhaustible fe-
cundity of reason' to which a 'great injury' is done by 'confining it to the
narrow limits of sense, fancy, or experience'.[54] While eighteenth-century
intellectuals implicitly suggested that 'a female's most salient characteristic is
her emotional responsiveness',[55] Wollstonecraft, influenced by Price and Locke,
sought to re-define the role of woman in an age of reason and enlightenment.

Following her marriage to Hugh Skeys in 1784, Fanny Blood moved to
Portugal where the weather was thought more suited to her frail health. In
1785, upon hearing of her friends' approaching confinement and deteriorat-
ing health, Mary travelled to Portugal only to witness her friends' death.
There followed a period of loneliness and depression, during which time her
school foundered and she turned to writing to make some money. Her *Thoughts
on the Education of Daughters* was published by Joseph Johnson in 1787, and it
earned her ten guineas which she gave to Fanny's impoverished family. Obliged
to pursue the only other respectable profession available to middle-class
women, Wollstonecraft sought a governessing position and upon the recom-
mendation of her friend Mrs Burgh she was directed to report to the Revd
John Prior at Eton College, to meet the children of Lord Kingsborough and
accompany them to Ireland. The few days spent at Eton made an impression
on Wollstonecraft, which would influence her later evaluation of the public
school system in her *Vindication of the Rights of Woman*. She found the masters
and their wives to be frivolous and superficial. From Eton she wrote to her
sister, Everina:

> In short I could not live the life they lead at Eton – nothing but dress and
> ridicule going forward – and I really believe their fondness for ridicule
> tends to make them affected – the women in their manners and the men
> in their conversation. . . . Vanity in one shape or another reigns trium-
> phant. . . . A false kind of politeness throws a varnish over every char-
> acter.[56]

Wollstonecraft then travelled to Ireland to begin her new position. From
the start she felt uncomfortable with the trappings of life at Mitchelstown
Castle, finding herself surrounded with women as superficial and silly as the
masters' wives at Eton. Her letters at this time reveal a heightened sense of
her predicament. Of her arrival she wrote:

> . . . I entered the great gates with the same kind of feeling as I should
> have if I was going into the Bastille – . . . I found I was to encounter a
> *host* of females – my lady, her step-mother, and three sisters, and Mrsus
> [*sic*] and Misses without number – who of course, would examine me
> with the most minute attention.[57]

Wollstonecraft was in charge of the education of three girls, the eldest in
whom she appears to have taken an interest, and her letters suggest the direction that her later writing will take as she discusses the aimless education she
is to offer to a bright girl:

> She has a wonderful capacity but she has such a multiplicity of
> employments it has not room to expand itself – and in all probability
> will be lost in a heap of rubbish miss-called accomplishments. I am
> grieved at being obliged to continue so wrong a system.[58]

Her stay at Mitchelstown was short: Lady Kingsborough found Wollstonecraft
too opinionated, and she dismissed her for insubordination. This did not
worry Wollstonecraft unduly. She had used her free time in Ireland to write
her first novel, *Mary, a Fiction* (1788), and she had maintained a correspondence with the London publisher Joseph Johnson, who had published *Thoughts
on the Education of Daughters*. Johnson, the patron of many young writers including William Blake, encouraged Wollstonecraft to return to England on
the promise of some work as a translator, reader, and eventually reviewer, for
the *Analytical Review*. Her years working for the *Analytical Review* spanned
from 1787 to her death, with a short break from 1792 to 1796 when she
travelled to Norway, Sweden and Denmark. She had a natural aptitude for
reviewing, with a perceptive and often devastating ability to slice through the
vast quantities of popular literature that appeared in the late eighteenth cen-

tury, exposing literary incompetence and lack of originality, and she was often harshly critical of her own sex. Reviewing *The Child of Woe*, by Mrs
Elizabeth Norman she wrote:

> *The Child of Woe*, having no marked features to characterize it, we can
> only term it a truly feminine novel. Indeed, the generality of them . . .
> are so near akin to each other, that with a few very trifling alterations,
> the same review would serve for almost all of them.[59]

Wollstonecraft went so far as to say that she opened a novel 'with a degree of
pleasure, when *written by a lady*, is not inserted in the title page',[60] and dismissed the novels of the famous Bluestocking Fanny Burney as 'a flimsy kind
of writing' which had influenced other women writers, adding that a 'varied
combination of the same events has been adopted, and like timid sheep, the
lady authors jump over the hedge one after the other, and do not dream of
deviating either to the right or left'.[61] Neither was her own skill as a novelist
without reproach. *Mary, a Fiction* (1788) with its autobiographical heroine
and sentimental plot, reflects self-pity and a certain lack of distance from her
years of hardship. It traces the personal development of a young woman who
runs away from an unhappy marriage and experiences poverty and hardship
as she wanders about administering to the poor. However, while *Mary* is an
imperfect novel, it shows Wollstonecraft exploring themes that will become
central to her writing. Mary's mother is presented as a foolish woman who is
despised by her husband because she is uneducated and therefore uninterest-
ing: 'Her voice was but the shadow of a sound, and she had, to complete her
delicacy, so relaxed her nerves, that she became a mere nothing. . . . Many
such noughts are there in the female world!'[62] She educates her daughter
'with the expectation of a fortune',[63] a practice which Wollstonecraft condemned in *A Vindication of the Rights of Woman*.

Wollstonecraft, now twenty-eight years old, had decided not to return
to teaching but to earn her living by her pen. Nonetheless, apart from her
reviews, most of her work was educational in theme. She became part of a
circle of liberal and intellectual young radicals which included Henry Fuseli,
the Swiss painter, William Godwin, the political philosopher, the poet William
Blake, and Thomas Paine, author of the *Rights of Man*, who gathered occasionally at rooms above Joseph Johnson's bookshop in London. Johnson published her next work, *Original Stories from Real Life; with Conversations, Calculated
to Regulate the Affections, and Form the Mind to Truth and Goodness*, in 1788.
Written for children, *Original Stories* belonged to the tradition of moral and
didactic children's literature which was popular in the eighteenth century,
and it illustrated her early conviction that the years of childhood were important in character-formation.

Her interest in the education of children was doubtless deepened by her reading of Christian Gotthilf Salzmann's *Elements of Morality for the Use of Children*,[64] which she had translated into English in 1790, and *Letters on Education* by the historian Catherine Macaulay[65] which she reviewed for the *Analytical Review* in the same year. In her review, Wollstonecraft emphasized Macaulay's pious and humanitarian ideas, concluding that Macaulay displayed 'a degree of sound reason and profound thought which either through defective organs, or a mistaken education, seldom appears in female productions'.[66] Macaulay's *Letters*, together with Dr Price's sermon 'On the Love of Country', delivered in 1789, laid the groundwork for her educational philosophy as seen in *A Vindication of the Rights of Woman*. Price's sermon congratulated the French National Assembly, rejoiced in the prospects of civil liberty for France, and advocated 'a doctrine of perfectability which justified one's tampering with the social order as if it were a series of cogs and wheels which could be put right with the skills of a mechanic'.[67] Edmund Burke, seeing the sudden upheaval of traditional values as hugely dangerous, replied to Price's sermon with *Reflections on the French Revolution* (1790), in which he denied the doctrine of perfectibility and the rights of man, and argued forcefully against disregarding tradition and experience. His view of humanity suggested that it was flawed and, by nature, brutish. Wollstonecraft reacted to this attack on the perfectibility and reason of humanity with the first of many pamphlets that would appear at this time in defence of the principles so dear to London's liberal reformers. She hastily wrote and published *A Vindication of the Rights of Men* (1790), vigorously attacking Burke's position, establishing herself at the forefront of the apostles of the Enlightenment and bringing herself fully into the public eye.

In the *Rights of Men*, she included in her attack the practice of primogeniture, supported by Burke as part of the natural social order, and she exposed the hypocrisy and selectivity of his extension of sympathy to the French Queen and a few other titled women while ignoring the thousands of ordinary women who suffered. These are but two examples of Wollstonecraft defending the position of her sex in this publication: in fact she wrote *The Rights of Men* to defend the position of working men whom she saw as the subordinate class in the contemporary debate. Failing to see her own sex as oppressed at this time, she later became critical of the Revolution when she realised that civil liberties did not necessarily extend to women. In France, the French National Assembly was considering a plan by Talleyrand to provide education for boys but limit it for girls, suggesting to Wollstonecraft, and to the Frenchwoman Olympe de Gouges, that 'the rights envisioned by the Assembly in its Declaration of the Rights of Men were indeed just that'.[68] Olympe de Gouges wrote an ironic commentary on the situation in *A Declaration of the Rights of Woman* at the same time that Wollstonecraft began *A*

Vindication of the Rights of Woman. Wollstonecraft optimistically dedicated her work to Talleyrand in the hope of influencing the situation in France, but it was in England that it would have its greatest impact.

Wollstonecraft's *A Vindication of the Rights of Men* is rightly described by Janet Todd as containing the embryonic ideas of *The Rights of Woman,* for while she had previously argued for civil and religious liberties for mankind, she now specifically demanded the same for woman, calling for a 'revolution in female manners' and an assertion of woman's right to reason, and acknowledging that this revolution, like the French Revolution, would have social and political consequences.

In December of 1892 she left for France, in the hope of seeing the effects of the Revolution close at hand. She was in Paris for the beheading of the King, and was appalled that so many people were guillotined merely because they were, in name, noble. She became disillusioned with the Revolution, and questioned the possibility of human perfectibility in the light of such brutality. Nevertheless, when she wrote *An Historical and Moral View of the Origin and Progress of the French Revolution* (1774), she indicated her belief that out of the 'chaotic mass a fairer government is rising. . . . But things must have time to find their level'.[69] This work outlined the principles of human equality and the role of government in establishing and protecting it:

> Nature having made men unequal, by giving stronger bodily and mental powers to one than to another, the end of government ought to be, to destroy this inequality by protecting the weak.[70]

She would equally make this demand of the government concerning the question of the equality of the sexes, believing it to be a political and social issue.

It is somewhat ironic that at this time Mary Wollstonecraft was involved in a romantic relationship with the American Gilbert Imlay, a writer of a sentimental novels who was interested in using the Revolution for financial gain.[71] She grew to rely almost totally on his company, and lived in virtual seclusion near Paris, depending upon his sporadic visits for company. Her letters to Imlay indicate that they shared few moments of happiness, and although she was widely known as Mrs Imlay, they were not married and he appears to have lost interest in the relationship at an early stage. The record of their relationship was published in a volume of letters included by Johnson in *Posthumous Works* (1798), and later in a controversial volume called *Love Letters of Mary Wollstonecraft to Gilbert Imlay* (1908). The reasons for contemporary public censure of the letters was twofold: few people could understand how Wollstonecraft's husband, William Godwin, could flaunt his wife's affair in public when he edited the volume, nor could they tolerate the pub-

lication of the love letters of a woman who had borne her lover an illegitimate child.

Wollstonecraft had often expressed her belief that a happy domestic environment was necessary for proper child-rearing, and she was anxious that
her daughter, Fanny, would never experience this while Imlay lived apart
from them. She followed him to England in 1795, to discover his infidelity.
Her attempted suicide by poison was followed by Imlay dispatching her to
Scandinavia to act as his business agent, although he did not join her there.
While there she compiled a travel journal, *Letters Written During a short Residence in Sweden, Norway and Denmark* (1796). It was arguably her best-liked
publication, displaying her pensive state of mind and an ability to produce
lyrical prose when describing natural beauty, and her usual detractors found
nothing to offend in this work. She returned to England in 1795, re-estab-
lished herself within her London circle of intellectuals, and began a sustaining
relationship with the author William Godwin. They married when she became pregnant in 1797, but Wollstonecraft died following complications
after the birth of a daughter, Mary, in August 1798.

Immediately following her death, Wollstonecraft continued to be the
object of discussion, vilification and abuse. Godwin published *Posthumous
Works* (1798) and his *Memoirs* of her life, and was ridiculed for his truthful-
ness about her life. His report of her death included reference to that fact that,
in keeping with their beliefs, nothing of a religious nature was said at her bed-
side and there was no clergyman present. He noted that during her whole
illness 'not one word of a religious cast fell from her lips',[72] only to be attacked in the *Gentleman's Magazine* (1798) for having triumphed in this cir-
cumstance. Of Godwin, the author wrote:

> . . . he has disclosed *some circumstances* which one might have supposed
> delicacy to the memory of the deceased would have prompted him to
> have concealed. . . . If Mr. G. proposes the subject of his *Memoirs* as a
> pattern to her lovely and amiable sex, I hope, and I firmly believe, few,
> if any, will be found who would wish to be endowed with the splendid
> talents of a Mary Woolstonecraft [*sic*], if they must part with that which
> alone can induce peace and serenity into the mind.[73]

In the same year Richard Polwhele published his poem 'The Unsex'd Females' in which he attacked her for her desire to unsex women by advocating
female reason, and described her life as one of dissipation, and licentiousness.
In 1801 the *Anti-Jacobin Review* published another vicious poem, 'The Vision
of Liberty', which castigated Godwin's *Memoirs* saying, 'With won-
drous glee and pride, this simple wight/Her brothel feats of wantonness sets
down. . . '.[74] and her life and works continued to provoke heated debate and

much condemnation, into the next century. The controversy which surrounded her personal life, and the association of her name with the emancipation of women, has eclipsed her very considerable contribution to female education. To date, her position as an educational theorist remains largely overlooked.

Because of the peripatetic life-style of her father, Mary Wollstonecraft was never in any one village long enough to have had a proper school education. While she attended some day schools around Beverly in Yorkshire, she was, like many other women mentioned in this study, self-taught. Despite the fact that she had neither the privacy for quiet study nor the books for reading, she developed an intellectual curiosity that sustained her until she left home in 1778, to earn her own living. She always wrote, although she did not earn her living by her journalism until 1787. Her first publication, *Thoughts on the Education of Daughters* (1787) reveals an early interest in education, and was influenced by her time spent running a small school at Newington Green. It was not an original piece of work: in it she criticised female vanity, but she did not question contemporary female ideology. The traditional Christian concept of the role of the woman was supported, and her first educational work sits easily among the eighteenth-century genre of conduct books which she would later condemn in *A Vindication of the Rights of Woman*. Questions thus present themselves to the Wollstonecraft reader. Why did her philosophy of education change so radically over a period of five years? To what extent was she representative of contemporary women? Why was her educational *magnum opus*, *A Vindication of the Rights of Woman*, received with such marked hostility? To trace the development of Wollstonecraft's educational writing is to attempt to understand Wollstonecraft. It is an endeavour to establish the degree to which she challenged the dominant ideology of female propriety in the light of political and religious constraints: constraints which she would increasingly ignore.

The most widely known of Wollstonecraft's works, *A Vindication of the Rights of Woman*, was devoted to a discussion of female education and the effects of its neglect. Her less well known writings show the genesis of this concern. Much of her reviewing for the *Analytical Review* was on pedagogical treatises and children's books, and at her death she left an unfinished manuscript, 'Letters on the Management of Infants'. She based her rationalist philosophy of education on a belief that character is determined by upbringing. Like More, she believed that the evils of society could be eradicated if infants were well raised. Her early works are pious in tone, as she confronts the evils of life in the light of divine purpose.

Thoughts on the Education of Daughters was written in six weeks in 1786, to illustrate the results of the inadequate education afforded to girls, and to propose a more rational one. Based on the theories of John Locke, it suggested that children should be treated as individuals. The mind, a *tabula rasa* at birth, should be filled with ideas, which the intellect will test in a search for Truth. Infants do not, Locke argued, 'bring many ideas into the world with them'.[75] He developed his theory of understanding on the basis of 'God having fitted men with faculties and means to discover, receive, and retain truths, accordingly as they are employed'.[76] Wollstonecraft extended this to women, accepting for them also the criticism that '. . . some (and those the most) taking things upon trust, misemploy their power of assent, by lazily enslaving their minds to the dictates and dominion of others. . . '.[77] In *Thoughts on the Education of Daughters*, Wollstonecraft advised parents that 'reason should cultivate and govern those instincts which are implanted in us',[78] adding 'Above all teach . . . [children] to combine their ideas. It is of more use than can be conceived, for a child to learn to compare things that are similar in some respects, and different in other. I wish them to be taught to think'.[79]

In *Thoughts on the Education of Daughters*, Wollstonecraft entered the erstwhile predominantly male domain of attacking female vanity. She condemned 'the whole tribe of beauty-washes, Olympian dew, oriental herbs, liquid bloom and . . . paint'[80] but, like Mary Astell, she blamed women's inability to amuse themselves constructively on their lack of education. 'Your *Glass* will not do you half so much service as a serious reflection on your own Minds',[81] wrote Astell; Wollstonecraft answered this one hundred years later as she wrote:

> Very frequently, when education has been neglected, the mind improves itself, if it has leisure for reflection, and experience to reflect on; but how can this happen when they are forced to act before they have had time to think, or find that they are unhappily married?[82]

Both Astell and Wollstonecraft used Platonic imagery to point out that women's inferior education was responsible for their inferior understanding of ideas:

> Whence is it but from ignorance, from a want of understanding to compare and judges of things . . . that we quit the substance for the Shadow, reality for Appearance . . . tho they have nothing of the Nature of those venerable Objects we desire and seek?[83]
>
> (Mary Astell, *A Serious Proposal*)

> Men have in some respects very much the advantage. If they have a tolerable understanding, it has a chance to be cultivated. They are forced to see human nature as it is, and are not left to dwell on the pictures of their own imagination.[84]
>
> (Mary Wollstonecraft, *Vindication*)

A comparison of Astell and Wollstonecraft reveals other shared similarities in thought. Both argued that virtue was dependent on knowledge. Astell wrote:

> That therefore women are unprofitable to most, and a plague and a dishonour to some men is not much to be regretted on account of the Men because 'tis the product of their own folly in denying them the benefits of an ingenuous and liberal Education, the most effectual means to direct them into, and secure their progress in the ways of Virtue.[85]

While Wollstonecraft wrote:

> . . . the most perfect education, in my opinion, is such as exercise of the understanding as is best calculated to strengthen the body and form the heart. Or, in other words, to enable the individual to attain such habits of virtue as will render it independent. In fact, it is a farce to call any being virtuous whose virtues do not result from the exercise of its own reason.[86]

Later in life, Wollstonecraft would become cynical about the church, the clergy, and the notion of providence. However, in her early works she shared with Astell a conviction that life was a preparation for 'immortal bliss' and that education would show women how to attain such bliss through a virtuous life:

> The main business of our lives is to learn to be virtuous; and who is training us up for immortal bliss, knows best what trials will contribute to make it so; and our resignation and improvement will render us respectable to ourselves, and to that Being, whose approbation is of more value than life itself.[87]
>
> (Mary Wollstonecraft, *Vindication*)

> A desire to advance and perfect its Being, is planted by GOD in all Rational natures, to excite them hereby to every worthy and becoming Action; for certainly, next to the Grace of GOD, nothing does so powerfully restrain people from Evil, and stir them up to Good. . . .[88]
>
> (Mary Astell, *A Serious Proposal*)

The emphasis on teaching females to attain virtue through reason provided Wollstonecraft with the central theme of her next work, *Original Stories from Real Life* (1788). Here she followed her own advice in *Thoughts*, as she argued for instructing children through tales, a practice also favoured by Hannah

More. *Original Stories* reflected both her time spent as a governess to the Kingsboroughs, and her reading of *Emile* in which Rousseau stressed the importance of experience in education.[89] In *Original Stories*, Mrs Mason, through a series of moral tales, brings her two charges to an understanding of virtue and vice, through the application of reasoned thought. It is very possible that *Original Stories* was influenced by Sarah Fielding's *The Governess, or Little Female Academy* (1749). Fielding's book, the earliest known full length novel written specifically for young people and the first school story for girls, has at its centre a Mrs Teachum to whom nine students tell their stories. Through each story Fielding highlights common weaknesses and prejudices, and Mrs Teachum suggests more progressive attitudes. Anticipating Wollstonecraft, she insists that 'Happiness must dwell in the Mind, and depends upon no outward Accidents'.[90] *The Governess*, still in print in 1903, influenced Maria Edgeworth, Charles and Mary Lamb, and Charlotte Yonge: it is not impossible that Wollstonecraft had both its format and its general theme in mind when she penned *Original Stories*. She did, however, acknowledge the influence on *Original Stories* of Salzmann's *Moralisches Elementarbuch*, which she had translated in 1790.

In *Original Stories*, Wollstonecraft discussed bad parenting, the development of good habits and the importance of virtue. Although these were themes in *Thoughts*, in *Original Stories* their significance was more successfully imparted by virtue of the fact that the young girls learn of them by experience. 'Knowledge', Wollstonecraft argues, 'should be gradually imparted, and flow more from example than teaching'.[91] By the fifth chapter, Mrs Mason is satisfied that her duty is done and she can, like Mary Poppins, move on to where she is next needed. Mrs Mason's parting words urge the girls to 'love truth' reflecting Wollstonecraft's personal philosophy at that time.

By the time she came to publish her next work, *A Vindication of the Rights of Men* (1790), she was committed to a love of truth, but her sense of religious duty had been supplanted by a belief that God was not to be dutifully served, but was a 'sublime power' with 'wise and good' motives:

> . . . I submit to the moral laws which my reason deduces from this view of my dependence on him. – It is not his power that I fear – it is not an arbitrary will, but to unerring reason that I submit.[92]

At this point, the seeds of Mary Wollstonecraft's mature philosophy of education take root. She established the primacy of reason in the quest for knowledge, even knowledge of God, and does not waver from this position again in her writings.

The primacy of reason provided Wollstonecraft with a basis for her refutation of some of the long-standing assumptions about the biological and moral inferiority of woman, as she attacked Burke's *Reflections*:

> You may have convinced them that *littleness* and *weakness* are the very essence of beauty; and that the Supreme Being, in giving women beauty in the most supereminent degree, seemed to command them, by the powerful voice of Nature, not to cultivate the moral virtues that might chance to excite respect, and interfere with the pleasing sensations they were created to inspire.[93]

Here Wollstonecraft replaced the 'Nature' argument for female behaviour with an argument for 'moral virtues' cultivated by reason.

A Vindication of the Rights of Men, written in response to Burke's *Reflections*, did not set out to define the female role. Nonetheless, in it Wollstonecraft attacked the practices primogeniture and arranged marriages as evils of society. The effects of these social practices on women shaped her thought as expressed in *A Vindication of the Rights of Woman*. She considered that inheritance was 'a barbarous, feudal institution, that enables the eldest son to overpower talents and depress virtue' arguing that 'the only security of property that nature authorizes and reason sanctions, is the right a man has to enjoy the acquisitions which his talent and industry have acquired; and to bequeath them to who he chooses'.[94] In 1792, she concluded that reason equally extended human rights to women when she wrote the work with which her name has become synonymous.

A Vindication of the Rights of Woman was the work in which all previous arguments for the inferiority of the female mind are synthesized, and new ground was broken as Wollstonecraft claimed for woman the 'power of improvement, the power of discerning truth'.[95] In it, Wollstonecraft questioned the contemporary definition of woman's social role, and established that it was wrong. She challenged an ideology that denied to woman the ability to perceive moral truth by an act of intelligence, arguing that since reason is an emanation of divinity, it must be the same in all. She agreed with Locke when he defined reason as 'natural revelation, whereby the Eternal Father of Light, and Fountain of all knowledge, communicates to mankind that portion of truth which he has laid within the reach of their natural faculties'.[96] To this she added in *A Vindication of the Rights of Woman* that the nature of reason must be the same in all, if it is truly an emanation of divinity. Hers was not the conventional position of those who supported a limited education for women to make them better wives and mothers: it was influenced by her liberal politics. She saw the education of woman as fundamental to the well-being of the state. Deprived of the education necessary for the cultivation of reason, the female position signalled a violation of divine law and human liberty.

Wollstonecraft was convinced that 'the neglected education' of her sex was responsible for their miserable position, and she attributed this neglect to 'a false system of education, gathered from the books written on this subject by men who, considering females rather as women than human creatures, have been more anxious to make them alluring mistresses than affectionate wives and rational mothers. . . '.[97] She did not doubt the fact that women and men were different, she simply questioned the way in which their differences had been interpreted by both men and uneducated women:

> In the government of the physical world it is observable that the female in point of strength is, in general, inferior to the male. This is the law of nature; and it does not appear to be suspended or abrogated in favour of women. A degree of physical superiority cannot, therefore, be denied – and it is a noble prerogative. But not content with this natural pre-eminence, men endeavour to sink us still lower, merely to render us alluring objects for a moment, and women, intoxicated by the adoration which men, under the influences of their senses, pay them, do not seek to obtain a durable interest in their hearts, or to become the friends of the fellow creatures who find amusement in their society.[98]

Her examination of the contemporary lamentable state of female education included a discussion of the best-known conduct literature of the day, and a sustained argument against the presentation of Sophie's education in Rousseau's *Émile*. In *A Vindication of the Rights of Woman*, Wollstonecraft also attacked the arguments of Fordyce,[99] and Gregory.[100] Of Fordyce's *Sermons* she wrote:

> I should not allow girls to pursue them, unless I designed to hunt our very spark of nature out of their composition, melting every human quality into female meekness and artificial grace.[101]

Against Gregory's advice to women to hide their learning from men lest they should appear unattractive, she retorted:

> Surely it would have been wiser to have advised women to improve themselves till they rose above the fumes of vanity; and then to let the public opinion come round – for where are rules of accommodation to stop?[102]

While she argued that she could have searched the 'annals of antiquity' for predecessors of Drs Gregory and Fordyce, and Rousseau, she chose to confine her discussion, almost entirely, to contemporary writers and educationalists to conclude that the 'grand source of female folly and vice . . . arise[s] from narrowness of mind; and the very constitution of civil governments has put almost insuperable obstacles in the way to prevent the cultivation of female understanding; yet virtue can be built on no other foundation'.[103]

In discussing the ethics which Rousseau taught girls in *Émile*, she argued that if 'virtue' was applied differentially to men and women then it was a 'sexual virtue'. Cunning and dissimulation, which Rousseau found charming in girls, were sexual virtues since he found them demeaning in a man. She believed such virtues to be immoral, dangerous and unnatural, and to encourage girls in unnatural behaviour was to encourage the development of 'non-reasonable' human beings. For Wollstonecraft, education was an imperative both to prevent the cultivation of sexual virtues and to foster the innate capacity for reason which she believed women had in equal measure to men.

When Wollstonecraft acknowledged the responsibility of motherhood in *A Vindication*, she again stressed the importance of women's education, linking its significance to the well-being of the state. Her vision of female education was wider than that of her contemporaries: she did not simply wish to render women attractive to men, as did Rousseau and the writers of conduct books, she wanted to educate women because education brought with it the possibility of financial independence and in this respect Mary Wollstonecraft broke new ground. The *Vindication* demanded that traditions and laws which prevented a woman from working in society should be changed:

> How many women thus waste life away the prey of discontent, who might have practised as physicians, regulated a farm, managed a shop, and stood erect, supported by their own industry, instead of hanging their heads surcharged with the dew of sensibility. . . . I have seldom seen much compassion excited by the helplessness of females, unless they were fair. . . . How much more respectable is the woman who earns her own bread by fulfilling any duty, than the most accomplished beauty![104]

The *Vindication* was arguably the most original contribution to the debate about women's education in England in the eighteenth century; it was also the work which contributed to Mary Wollstonecraft becoming one of the most vilified writers in the English language. As Miriam Brody (1992) has pointed out, 'no woman's revolt followed the publication of the *Vindication*. . . . Her own contemporaries called her a shameless wanton. . . . Early twentieth-century readers have called her an archetypal castrating female.'[105] Until recently, feminists shrank from association with what Brody calls 'their notorious progenitor', perhaps to disassociate themselves from the very attacks which her contemporaries made. But as historians increasingly rewrite and reinterpret the past in an endeavour to understand the role of women in society, Mary Wollstonecraft has been accorded her rightful position as the woman who dared to assume the doctrine of human rights for her own sex, and who wrote what may be seen as the first declaration of female independence. Her abiding commitment was to establish that human reason was the same in man and woman and, from this point, to argue that all humans are equal. She was, first and foremost, an educationalist. She saw education as the great liberating force which had been denied to her sex, and she continues directly from the seventeenth-century writer Mary Astell in both her analysis of the position of women in society and her conclusion that in education lay the key to equality.

STRICTURES: HANNAH MORE AND THE IDEOLOGY OF FEMININITY

The childhood and youth of Hannah More contrasts starkly with that of Mary Wollstonecraft. More was born into a family which, if not wealthy, was comfortably off and happy. Her father, Jacob More, a Tory and High Church man who doubtless exerted great influence on her intellectual development, was born around 1700 at Thorpe Hall, in Norfolk. It was assumed that he would take Holy Orders, but, on failing to inherit an estate which would have furnished him with financial means, he moved to Bristol. There he worked as a supervisor of the excise, until appointed to a school at Fishponds, in the parish of Stapleton, Bristol. He married Mary Grace, a girl from a farming family, and they raised five daughters at the school house in Manor Road, Fishponds. Hannah was their fourth child, born on 2 February 1745.

It would seem that Jacob More did not share the contemporary belief in the inferiority of the female mind, nor did he assume that his daughters would not need to earn a living. Hannah's memoirs record that 'it was the wish of the parents that their children should be qualified to procure for themselves a respectable independence by the establishment of a boarding school',[106] and he educated them thoroughly, and sent his eldest daughter, Mary, to a French school in Bristol so that she could then teach the younger girls, Elizabeth, Sarah, Hannah and Patty. At home, Hannah was taught Latin, Greek, English and mathematics by her father, although he stopped her mathematics lesson, fearing that her brain might be damaged by over-work. When the family moved into Bristol, the nineteen year-old Mary opened a school, with Elizabeth as housekeeper and the three younger sisters enroled as pupils. On 11 March 1758, a Bristol paper noted:

> At No. 6 in Trinity Street, near the College Green. On Monday after Easter will be opened a School for Young Ladies by Mary More and Sisters, where will be carefully taught French, Reading, Writing, Arithmetic, and Needlework. Young Ladies boarded on reasonable terms.[107]

The school was funded in part by subscriptions raised from a number of wealthy subscribers, including the Dowager Duchess of Beaufort. The prosperity of the school allowed the girls to move location to 43 Park Street, a fashionable shopping street, and there they remained until 1790, by which time the reputation of the school benefitted from the growing fame of its former under-governess, Hannah. At the age of sixteen, she wrote her first work, a play called *The School for Happiness*, which sold 10,000 copies. In it she suggested that girls would not make poorer wives and mothers because of a little education.

It is arguable that her writing career might have been cut short if she had chosen to become a wife and mother; as it happened, the jilting of Hannah More by her fiancé, Edward Turner, resulted in his settling an annuity on her which gave her the financial independence to move to London and join the best literary circles. Turner, a middle-aged squire from Wraxall, postponed their wedding on two occasions, and on the third he jilted her at the altar. This did not prevent them from remaining friends, and in addition to her £200 annuity, he left her £1000 in his will.

On the strength of her financial independence, she and her sisters, Patty and Sarah, went to London in 1773-4. Her *Memoirs* indicate that she was an immediate social success. She met and became great friends with the celebrated actor David Garrick, who invited her to his home to meet the celebrated Bluestocking, Mrs Montagu, and at the home of Sir Joshua Reynolds she was introduced to a man who would become one of her greatest admirers: Dr Johnson.[108] Sarah's letters home indicate that she was proud of Hannah's popularity:

> Since I wrote last, Hannah has been introduced by Miss Reynolds to Baretti, and to Edmund Burke (the sublime and beautiful Edmund Burke!). . . .[109]

> Tuesday evening we drank tea at Sir Joshua's with Dr Johnson. Hannah is certainly a great favourite. She was placed next to him, and they had the entire conversation to themselves.[110]

Hannah's own letters home equally suggest the awe and delight with which she entered into her new circle of admiring luminaries. She frequently listed names of guests at parties she attended, and lavished praise on their wit, and conversation:

> I had yesterday the pleasure of dining in Hill Street, Berkely Square, *at a certain Mrs Montagu's, a name not totally obscure* [her italics]. The party consisted of herself, Mrs. Carter, Dr. Johnson . . . Mrs Boscawen, Miss Reynolds, and Sir Joshua, (the idol of every company;) some other persons of high rank and less wit, and your humble servant.[111]

A year later, she is securely at the centre of this circle, and her tolerance of people lacking in 'sentiment' is more pronounced:

> Just returned from spending one of the most agreeable days of my life, with the female *Maecenas* of Hill Street; she engaged me 5 or 6 days ago to dine with her, and had assembled half the wits of the age. . . . I spent my time going from one to the other of these little societies, as I happened more or less to like the subjects they were discussing. . . . Mrs Scott, . . . Mrs Carter, Mrs Barbauld . . . Mrs Montagu, Dr Johnson, the Provost of Dublin, and two other ingenious men . . . [were] interesting . . . it was amusing to see how the people of sentiment singled out each other, and how the fine ladies and pretty gentlemen naturally slid into each other's society.[112]

Her admiration for these people was reciprocated. Dr Johnson knew her verses by heart, inviting himself to her house to drink tea and read her poetry aloud. Her circle also praised her plays, the most successful of which was *Percy* (1777). *Percy* played for twenty-two full nights at the Theatre Royal in Drury Lane, and her royalties came to £600,[113] a fortune in her time, and the celebrated hostess Mrs Montagu booked boxes for three nights. Hannah More's plays and poetry have not withstood the test of time; so obvious are her rhyming verses that it is difficult to imagine how Garrick, Johnson and Montagu found merit in them. However, as R. Brimley Johnson (1925) has argued, 'Flattery was then the habit, and . . . she expressed with direct and vigorous simplicity, a number of feelings and thoughts that were in the air.'[114] She was, in this sense, a good journalist and a clever business woman. Her output was astonishingly rapid, and she could turn her hand with equal facility from verse to drama. It is hardly surprising to find that she experimented successfully with the popular genre of conduct literature in 1777, when she published *Essays on Various Subjects Principally Designed for Young Ladies*. It was dedicated to Mrs. Montagu, and it presented a conservative opinion of the role of woman in society, reflecting a common belief in the civilizing influence of women but limiting their involvement in worldly affairs. It is, essentially, the viewpoint of the *Bas Bleu*, and while the Bluestocking circle may have influenced the public perception of the intellectual ability of upper-class women, they cannot be accused of having revolutionised the system of female education in any way. In the title of *Essays . . . for Young Ladies*, More has limited her concerns in class terms. Then in the opening pages she limits *their* concerns in gender terms:

> Besides those important qualities common to both, each sex has its respective, appropriated qualifications, which would cease to be meritorious, the instant they ceased to be appropriated. Nature, propriety, and custom have prescribed certain bounds to each; bounds which the prudent and the candid will never attempt to break down.[115]

The years spent among London's literary élite, and the letters she wrote to her sisters during this period indicate little interest in either education or evangelicism, yet it is for these that Hannah More gained a place in English history. In 1796, a year of food shortage, it is reported that the singing of her ballad 'The Riot, or Half a Loaf is Better than no Bread' quelled a riot in Bath; the educationalist J.C. Colquhoun considered that the great improvement in religion and morals since the beginning of Victoria's reign was, to a very large degree, due to her writings,[116] and upon her death the woman who William Cobbett called the 'Old Bishop in Petticoats' left £30,000 to various charities and schools. These facts become more understandable in the light of her correspondence between 1785 and 1798, the years during which she gradually withdrew from society and developed a love of scripture which dictated the course that the second half of her life should take.

The death of her close friend Garrick in 1779 precipitated her complete loss of interest in the theatre. Her last play, performed in the year of Garrick's death, indicated in the preface that she had come to view with circumspection the role of literature in life:

> For if to govern realms belongs to few,
> Yet all who live have passions to subdue.
> Self-conquest is the lesson books should preach,
> Self-conquest is the theme the stage should teach.[117]

Her personal experience of self-conquest would appear to have been built upon the conflict between flattery and 'polished society', which left one spiritually impoverished, and the pursuit of truth and virtue, which promised eternal rewards. Around 1784 she retired from London to a cottage at Cowslip Green, under the Mendip Hills near Bristol. There she began her efforts to reform the fashionable society to which she had belonged, with *Thoughts on the Improvement of the Manners of the Great to General Society* (1788), and *An Estimate of the Religion of the Fashionable World* (1790). Her letters betray her increasing frustration with the society in which she was implicated. Shortly after the publication of *Manners of the Great*, she wrote:

> All one can do in a promiscuous society is not so much to start religious topics, as to extract from common subjects some useful and awful truth, and to counteract the mischief of a popular sentiment by one drawn from religion. . . . Fine people are ready enough to join you in reprobating vice; for they are not at *all* vicious; but their standard of vice is low; it is not the standard of the gospel.[118]

More's diaries indicate a period of soul-searching, as she tried to jettison her famous past. In 1794 she writes:'Many temptations this week to vanity. My picture asked for two publications. Dedications – flattery without end. God be praised, I *was* not flattered but vexed. . . .'[119] and subsequent entries indicate her continued concern with spiritual matters. 'How much better I might be', she reflects, 'had I fewer interruptions, more opportunity of vital preachers, more pious friends, less worldly company',[120] and one month later her thoughts anticipate the turn her life will take as she writes:'Lord, send more labourers into thy vineyard! Increase the number of those who preach Christ Jesus, and salvation through him only'.[121] Together with her sister Martha, she accepted a challenge from her friend William Wilberforce to 'do something for Cheddar', and began the Mendip Scheme, a programme of elementary education, religious instruction, and social welfare.

It would seem that Hannah More was destined to be famous, for even her moral tracts drew lavish praise. *Manners of the Great* went through seven editions, the third of which sold out in four hours. *Strictures on the Modern System of Female Education* prompted letters of admiration from Mrs Carter, Hester Chapone, Charles Burney, Mrs Barbauld, Mrs Montagu, Samuel Pepys, and the Bishop of Durham, and went through at least nine editions in two years, selling over 19,000 copies. Her *Cheap Repository Tracts* were so popular that by March 1796, over two million copies had been distributed through booksellers, pedlars, and friends of the repository. She was a publishers delight, never failing to produce material that would sell well, and attract the attention of important reviewers in fashionable magazines. However, while the fashionable world supported and applauded her work, it did not necessarily pay heed. Her own friends formed part of a society that thought religion was venerable, but did not necessarily see it as central to their lives. More was deeply frustrated by this, arguing repeatedly that it was the duty of the upperclasses to lead by example. She eventually turned her attention exclusively to the development of the Mendip Schools, and the Women's Friendly Societies. These were welfare clubs which collected small subscriptions from women and then offered them financial benefits in time of sickness, maternity, and funerals. The women were given religious and moral instruction, taught house-keeping skills, and encouraged to attend church. Each year she organised a Mendip Feast in the hills, attended by upwards of 4,000 people. Children were examined in scripture, Hannah gave a speech in which she pointed out the changes which were transforming the community, and the picnic which she provided was enjoyed by all.

The Mendip Scheme and her writing, took up all Hannah More's time and energy. In addition to writing forty-nine Cheap Repository Tracts, she published *Hints Towards the Education of a Young Princess* in 1805, her only novel, *Coelebs*, in 1808, and *The Spirit of Prayer* in 1825. Her work-load, together with occasional bursts of abuse received from those who accused her of preaching Methodism and Calvinism in her schools, weighed heavily on More as she got older. In 1801 she sold Cowslip Green and, together with her sisters, moved to a house she had built at Barley Wood, in Wrington. Her popularity did not wane: she was visited endlessly by missionaries, bish-ops, and literary figures such as Wordsworth and Thomas Babington Macaulay. Between 1813 and 1819 all of her sisters died, leaving Hannah at the mercy of some unscrupulous servants, who stole from her. She moved to Clifton in 1828, settling at a smaller house at 4 Windsor Terrace, and continued to over-see her charities. When she died, aged eighty-eight, on 7 September 1833, her funeral was attended by hundreds of mourners, and the churches of Bristol tolled their bells.

More has been criticised for the narrowness of her educational princi-ples; she did not see any alternative to the hierarchical order of society and therefore did not believe in educating people above what she perceived was their station in life. An academic education could, she believed, only arouse in the Mendip children expectations which society would not be able to satisfy. She wrote of her aims:

> My plan for instructing the poor is very limited and strict. They learn of weekdays such coarse work as may fit them for servants. I allow of no writing. My object has not been to teach dogmas and opinions, but to inform the lower class to habits of industry and virtue. . . . To make good members of society . . . has been my aim. . . . Principles, and not opinions, are what I labour to give them.[122]

When she wrote specifically about female education, she directed her words to the upper classes. She addressed women and girls from a class who had already proven that female learning was fashionable and laudable, a class of woman with whom she must surely have identified. Hers had been a thorough education which rendered her capable of earning a large income during her life, and she enjoyed stimulating company and good literature. To analyse her educational writing is to attempt to understand why such a woman could circumscribe the role of her sex with 'strictures' on their education; it is also to come to an understanding of an ideology which was the antithesis of that of Mary Wollstonecraft, an ideology which shaped the education of women into the next century.

Hannah More's life falls into two clear halves: the years spent at the centre of London's literary and social life, and those spent at Cowslip Green and Barley Wood when her time was devoted to educational, charitable and evangelical work. Her writing reflects these two 'lives' and thus it is the work published after 1777 with which we are concerned. In 1777, with the Publication of *Essays on Various Subjects Principally Designed for Young Ladies*, Hannah More entered the contemporary debate as to the appropriacy of female education. Her position was conservative; she considered that 'it would be highly impolitic to annihilate distinctions from which each [sex] acquires excellence, and to attempt innovations, by which both would be losers'.[123] She believed that the sexes were fundamentally different, writing that 'Women have generally quicker perceptions; men have juster sentiments. Women consider how things may be prettily said; men how they may be properly said. . . . Women admire what is brilliant; men what is solid'.[124] Her *Essays* were based on personal opinions, rather than empirical fact. She observed women within her social circle, drew conclusions, and gave them great weight by publishing them. Because of her popularity, it is not hard to conclude that the sentiments in her *Essays* held a certain appeal for the class of woman to whom they were directed, and she argued that the civilizing influence of 'ladies' gave them their *raison d'être*:

> The prevailing manners of an age depend more than we are aware, or
> are willing to allow, on the conduct of women: this is one of the prin-
> ciple hinges on which the great machine of human society turns. . . .
> How much it is to be regretted , that the British ladies should ever sit
> down content to polish, when they are able to reform; to entertain,
> when they might instruct; and to dazzle for an hour, when they are
> candidates for eternity.[125]

Hannah More's is considered to be the voice which first galvanized up-per-class women into forming charitable organisations, adopting for them-selves the role of social worker, a role which they would retain into the next century. She considered that this was their societal function, and never sup-ported the idea that they should engage in industry, politics or the profes-sions. Her endeavours to influence fashionable society were continued in *Thoughts on the Improvement of the Manners of the Great to General Society* (1788). In it she articulated a life-long belief in *noblesse oblige*, a belief which coloured her perceptions of the role of education in society. She wrote vehemently that the moral and intellectural 'reformation' 'must begin with the GREAT, or it will never be effectual. *Their* example is the fountain whence the vulgar draw their habits, actions and characters'.[126] In keeping with her Tory belief in the established order in government and church, she continued a two-pronged attacked on the vices of society by establishing the Mendip Scheme, giving a limited education to the poor, and instilling in 'the lower orders of mankind' a fear and a love of God. Between 1790 and 1798, she opened eight schools. The Greater Schools, at Cheddar, Shipham and Nailsea, had a practical curriculum including industrial, agricultural and domestic training for boys and girls. Farmers' sons could, for a small fee, have additional tuition in reading, writing and arithmetic. All the children attended Sunday School, where the poorer children could learn reading as well as the Scriptures. Writing to Dr Beadon, Bishop of Bath and Wells, some ten years after the Scheme had been founded, More stated:'I allow of no writing for the poor. My object is not to make fanatics, but to train up the lower classes in habits of industry and piety'.[127]

More had, on occasion, to rebuke suggestions that she was teaching the poor the means for Revolution. In fact, this was far from the truth. She desired social amelioration, achieved by each class performing their God-given duty. It was the duty of the ruling class to govern with benevolence and philanthropy, just as it was the duty of the lower classes to work hard. Her view on the development of education is best expressed in a letter to Sir William Pepys, in which she stated that she had prevailed upon her 'parliamentary friends, to steer the middle way between the scylla of brutal ignorance, and the charybdis of a literary education. The one is cruel, the other preposterous'.[128]

So far were her sentiments from those expressed by supporters of the French Revolution, that it could be said that she began the Cheap Repository Tracts to counter its influence. Tom Paine's *Rights of Man* had spread alarm among the governing classes, and the Bishop of London appealed to Hannah More to write an antidote to it. More's response contrasted dramatically with that of Mary Wollstonecraft, who had penned her own *Vindication of the Rights of Man*. She wrote a pamphlet called *Village Politics,* consisting of a dialogue between Jack Anvil, the blacksmith, and Tom Hood, the village mason. The latter was attracted by the cries for liberty and equality, while the former defended the status quo. The enormous popularity of *Village Politics* was not expected by More, and her own opinions of it suggest that it was not inspired by the kind of passion which had consumed Wollstonecraft when writing the *Rights of Man*. More wrote in her diary that Village Politics was 'as vulgar as heart can wish; but it is only designed for the most vulgar of readers. I heartily hope that I shall not be discovered; it is a sort of writing repugnant to my nature.'[129]

Whether or not this sort of writing was repugnant to her nature, Hannah More was so impressed by the success of *Village Politics* that she began what would quickly become a cottage industry: the publication of Cheap Repository Tracts. The popular author Charlotte Yonge, in her biography of More (1888), estimated that for twenty years they were the staple fare of the village libraries, and in addition to their market in England, they were shipped to America and overseas, where they were distributed in schools, hospitals and prisons.

More turned her hand to writing for people of 'rank and fortune' once again in 1799, when she published her *Strictures on the Modern System of Female Education*.[130] Unlike Wollstonecraft's *Vindication of the Rights of Woman*, More's educational *opus* was not designed to challenge the contemporary view of woman's role in society; it reinforced the traditional model, but emphasised that women of rank could exercise a civilising influence on men, and on the manners of society in general:

> Among the talents for the application of which women of the higher class will be peculiarly accountable, there is one, the importance of which they can scarcely rate too highly. This talent is influence. . . . The general state of civilized society depends . . . on the prevailing sentiments and habits of women, and on the nature and degree of the estimation in which they are held.[131]

She criticized the prevailing system of female education for paying too much attention to the 'frenzy of accomplishments', which – to her dismay – was 'no longer restricted within the usual limits of rank and fortune'. Instead, she continued, 'the middle orders have caught the contagion, and it races downward with increasing and destructive violence'.[132]

More saw no purpose in educating the 'lower orders' in languages, arguing that 'those humbler females, the chief part of whose time is required for domestic offices, are little likely to fall in the way of foreigners'.[133] The purpose of education, as she saw it, was to make good 'daughters, wives, mothers and mistresses of families', women who could 'reason, and reflect, and feel, and judge, and discourse and discriminate', and both 'comfort and counsel' their husbands, and educate their children.[134] Her view of the role of women was framed by her Christian beliefs. Like many before her, she could argue that 'Christianity has exalted woman to true and undisputed dignity; in Jesus Christ . . . there is neither 'male nor female. . . ';[135] but she did not extrapolate from her argument that man and woman were therefore equal in all things. She believed that the female mind was inferior to that of the male, and that female education should restrict its aims to practical purposes, concluding that 'the great uses of study to a woman are to enable her to regulate her own mind, and to be instrumental to the good of others'.[136] *Strictures* clearly limited the uses of female knowledge, and, in the light of More's own life, it seems very harsh indeed. Perhaps speaking from personal experience, she believed that 'women . . . become ridiculous by the unfounded pretensions of literary vanity', and that they might become 'puffed up with the conceit of talents'. She did not allow that women should compete with men, and never acknowledged that her charitable 'empire' had been built on earned money and an industrious writing career.

It is possible that Hannah More, who enjoyed a full life, throughout which she remained financially independent, had some vague reservations about limiting female experience and education. In the opening chapter of *Strictures* she had warned, 'I am not sounding an alarm to female warriors, or exciting female politicians: I hardly know which of the two is the most disgusting and unnatural character',[137] yet by the end of chapter fourteen she comforts women for the deprivations which they must suffer:

> If we have denied them the possession of talents which might lead them to excel as lawyers, they are preserved from the peril of having their principles warped by that too indiscriminate defence of right and wrong to which the professors of the law are exposed. If we should question their title to eminence as mathematicians, they are happily exempt from the danger to which men devoted to that science are said to be liable, namely, that of looking for demonstration on subjects which, by their very nature, are incapable of affording it.[138]

The transparency of this argument cannot have escaped More, who wrote, six pages earlier, of man's 'firmer texture of mind': the scholar of More's works must remain frustrated by the consummate irony of a writer and a businesswoman denying educational and vocational opportunities to her own sex, while endeavouring to understand her in the light of her religious and political beliefs.

For Hannah More, then, female education was linked with appropriate female behaviour. Such behaviour was guided by moral sense which, in turn, was based upon religious belief. For her close contemporary, Mary Wollstonecraft, the existence of God was a fundamental truth, based upon a reasoned perception of the harmony of the attributes of God. She did not accept the doctrine of original sin, or believe in the punishment of hell. Wollstonecraft did not use the principles of Christianity to serve as allies in vindicating the rights of woman. While More believed in the 'controlling hand of Providence in the direction of events',[139] Wollstonecraft believed that reason would direct people to 'attain such habits of virtue as will render it independent'.[140] Blind submission to religious and political instruction was anathema to Wollstonecraft, hence her reiterated demands for the cultivation of female reason.

Hannah More claimed not to have read Wollstonecraft's *Vindication of the Rights of Woman*. Her refusal to do so betrays an unwillingness to form her own opinion about a controversial work. She wrote to Horace Walpole, who had labelled Wollstonecraft a 'hyena in petticoats' :

> I have been pestered to read the 'Rights of Woman' but am invincibly resolved not to do it. Of all jargon, I hate metaphysical jargon; beside, there is something fantastic and absurd in the very title. I am sure I have as much liberty as I can make a good use of, now I am an old maid; and when I was a young one I had, I daresay, more than was good for me . . . there is, perhaps, no animal so much indebted to subordination for its good behaviour as woman.[141]

Walpole's reply serves as an index of contemporary hostility to Wollstonecraft:

> I am glad you have not read the tract of the last mentioned writer. I would not look at it, though assured it contains neither metaphysics nor politics. . . . We have had enough of new systems, and the world a great deal too much already.[142]

Despite their many differences, More and Wollstonecraft shared some opinions on education. Both argued that girls should not waste time on accomplishments, and that teachers spent too much time drilling facts into their charges in order to illicit a favourable response from parents. Both believed that an educated mother was a better one, yet while Wollstonecraft supported the Lockean notion that a child's mind was a clean slate onto which ideas should be placed by virtuous parents, More argued that children were not 'innocent beings' but instead 'bring into the world a corrupt nature and evil dispositions, which it should be the great end of education to rectify'.[143]

It is not difficult, however, to conclude that political and religious allegiances shaped their differing thoughts. While Wollstonecraft dismissed marriage as an unnecessary contract between consenting adults, More believed that while a man who was a 'free-thinker' might treat conventional morality with scorn, he would not find liberality attractive in a woman. More considered England to be ' a country where [her] sex enjoy[ed] the blessings of liberal instruction, of reasonable laws, of a pure religion, and all the endearing pleasures of an equal, social, virtuous, and delightful intercourse'.[144] Mary Wollstonecraft examined the facts and concluded that this was far from the case.

In their respective lifetimes, Hannah More was a wealthy and very popular writer, whose charitable works won her rightful praise. Wollstonecraft lacked emotional and financial security most of her life, and her writing drew upon her a small amount of acclaim and an abundance of abuse. History has, however, shown that in time More would fade from public memory as her ideas became rapidly out-moded, while Wollstonecraft would be hailed, two centuries later, as the founder of the movement for female emancipation.

Comparing More's and Wollstonecraft's respective demands for female education, it is impossible to ignore the impact of background and intellectual milieu. Both Wollstonecraft and More would have read educational philosophy, and their works clearly indicate their greatest influences. Wollstonecraft drew on Locke and Rousseau, and devoted much of *A Vindication of the Rights of Woman* to a rational deconstruction of his version of female education as presented in *Émile*. His Sophie, created as the ideal mate for Émile, was the antithesis of her rational women. Rousseau stated:

> A woman's education . . . must be planned in relation to man. To be pleasing in his sight, to win his respect and love, to train him in childhood, to tend him in manhood, to counsel and console, to make his life pleasant and happy, these are the duties of woman for all time, and this is what she should be taught while she is young.[145]

Wollstonecraft found the idea that woman was created for man's entertainment particularly offensive, but she agreed with him on certain points. When Rousseau argued that women were given to levity, dissipation and inconstancy, Wollstonecraft agreed. However, while Rousseau proposed that these flaws were in the very nature of women, and that the cure was to restrain them and make them dependent on men, Wollstonecraft – like Astell before her – blamed their defective education for their faults.

Hannah More, on the other hand, accepted that women were naturally inferior. She hoped that education would lead them to a virtuous life. Her primary motive was their moral, rather than intellectual, development, and she was limited in her vision of what a woman could contribute to society in political and economic terms. Additionally, she supported the Burkite position that society was ordered in class terms, and that it was the duty of the upper classes to act as benefactors to the poor. Her vocation to educating the poor stemmed from a sense of duty towards her inferiors, and an examination of her educational writings reveals that her view of the amount of education they should receive was strictly limited by a belief that too much learning could incite them to desire that to which they had no birthright.

Wollstonecraft and More were two writers whose sharply divergent positions on education reflect the polarities of thought on the education of

women in eighteenth-century England. They contrasted in so many ways –
literary style, political point of view, religious beliefs, family background –
that it seems impossible that they should now be considered together. Yet it
is for their differences that they have demanded attention: they force the
literary historian to acknowledge that from dichotomous viewpoints we can
come closer to truth.

3

The Education of Women in
English Literature

WOMEN AND EDUCATION IN POPULAR NARRATIVE
PUBLICATIONS

The debate about the suitability of women for education, and the nature of that education, featured in non-fiction English print culture throughout the long eighteenth century. The pattern continued into the nineteenth century: with the growth of the popular periodical, and developments in publishing, there was a corresponding growth in the number of publications which continued Anna Van Schurman's debate about whether or not 'a maid may be a scholar'. The eighteenth and nineteenth centuries also witnessed the growth of the most popular literary form: the novel. Serialised or published whole, the widespread popularity of the novel owed much to the increase in literacy in England in the late eighteenth and nineteenth centuries. Additionally, greater numbers of readers had access to such literature with the growth of the circulating libraries during this period. Just as print culture and the female readership grew, so to did literary representations of learned women become more commonplace in fiction, verse and drama. While it is not possible to conclude that such publications directly influenced developments in women's education, it can be said that this literature echoed strongly the tensions evident in non-fictional debates about women and learning. For example, learned women in popular fiction of the late eighteenth and nineteenth centuries were often portrayed as having compromised their femininity: the stereotypes of the plain spinster and the female pedant were frequently reverted to by writers who chose to include a bookish or intellectual female character. The fate of such women was rarely presented as desirable or laudable, and they invariably suffered ridicule, poverty and loneliness. The learned woman in literature, then, served as a warning to female readers of the dangers of scholarly pursuits.

The fate of the uneducated heroine was often as unfortunate as that of the learned heroine. Many female characters suffered precisely because of fool-hardy behaviour, ill-informed decisions, or the want of useful occupation. But while the novel of the heroine's education was a popular genre, college education for women was not treated directly in the novel until the late nineteenth century, with the growth of the genre of schoolgirl fiction.[1] However, the gathering together of a community of women for the purpose of learning was the theme of a small number of works which pre-date the growth of schoolgirl fiction. As early as 1405, a prose work in which a woman made a plea for the female intellect, was published. This was Christine de Pizan's *Le Livre de la Cité des Dames*, translated to English by Bryan Anslay in 1591 as *The Boke of the Cyte of Ladyes*.[2] In writing it, de Pizan elected to use the popular medieval convention by which the author converses with allegorical figures. Christine talks with women named Reason, Justice, and Rectitude ('Right-thinking', 'Right-doing'), and casts herself in the role of tutor rather than poet: it is her intention to instruct the reader as to how women should think and do what is right. Like Mary Astell (1694), her plea for the education of women is based on her belief that it will lead to good conduct. As Marina Warner (1982) has observed, in her creation of Reason, Justice and Rectitude, de Pizan brings back to memory 'the lives and deeds of virtuous women embodying those qualities, who have been neglected by history . . . [and] breaks the narrow moulds of female stereotypes'.[3]

Christine de Pizan is now considered to be 'one of the outstanding writers of the world of literature and one of the most neglected'.[4] Born in Venice in 1365, she lived most of her life in France and had a good education at the court of Charles V where her father was court astrologer. She made a happy marriage at the age of fifteen, but was widowed by the age of twenty-five. She then turned to writing to support her children and was soon recognised as an accomplished poet. In addition, de Pizan was the official biographer of Charles V, and she also wrote widely on the status of women. Both a scholar and a popular writer, she left a vast *corpus* of work, and the fact that manuscripts of her work have survived owes much to her close supervision of the copying and illuminating of her own books. The particular legacy of *The Book of the City of Ladies* to learned women is that it presented a scholarly yet very readable defence of the female intellect, and it linked female learning with salvation. In Book 1, Christine asks Reason 'whether God has ever wished to ennoble the mind of woman with the loftiness of the sciences'.[5] Reason assures her that it is not God, but society and custom that deprive women of 'high understanding and great learning:'[6]

> . . . if it were customary to send daughters to school like sons, and if they were then taught the natural sciences, they would learn as thoroughly and understand the subtleties of all the arts and sciences as well as sons.[7]

Reason advises Christine that women know less simply because their minds are not trained. She then instructs Christine (and the reader) in the history of learned women from the past. Medea, Sappho, Circe, Ceres, and Minerva, are among the many women introduced. In its presentation of a catalogue of illustrious women, the *City of Ladies* invites comparison with Boccaccio's *De mulieribus claris*, available to de Pizan both in the original and in French translation.[8] But, as Richards (1982) has clearly illustrated, Boccaccio's purpose was simply to write about famous women, regardless of their moral stature, whereas 'Christine writes only about *good* women',[9] and she therefore corrects and reorganises Boccaccio's work.

The 'city of ladies' is built to glorify feminine virtue. Elaine Beilin (1987) has noted that because the English translation of the *Book of the City of Ladies* appeared in 1591, it very likely had some influence on learned Renaissance women who, as noted earlier, equated virtue with salvation. Beilin has also argued that the building of the city is 'a metaphor profoundly appropriate to the architects of a women's literary tradition in English'.[10] However, the city is arguably the earliest known metaphor for a community of women in pursuit of truth: that is to say, a metaphor for a female college. In the book, Reason advises Christine to 'lay the sturdy foundations and to raise lofty walls all around . . . set the foundations deep to last all the longer . . . ',[11] Justice says that she will 'populate the City . . . with worthy ladies'[12] and Rectitude, reminding the reader that the city is a metaphor for the dwelling-place of ladies 'filled with wisdom', advises Christine to 'mix mortar in [her] ink bottle . . . [to] fortify the City with [her] tempered pen'.[13]

As already noted, the English translation of the *Book of the City of Ladies* appeared in 1591, although the original had appeared in 1405. In the years which lapsed before the publication of the English translation, some prose and poetry appeared which treated broadly of women and learning. Of particular interest to Renaissance scholars is *The Schole house of Women* (1541), a mysogynistic verse publication (see fig. 7).[14] With it, the author (probably Edward Gosynhill)[15] began a controversy about women which was played out in one of the several Pamphlet Wars of the period.[16] It contained a catalogue of charges against women, arguing that they are 'evil to please and worse to trust'.[17] The charges were those that Mary Astell had to repudiate in her *Proposal* (1694). For example, the *Schole house* alleged that women were 'crabbed and cumbersome', 'loud and shrill', and too fond of 'gossip'.[18]

Much of the *Schole house* comprises the complaints of a young woman about her husband. She is then 'schooled' by on older woman:

> Then saith the elder, 'Do as I do;
> Be sharp and quick with him again.
> If he chide you, chide you also,
> And for one word you give him twain'.[19]

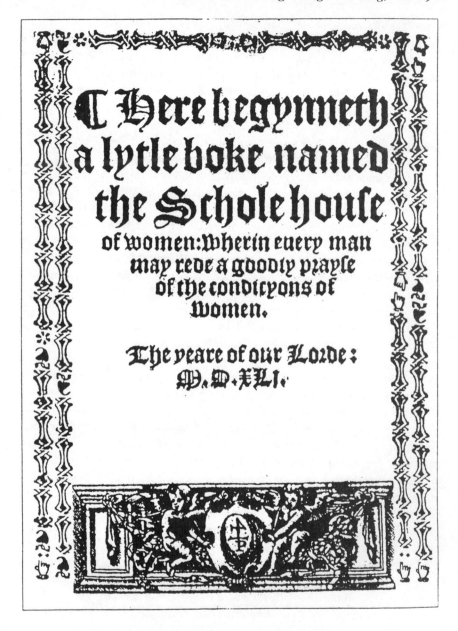

Fig. 7 Title page from *The Schole house of women*, 1541

The teachings of the elder continue thus, and the author laments that these 'schole houses' of women are the cause of men's misfortune:

> Thus among they keep such schools,
> The young to draw after the old,
> Moting[20] ever upon their stools
> Of every matter that they have wold,[21]
> By mean[s] whereof the young wax bold,
> So that within a month they be
> Quartermaster, or more than he.[22]

Allowing women to gather together for 'gossip' or schooling is presented as threatening to men. The elder advises the young woman not to suffer abuse, or to allow her husband to 'game' with prostitutes. The author then interjects to establish once again that women are, by nature, without virtue. Here he reverts to what will become a common motif of listing women of ill-repute in support of his point. Thus, much as de Pizan had offered lengthy examples of virtuous and wise women in defense of her sex, the author of the *Schole house* lists women who have betrayed or seduced men. Jezebel, Mirrah, the daughters of Lot, Eve, Samson's wives, and Job's wife are among the examples of malicious and cruel women, whose existence suggests to the author that women are 'frail of disposition,/So crooked, so crabbed, with that so ill,/So lewd, so shrewd, light of condidtion,/That sure it were impossible/To let them of their own self will'.[23]

In 1615, Joseph Swetnam published *An Arriagnment of Women*,[24] starting yet another Pamphlet War. Of the many replies which it provoked, Rachel Speghts' *Mouzel for Melastomous* (1617) was the first. She followed it with *Mortalities Memorandum, with a Dreame Prefixed* (1621). This is possibly the earliest English verse work in which a woman laments her lack of learning, and recognises that ignorance keeps women in submission. Little is known about Speght, other than the facts of her publications. She was born in 1597, and her father, James, was a rector in London. She married a William Proctor in 1621. Nothing is known of Rachel Speght's life after her marriage.[25]

> In *The Dreame*, Speght writes:
> My griefe, quoth I, is called *Ignorance*,
> Which makes me differ little from a brute . . .
> I feele disease, yet know not what I ayle,
> I find a sore, but can no salve provide;
> I hungry am, yet cannot seek for food;
> Because I know not what is bad or good.[26]

The Dreame, which appeared some fifty years after the publication of the
English translation of de Pizan's *City of Ladies* uses a similar device of personi-
fying human virtues such as Experience, Erudition, Truth and Industry, and
allowing them to teach the narrator how to cure her illness. It is impossible to
guess whether or not de Pizan's work influenced Speght; certainly there are
similarities in their arguments but The *Dreame* is inferior in style and com-
plexity of argument. It is important, however, to note the thread of the argument since, given her involvement in the Pamphlet Wars Speght's work was
probably widely read.

Speght uses biblical and classical references in support of her thesis that
women should be educated. In stanza fifteen, Truth argues:

> Both man and woman of three parts consist,
> Which *Paul* doth bodie, soule, and spirit call:
> And from the soule three faculties arise,
> The mind, the will, the power; then wherefore shall
> A woman have her intellect in vaine,
> Or not endeavour *Knowledge* to attaine.[27]

Speght, like Astell, argues that the cultivation of the female intellect was
divinely ordained, since the 'talent God doth give, must be imploy'd' and
'The God of *Knowledge* nothing gave in vaine'.[28] She then adopts the literary
device of listing learned women in support of her point that female learning
is not unnatural. The poets Cleobulina, Demophilia and Telesilla, together
with the astronomer Hypatia and the rhetorician Aspatia, were listed.

The classical references in both de Pizan and Speght suggest a familiarity
on their part with Greek and Roman history. It was such a familiarity that
would, however, cause women to be lampooned in seventeenth and eighteenth-century literature. Katherine M. Rogers (1966) has noted that Jonson's
particular dislike for intellectual women 'reflected the general trend of his
period'.[29] In *Volpone* (1606) is found his best known female intellectual,
Lady Politick Would-Be. Her vanity and intellectual conceit cause her to
proclaim on a variety of subjects, though she fails to recognise Sophocles
(*Ajax*) when Volpone reflects that the 'highest female grace is silence'. The
catalogue of possible sources which she lists is intended to make her appear
ridiculous, rather than wise, as she wonders who the author could be:

> Petrarch, or Tasso, or Dante?
> Guarini? Ariosto? Aretine?
> Cieco di hadria? I have read them all. . . .[30]

In addition to the female pedant, Jonson included other stereotypes of learned women in his plays. As Rogers has noted, the Collegiate Ladies in *Epicone* (1629) are 'masculine' and 'hermaphroditical', while in *Catiline* (1611), the learned Sempronia has a 'very masculine' wit.[31] In his ridiculing of intellectual women, Jonson reflected the trend of the day. Sir Thomas Overbury's poem 'A Wife' (1614) emphasised the dangers of learning in women:

> *Learning* and *pregnant wit* in woman-kinde,
> What if findes malleable, makes fraile,
> And doth not adde more *ballast*, but more saile.[32]

The intellectual frailty of women continued to be a theme in literature throughout the late seventeenth and early eighteenth centuries. Translations of Molière's plays brought the ridiculing of the *femme savante* to England. Between 1659 and 1672 he produced a series of plays which made a mockery of the over-educated female yet developed 'une thèse morale en faveur de l'éducation des filles par la douceur dans la liberté'.[33] *Les Précieuses Ridicules* was his first success, presenting a caricature of the self-consciously intellectual female who would contrast with the virtuous and wise Henriette in *Les Femmes Savantes*, and with the naive Agnès in *L'École des Femmes* who was reared for marriage by her future spouse who demanded of her 'une ignorance extrême;/Et c'est assez pour elle, a vous bien parler,/De savoir prier Dieu, M'aimer, coudre et filer' (*L'École de Femmes*, Act I, sc.i.).

Molière expressed his theory of female education with a delicate irony which was largely misunderstood by English readers and, indeed, he was read in the original by few English. Dorothy Gardiner (1929) has commented on crude adaptations of his plays which were produced in England, in which contemporary boarding schools were ridiculed and women with intellectual pretensions were derided.[34] One such play, the popular *Female Virtuoso* (1693) by Thomas Wright, caricatures contemporary intellectual noble women in its presentation of Lady Meanwell who had 'more sentences in her mouth than teeth' causing her husband to address her: 'My Walking University, my puzzling/Library of Flesh'.[35] Wright can be numbered among the group of wits and writers who joined in the 'querelle des femmes' in England purely to toy, half-gallantly, with ideas concerning women. At this time the mentality and morals of women was a stock subject in literature of wit, and the discussions included 'cynical, libertine denunciations of woman's inferior mentality and her depravity'[36] (as in Robert Gould's *Love Given Over: or a satyr against the Pride, Lust and Inconstancy of Women* (1690) and gallant defences of women, idealising the feminine virtues of what was widely referred to as 'the fair sex'.

There were contradictions, however, in such literature. For some writers a truly feminine and 'fair' woman was idle, and enjoyed leisurely rather than scholarly pursuits, while other authors chose equally to ridicule this type of woman. Swift's account of the 'Annals of a Female Day' in *The Journal of a Modern Lady* (1729), and Alexander Pope's *The Rape of the Lock* (1714) described the emptiness and triviality of a woman's day, yet for a woman to fill her day with learning was equally ridiculous.

Against these conflicting versions of women's lives, some writers chose to explore the possibility of creating educated female characters whose femininity was not compromised by their erudition. The ideas of Astell and de Pizan, who allowed that learning might make women more virtuous and wise, were shared by such writers. With its vision of a community of learned and wise women, the *Book of the City of Ladies* anticipated Sarah Scott's *Millenium Hall* (1762) and Tennyson's 'The Princess' (1847), just as it anticipated Astell's non-fictional *Proposal*. It is possible that Astell read the English translation of the *City of Ladies*, and certainly there are some similarities in arguments. In particular, Astell's blaming of women's inferior position on custom recalls de Pizan. Astell, however, moved from a figurative representation of a group of learned women to an actual proposal for a female college or 'monastery'. In a handful of successive publications by various authors over the next two centuries, the theme re-emerged. For example, Swift satirised Astell's female college in the *Tatler* (No. 32), describing it as though it already existed. It was presented as a kind of protestant nunnery, to which a rake and his companions pay a visit, only to conquer the college. As shall be seen, this anticipates to some degree the plot of both Sara Scott's *Millenium Hall*, and Tennyson's *The Princess*. In 1709, the famous comic playwright Mrs. Centilivre used Astell as a specific instance of a learned lady in her play *The Basset-Table*, in which the studious young Valeria resists her father's wishes to marry a sea Captain. Her aunt, Lady Reveller, advises in despair that she should perhaps use her fortune to found a college for women. Almost immediately following the publication of Astell's *Proposal*, Defoe published a proposal for a female college in his *Essay upon Projects* (1697).

The general idea, then, of a protestant community or college for women, had appeared in print a number of times in the late seventeenth century, and doubtless the idea of a female college had supporters whose opinions have not survived in print. The biographer of Lettice, Lady Falkland wrote in 1653, that her subject had long held a wish that 'there might be places for the education of young gentlewomen, and for the retirement of widows (as Colleges and Inns of Court and Chancery are for men) in several parts of the Kingdom', and in 1698, 1715 and 1722 there appeared in three publications brief but supportive references to Astell's *Proposal* which suggest that it continued to be the subject of discussion.[37]

The argument about women's suitability for education, and the nature of such an education, had thus appeared in popular narrative many times before the eighteenth century. With the development of the novel, it would continue to be the subject of much writing. In particular, it received the attention of writers of epistolary fiction. Given the circumstances in which English epistolary fiction emerged, it is not altogether surprising to find that woman's quest for self-hood through learning should have received some attention by writers. As Ruth Perry (1980) has observed, early novels charted 'the private voyages of individual minds': subject matter which only became appropriate and relevant in post-Reformation England, when the separate struggles and salvation of each single person was deemed worthy of attention.[38] This was, too, a time in which sufficient numbers of people were reading and writing, 'so that private acts of consciousness were a substantial part of life for a sizeable portion of the population'.[39] As will be seen, women writers used the novel to tease out meaning for their lives, and a number of these women focussed on education as a key to such meaning.

Additionally, they wrote fictions which 'perpetuated the myths of romantic love'.[40] These stories, told according to the conventions of realism, were assumed to be about living people. As Perry has noted, because of 'the residual Puritan distaste for 'falsehood', as well as the new craze for scientific objectivity, the contemporary preference for stories of 'real people' dictated that much fiction be framed as first person writing'.[41] There emerged, therefore, a genre of fictional writing that embraced diaries, journals, confessions, memoirs, travelogues, autobiographies and letters.

Epistolary fiction, that is works written in the form of letters, are of particular interest here. Letters were a very significant part of the culture of the time, and it would seem that women had 'a special affinity for this one-to-one format'.[42] In his study of epistolary fiction Robert Adams Day (1969) indicates that between 1660 and 1740 some two hundred publications of 'English letter fiction' appeared.[43] Fifty-four of these were by women, and seventy-two were by men, while the remainder were published anonymously. Of those by women, a number were by writers examined below. Eliza Haywood penned twenty-eight works of epistolary fiction, while Mary Delariviere Manley and Elizabeth Singer Rowe were also very popular. These three writers, examined in greater depth by John J. Richetti (1969), wrote stories which anticipate the novel as popular narrative. They allowed their readers to live vicariously through the lives of their characters, providing them with synthesized versions of fictionalized experiences. Human conduct and its consequences were held up to a microscope, and as a consequence the market rapidly expanded for 'books of advice on how to behave in even the most intimate moments of one's life'.[44] As Clive T. Probyn (1987) has noted, by the middle of the century 'the possibility of self-education through books became a reality for the modestly welltodo'.[45] As a proportion of all publications, the production of works of fiction rose from 7% per annum (1700-40) to 20% per annum after 1740, to 40% per annum in the period between 1770-

1800.[46] This would have particular significance for middle and upper class women who, deprived of public school and college education, educated themselves through reading. It would also have implications for women's writing: the subject of their education received increased attention in eighteenth-century epistolary fiction, in poetry and other forms of popular narrative.

The increase in production of published works on women and education corresponds to the general increase in publications by women themselves. The most extensive and authoritative research on the history of British women writers includes that of Janet Todd, Dale Spender and Patricia Crawford.[47] These literary historians have rescued from obscurity a body of literature which indicates that while female literacy was not widespread in the seventeenth century, a substantial proportion of upper-class women who could read and write chose to publish. While the mere act of writing challenged seventeenth-century ideas about the role of woman in society, some women chose to challenge convention explicitly by writing about the social injustice which deprived them of education and kept them in an inferior position. Equally important to the growing perception of female rationality were those women who published on other areas of interest. In the seventeenth century much of this material was ignored, some works were not recorded or catalogued correctly, and some were, either deliberately or accidentally, attributed to male authors.[48] These publications give some insight into the ideas of seventeenth-century women, and, since writing for publication was not an approved activity, they give an indication of contemporary women's needs to express their opinions and have a voice in society. A comparatively small corpus of work was produced by women before 1700: 231 named women wrote most of the 653 first editions.[49]

Nevertheless, considering the pyramid structure of English society by the end of the seventeenth century, and considering the dearth of educational opportunity for women other than those of the upper ranks, these publications marked a foray into erstwhile male territory. As David Cressy (1980) noted, the structure of English society during the seventeenth century was such that reading and writing skills were required by few for daily survival.[50] Only the upper-middle and upper ranks actually needed education in order to maintain their social status, and they formed a small, if powerful, percentage of the population (see Table 1). The Civil Wars and Interregnum marked a considerable increase in women's publications, and influenced a change in the content of women's writings. While published work in the first half of the century shows a preoccupation with maternal advice, the later decades of the century saw increased interest in politics, literature and biography. The Civil Wars had forced women into new roles as defenders of their homes, with increased responsibilities and increased interest in political controversy. As Crawford has noted, their 'experience of opposition and hostility forced

TABLE 1 English Society at the End of the Seventeenth Century

1.2%	landowners
24.3%	farmers & freeholders
3.4%	professionals, including clergy
3.7%	merchants & shopkeepers
4.4%	artisans & handicraftsman
26.8%	labouring people & out-servants
29.4%	cottagers & paupers
6.8%	the armed forces

Source: Roy Porter, *English Society in the Eighteenth Century* (London: Allen and Lane, 1982).

them to refine their arguments, and so led to further publications'.[51] However, the range of what women could write about was restricted by their lack of education. Virtually all of them were ignorant of Latin, the language of professional discourse, and they frequently apologised in their works for their lack of education. Those who did not apologise for their position were, like Mary Astell, expressing frustration that women did not have access to such an education. She, like many of her contemporaries who wrote pious works, tried to direct her work to a female audience. For Astell, this was a genuine endeavour to encourage women to seek education and to improve their spiritual and intellectual worth, but for many other women writers it was simply a device to avoid the scorn of male critics. Those who adopted the values of their critics simply used their gender as an excuse for any inadequacies in their works. Others published anonymously so that their works would be taken seriously. Astell originally opted for this ruse, and Bathsua Makin, in her Preface to her *Essay to Revive the Ancient Education of Gentlewomen* (1673), wrote: 'I am a Man my self, that would not suggest a thing prejudicial to our Sex.'[52]

Nor was admitting one's sex a guarantee that it would be believed: the better works were often assumed to be by men who had chosen a female pseudonym. Nevertheless, research has unearthed a *corpus* of women's published writing before 1700 that anticipates the huge increase in the number of 'literary ladies' that gradually came to prominence in the world of publishing by the second half of the eighteenth century. Research on seventeenth and eighteenth-century women writers reveals that the majority of these were women of the middle and upper-middle ranks, and most of them had some education.[53] Aristocrats were also well represented: they usually enjoyed exceptional educational advantages and had money with which to support their literary interests. They were also in a better position to pay for publication of their works, or to seek sponsorship from other titled and moneyed friends.

These women were usually educated by male relatives or friends, or by a male tutor employed to teach the sons of the household. Among the more privileged were Lady Masham and Viscountess Conway. The former was instructed by John Locke, while the latter had her brother's tutor, Henry More, as her teacher.[54] Clergymen relatives were also often responsible for female instruction, and many girls were taught by their fathers. Catherine Macaulay Graham, the historian whose educational writings are examined below, was taught by her father, as was the educational writer Hannah More whose father trained his daughters to be teachers, knowing that he could not afford dowries for them. Other women writers in this study were self-taught. Sarah Fielding (1710-68), author of a fictional call for female education in *The Governess* (1749), the first full-length novel for young people and the first ever school story for girls, learned Greek and Latin through private study, while it is a well-documented fact that Mary Wollstonecraft taught herself to translate for publication from dictionaries.

Religious background had a significant influence on the amount of formal female education that was allowed. While the Anglican church did not stress women's education, the liberal Quakers encouraged it in all classes, thus a large number of English and American women writers were Quakers. Methodists encouraged the writing of spiritual records, but 'only the older Dissenters emphasized education tending to a life of letters beyond religious polemics and autobiography'.[55]

The first woman to write and publish for money was Lady Mary Wroath (1586-7), although that title is often given to the playwright Aphra Behn (1640-89). Wroath, however, published *Urania* in 1621, some nineteen years before Aphra Behn's birth. She was the niece of the poet Sir Philip Sydney, and her work was a variation on his *Arcadia,* which had been published to great acclaim in 1590. Her most renowned female contemporaries were the poet Katherine Philips (1631-64), known as the 'Matchless Orinda', and Margaret Cavendish, Duchess of Newcastle (1623-73). Katherine Phillips is recorded as having been educated at a Miss Salmon's school in Hackney although upon the remarriage of her widowed mother to Sir Richard Phillips she was moved to Wales and was married at the age of sixteen to fifty-four year-old James Phillips. She began to write poetry for a small literary circle of friends in which all had romantic pseudonyms. Her husband's rise to prominence in Cromwell's parliament allowed her opportunity to participate 'in the literary renaissance emanating from the court of Charles II'[56] and her admirers included Dryden and Cowley. Her literary reputation was built on a translation of Corneille's *La Morte de Pompey*, which she undertook on a trip to Dublin in 1662, although she was reluctant to put her name to it, or to publish her poetry, so great was her fear of public censure.

On the other hand, Margaret Cavendish, Duchess of Newcastle, was fearless in her pursuit of literary fame. She wrote poetry, prose, philosophy, and scientific works, and frequently aired her views on female education. In her time she was looked on with some distaste, even horror, because she openly pursued knowledge and fame. Virginia Woolf wrote that Cavendish became a 'bogey to frighten clever girls with',[57] But still she insisted that women were intellectual beings, and she condemned their lack of education for giving them a sense of inferiority. In the Preface to her *Observations on Experimental Philosophy* (1666) she wrote:

> As for Learning, that I am not versed in it, no body, I hope, will blame me for it, since it is sufficiently known, that our Sex is not brought up to it, as being not suffered to be instructed in Schools and Universities . . . I will not say but many of our Sex may have as much Wit, and be as capable of learning as well as Men; but since they want instructions, it is not possible they should attain to it; for Learning is Artificial, but Wit is natural.[58]

Research indicates then, that there was a dramatic increase in the number of published women writers after 1640. Aphra Behn earned a living exclusively from her writing, and was followed by Delariviere Manley (1663-1724), Mary Griffith Pix (1666-1720), Catherine Trotter Cockburn (1679-1749), Lady Chudleigh (1656-1710) and Elizabeth Elstob (1683-1756). Not all gained financial independence through their writing; aristocratic women such as Lady Chudleigh rarely needed to earn a living and often published without payment, while Elizabeth Elstob relied partly on the generosity of her brother, and later supported herself by working as a governess. Lady Chudleigh produced two early eighteenth-century volumes of essays and poems, a number of which treated of the need for female education. She is numbered among the most influential of the polemical poetesses, along with Sarah Fyge (1669/1672 – 1722/1723) who also advocated female education, and Anne Finch, Countess of Winchilsea (1661-1721) whose poetry 'addressed the rights of women to their own creativity and autonomous thought'.[59]

By the middle of the eighteenth century, with the launch of the 'Bluestocking' salons, there was a widening of women's intellectual interests, and an increase in the number of women writers. Both factors popularized the idea of the learned lady, who became the subject of novels, popular journals, plays, poetry, and even art.[60] The Bluestocking circle of literary women was centred around the major salon hostesses, Mrs Montagu and Mrs Vesey.[61] It would be incorrect to suggest that these women merely imitated the earlier French *salonières*. Their underlying motives were to replace the limited social events of dining and card-playing with stimulating conversation, and they encouraged serious writing.

The lasting influence of the Bluestockings was to provide examples of virtuous, intellectual women, and to challenge the contemporary idea of women's intellectual inferiority. Montagu, known as the 'Queen of the Blues', was well known and wealthy. As Myres (1990) notes, it was Montagu who coined the term 'Bluestocking' in a letter in which she referred to Benjamin Stillingfleet, scholar and botanist, who had appeared wearing blue worsted wool stockings, those of a working man, rather than the silk hose which were the habitual dress of a gentleman. The term was applied by Montagu to learned men whose friendships were valued by the women in her salons, men who often acted as mentors through conversation and correspondence. A further reference to 'blue stocking philosophers' in her correspondence with Lord Lyttleton in 1763 indicates that the term was known to her friends. It came to imply a point of view, and as late as 1791 Hester Chapone was still using the term to signify the intellectual companionship of men and women. The term was not exclusively associated with women until late in the eighteenth century, when it was often used by those who wanted to ridicule the extended group of female intellectuals. The 'first generation' of Bluestocking women included Elizabeth Carter (1717-1806), Catherine Talbot (1721-70) and Hester Chapone (1727-1801), while the 'second generation' included Fanny Burney (1752-1840), Hester Thrale Piozzi (1741-1821) and Hannah More (1745-1833). While the early Bluestockings did not produce a huge volume of published work, their publications were of significant merit and lead to their growing fame as scholars. They were written about in periodicals and newspapers, and many other women imitated their literary activities.

The Bluestockings, doubtless, contributed favourably to the image of the learned woman. Because few of them pursued learning at the expense of their families or reputation, their literary out-put was often received favourably, and their social class ensured that they were members of the first circle of polite society. Many of them were directed by male mentors, husbands or friends, and they emphasised virtue and the value of friendship.

A number of Bluestocking women, noted for their wit, conversation and literary publications, were supporters of the female interest in science. This development in women's intellectual pursuits further demonstrated their capacity for rational thought as they studied and wrote on mathematics, experimental physics, botany and astronomy in increasing numbers. They also addressed the question of the development of female reason in epistolary works. Of the epistolary fiction which treated of the education of women, the most important works include Hester Chapone's *Letters on the Improve-*

ment of the Mind, addressed to a Young Lady (1773), Catherine Macaulay Graham's *Letters on Education* (1790), and Laetitia Matilda Hawkins's *Letters on the Female Mind* (1793). These works were didactic in tone, and resembled advice books. Chapone's letters were addressed to a 'Young Lady', while Macaulay addressed hers to 'Hortensia': both were thus directed to imaginary young women in need of guidance. Hawkins addressed hers to Miss H. M. Williams, a poet and novelist, in response to Williams's *Letters form France* (1790). In adopting either an anonymous or a fictitious recipient of the 'letters', Chapone and Macaulay utilised the popular epistolary device, but their works were more serious in intent than earlier publications which adopted this format. For example, Elizabeth Singer Rowe's *Letters Moral and Entertaining, in Prose and Verse* (1728), which comprised an exchange between Belinda and Silvia, and Wetenhall Wilkes's *A Letter of Genteel and Moral Advice to a Young Lady* (1740), offered readers a light treatment of issues of appropriate female conduct, but did not examine appropriate female education. Chapone, Graham and Hawkins, though writing in a popular style, invited readers to analyse the deficiencies in contemporary female education.

Hester Mulso Chapone was a self-educated woman who became one of the Bluestocking circle, and was a particular friend of Elizabeth Montagu, Fanny Burney, Elizabeth Carter and Samuel Richardson. Through Richardson she met John Chapone, a lawyer, whom she married in 1760. With Richardson she carried on an epistolary debate (published posthumously) about filial obedience, and she also wrote letters to a favourite niece outlining a practical course of self-education. Mrs Montagu advised her to publish the letters, and from them she produced *Letters on the Improvement of the Mind* (1773). The letters offered advice on social behaviour, and on the pursuit of personal happiness, in addition to proposing an extensive reading programme which should include the Bible, British and European history, the natural sciences, moral philosophy, selected literary works and geography. From the start, the importance of independent judgement and a developed reason were stressed. Rejecting the contemporary fashion for witty and superficial conversation, Chapone argued:

> . . . the faculties that please for an evening may not please for life..the wit, by constantly repeated flashes, confounds and tires ones intellect . . . but good sense can neither tire nor wear out; – it improves by exercise – and increases in value the more it is known.[62]

Chapone's *Letters* suggest that she sought a balance between proposing that the recipient should follow the contemporary curriculum for men, and proposing that she should merely settle for the usual round of accomplishments. Certain contradictions thus emerge: on the one hand, she wrote of

the 'dangers of pedantry and presumption in a woman [and] of her exchang-
ing the graces of imagination for the severity and preciseness of a scholar',[63]
and she considered that 'the labour' required to learn languages might be
'generally incompatible' with the female nature. On the other hand she emphasised the importance of 'a competent share of reading' and argued that
history would 'strengthen [the] judgement' and develop 'a liberal and comprehensive view of nature'.[64] It is possible that Chapone was anxious that her
work should be received favourably, and that it should not be ridiculed as
radical, thus she included occasional conventional words of caution to the
reader concerning female pedantry. Yet at the same time she ridiculed members of her own sex for their ignorance as she concludes that 'a woman makes
a poor figure who affects . . . to disclaim all knowledge of times and
dates . . . but the highest folly is to be proud of such ignorance – a resource in
which some of our sex find consolation'.[65]

In Chapone's *Letters* there was no proposal for a formal system of education for women. Instead, possibly influenced by her own circumstances, she
proposed a system of self-education suited to women's needs, and the *Letters*
were to act as a guide to such as system. In this sense, they took the place of
a formal institute or system of female education, and they did not offend
contemporary sensibilities concerning the female sphere. Chapone suggested
that an appropriate mentor or tutor would be an older woman 'of good sense
and good principles'[66] and that instruction would essentially be conducted
within the domestic sphere. In defining a curriculum specific to women, and
in allowing that women should be educated with or by other women,
Chapone's position contrasted with that of Catherine Macaulay Graham in
her *Letters on Education* (1790).

Catherine Sawbridge Macaulay Graham was educated privately with her
brother at their home in Kent. Both read extensively in Roman history and
developed an interest in republican values. In 1760, Catherine married Dr
George Macaulay, a middle-aged Scottish doctor working in London. She
began research at the British Museum, and in 1763 produced the first volume of her celebrated *History of England*. The second volume was published
in 1765, and in 1766 Catherine Macaulay was widowed. She and her young
daughter continued to live in London, where her home became a radical
salon. She completed three more volumes of her history, and became a prominent pamphleteer, criticizing Hobbes and Burke. Tributes to her writing
testify to her considerable ability as a historian and a writer on contemporary
concerns. Her *Letters on Education* were reviewed by Wollstonecraft,[67] who
acknowledged her debt to this historian, calling her a 'woman of the greatest
ability, undoubtedly, this country has ever produced'.[68] Doris Stenton (1977)
has noted that Macaulay Graham 'was one the first to attempt the writing of
history on a large scale, based on materials, in manuscript as well as in print',[69]

and W.E.H. Lecky considered her to have been 'the ablest writer of the New Radical School'.[70] Although Macaulay achieved a measure of influence unusual for her sex, her works had disappeared from public attention by the nineteenth century. Like Wollstonecraft, she was considered to have committed indiscretions in her personal life which may well have accounted for public rejection of her ideas. [71]

In *Letters on Education*, Macaulay began an argument which Wollstonecraft would continue, establishing the absurdity of separating the male and female children at home during their formative years of education. She then quickly launched into an attack of the system whereby such a separation deprived girls of education:

> Confine not the education of your daughters to what is regarded as the ornamental part of it, nor deny the graces to your sons. . . . Let your children be brought up together; let their sports and studies be the same.[72]

Her assertion that there were no natural or innate sex differences lead easily to the argument that male and female education should be the same. In this respect, Macaulay's *Letters* challenged the theories of female education expressed by Rousseau in *Émile*, a work to which she directly referred. The ideas of appropriate female behaviour, as seen in *Émile*, were rejected. For example, coquettish behaviour which Rousseau suggested was an appealing and typical female characteristic was dismissed as 'dangerous' and 'dishonourable'.[73] Macaulay wrote:

> How much feebleness of constitution has been acquired, by forming a false idea of female excellence, and endeavouring, by our art, to bring Nature to the ply of our imagination.[74]

Macaulay blamed the faulty system of education which prevailed for the poor self esteem of women and the inflated sense of importance of many men. She attacked the custom whereby women were prevented from pursuing a classical education, and used the familiar argument that educated women were better wives and mothers:

> . . . it must be obvious to all those who are not blinded by the mist of prejudice, that there is no cultivation which yields so promising a harvest as the cultivation of the understanding. . . . The social duties in the interesting characters of daughter, wife, and mother, will be but ill performed by ignorance and levity; and in the domestic converse of husband and wife, the alternative of an enlightened, or an unenlightened

> companion, cannot be indifferent to any man of taste and true knowledge.[75]

Macaulay's *Letters*, although addressed to 'Hortensia', were clearly prescriptive rather than discursive. The author was not simply giving information, nor even describing an appropriate female curriculum: it was a work written to expose what the author views as a flawed system. In particular, it attacked as reductive the Rousseauesque notion of a female 'nature' which precluded moral and intellectual development, and it posited that male and female reason were cultivated in precisely the same ways.

In a publication which appeared three years after Macaulay's *Letters*, Laetitia Matilda Hawkins also used the epistolary form with which to make suggestions as to an appropriate female curriculum in *Letters on the Female Mind, Its Powers and Pursuits* (1793). Hawkins was the daughter of the musicologist Sir John Hawkins, and the wealthy heiress Sidney Storer. Sir John, the biographer and friend of Samuel Johnson belonged to a circle of eighteenth-century intellectuals, and brought his daughter up in a literary environment. She started writing at an early age, although she did not publish until 1793. Her first publication, the *Letters*, indicates that she saw women's capacity as limited, but that their education was of great importance. In the first letter she argued that Nature 'certainly intended a distinction'[76] between the intellectual powers of men and women, and this distinction helps to define the 'female province':

> In general, and almost universally, the feminine intellect has less strength but more acuteness; consequently, in our exercise of it, we shew less perseverance and more vivacity. . . . The peculiar properties of the female mind . . . [are] acuteness of perception, [and] vivacity of imagination.[77]

Hawkins advised that an appropriate curriculum for women should include 'arithmetic, geography, natural philosophy, natural history, civil history [and] biography',[78] but concluded that religion and politics need not be studied since women are 'in religion and politics, in general, what [their] parents are'.[79] Certainly, Hawkins shared the conservative politics of her own father, and wrote the *Letters* to counter the claims made by Helen Maria Williams, poet and novelist, whose *Letters from France* had appeared in 1790. Williams's *Letters* gave a sympathetic first-hand account of the events of the French Revolution. They were very popular, but also widely criticized. Hawkins began her own *Letters* by writing that politics was an area in which women could not engage with 'propriety or success'.[80] Her advice to women on appropriate female education was influenced directly by her view of their essentially limited public sphere. In contrast, Catherine Macaulay shaped her theories of female education out of her belief that custom and not justice had limited the female sphere.

Epistolary works, therefore, discussed appropriate forms of education for women, but they did not deal directly with the issue of founding an institution or college for such an education. It was not until the end of the century that an epistolary work explicitly proposed the opening of a university or college for women. Written by Mary Robinson (1758-1800), *A Letter to the Women of England on the Injustice of Mental Subordination,* appeared in 1799. Written for an imagined audience, it is arguably one of the most direct and open discussions on women and education to appear in this period. Robinson was an actress and best-selling author, who had been educated at the Bristol school run by Hannah More's sisters. She moved broadly in the circles of both Macaulay and Hawkins, numbering among her friends and admirers Coleridge, William Godwin, and Mary Wollstonecraft, and had a romantic affair with the young Prince of Wales. Her great beauty, rather than her limited literary ability, brought her lasting fame, as her face was painted into works by Reynolds, Romney, Gainsborough and a number of miniaturists. Although her novels and plays are now considered sentimental and theatrical, the *Letter* is a lucid and forceful argument for the higher education of women.

She opened with an attempt to establish why women suffered various forms of domestic and social oppression, and concluded that they lacked 'the first privilege of nature, the power of Self-Defence'.[81] However, given that they were 'permitted to plough; to perform the laborious business of the dairy . . . to brew, and to bake, while men are employed in measuring lace and ribands'[82] then she could not accept the argument that they are the 'weaker sex'.[83] She argued that their weakness was their lack of learning, and she added that men had preserved learning for their sex by associating it with masculinity. This had thus given rise to the image of the masculine female pedant:

> Prejudice (or policy) has endeavoured, and indeed too successfully, to cast an odium on what is called the *masculine* woman; or . . . a woman of enlightened understanding.[84]

She argued that women would only 'become citizens of the world' when they expanded their intellects, and that she would like to build 'an University for Women' to develop their 'mental powers'.[85] In an original conclusion, she suggested that the University should eventually be run by 'learned women' graduates. No earlier proposal had made such a suggestion, and it would not come to fruition until the founding of Elizabeth Jesser Reid's Bedford College in the middle of the nineteenth century.

It is possible that Mary Robinson had read Sarah Scott's novel *Millenium Hall* which appeared in 1762, presenting a community of women living and studying together very much as Astell had envisaged. If so, this may have influenced her to write a concrete argument for the founding of an institution, run by women for women. Scott's novel did not explicitly argue for higher education for women, but it offered the earliest fictional representation of a community of learned women in novel form, and it has resonances of Astell's *Proposal*. Given that the *Proposal* was known to the Bluestocking circle with which Sarah Robinson was associated, it is in turn possible that Scott had read Astell, though there is no way of confirming these connections.

Sarah Robinson (later Scott) was born in Yorkshire in 1723 and, together with her sister Elizabeth Robinson, benefitted from the tuition of her step-grandfather, the Cambridge classicist Professor Conyers Middleton. Elizabeth married Edward Montagu, a distinguished MP, and became a leading society hostess and patroness of the Arts: she was known as the Queen of the Bluestockings. Sarah had a short and unsuccessful marriage to the mathematician George Scott, after which she moved to live with her close friend Lady Barbara Montagu, at Bath, until Lady Barbara's death in 1765. Financial necessity lead Sarah Scott to write, and she published a number of novels and historical works before writing her most famous novel, *Millenium Hall*, in 1762. The novel, which took her a mere month to complete, went through four editions by 1778, though it earned her no more than thirty guineas.

Like many eighteenth-century novels, it contains the separate histories of various characters. In this case they are all the female inhabitants of Millenium Hall. They present chastity, self-abnegation and duty to one's elders as the most desirable female virtues, and live a harmonious life pursuing their intellectual interests and doing good in the local community. However, as Jane Spencer (1985) has noted, the book is less an attempt to educate young women readers, than an attempt to educate men.[86] The narrator, a man who happens upon Millenium Hall while on his travels, is at first sceptical about the female utopia that he discovers. The novel, essentially, consists of the tales he is told there which gradually convince him of the uniqueness and importance of a community, or Hall of Residence, for intellectual and virtuous women. Thus, far from conquering the heroine as Swift's rake and Tennyson's prince did in varying degrees, the narrator and his companion, the coxcomb Lamont, are determined to engage in founding a similar scheme.

He is told that the occupants who had come to reside there were 'women who from scantiness of fortune, and pride of family, [were] reduced to become dependent'[87] and it had been founded by one occupant, Mrs Morgan, with the inheritance left to her by her tyrannical husband. The occupants of Millenium Hall draw up a set of rules which echo those of Clement Barksdale and of Mary Astell[88] in their respective designs of female colleges. At Millenium Hall, occupants conformed to regular hours, were provided with books and musical instruments, and could leave freely to marry. It also had much in common with conventual life: women at the Hall were obliged to contribute their fortunes to the community upon joining it, they dined at table together, and their dress was to be plain and neat.

Millenium Hall provided a non-threatening image of a female community, and suggested that the pursuit of learning within community life could provide a temporary occupation for single women, and a safe haven for widows and older women. As Jane Spencer has noted, this community for unmarried gentlewomen must have struck a special chord in eighteenth-century hearts.[89] At a time when more women than before were remaining unmarried, the spinster was seen as a problem and protestant England did not provide the alternative community of the convent. Astell's *Proposal* and Scott's *Millenium Hall* both presented community life for protestant women as an alternative to unhappy or forced marriage, but both clearly allowed than a happy marriage was preferred even to life at Astell's college or Scott's Hall. Neither work was designed to give offence to men who might have accused Astell and Scott of dispensing with men and marriage altogether. In Scott's novel, we see female communities and female learning treated in a fictional narrative. In the nineteenth century, with the development of the novel, these themes re-emerge. In addition, there are a number of treatments of the heroine's education, and of the consequences to women of poor education.

EDUCATING HEROINES: BURNEY, AUSTEN, ELIOT AND TENNYSON

The late eighteenth century witnessed not only the growth in popularity of the novel, but the dominating of this genre by women writers. The *Monthly Review* (1890) went so far as to state:

> Of the various species of composition that in course come before us, there are none in which our writers of the male sex have less excelled, since the days of Richardson and Fielding, than in the arrangement of a novel. Ladies seem to appropriate to themselves an exclusive privilege of this kind of writing; witness the numerous productions of romantic tales to which female authors have given birth.[90]

The popularity of the novel was directly influenced by the growth in literacy: it has been estimated that the years 1770-90 saw literacy increase four-fold.[91] Additionally, with the growth of the circulating libraries, which began lending novels for as little as twopence each, the market for fiction expanded.[92] It is calculated that between 1740 and 1800 there were at least 112 circulating libraries in London, and 268 in the provinces, distributed over thirty-seven counties.[93] Catalogues of twelve eighteenth-century circulating libraries examined by Cheryl Turner (1992) record the popularity of female novelists including Eliza Haywood, Sarah Scott, Sarah Fielding and Fanny Burney.[94] In addition to the circulating libraries, subscription libraries and book clubs also contributed to the expansion in women's reading. The stock of such libraries and clubs indicate that serious texts, designed for the self-education of women were also popular.

The prominence of women writers in the eighteenth century owed much to the sheer quantity of their published work, and recent scholarship has attempted to assess the scale and pattern of the development of fiction by women.[95] Turner (1992) has argued that historians have seriously underestimated the number of novels and books written by women in the eighteenth century, and in particular have overlooked serialized novels that were published in magazines. While Turner catalogues 446 works by 174 women writers between 1696 and 1796, she argues that these figures do not reflect the true growth in the number of women writers, as they do not take account of serialised fiction, or of autobiographical fiction.[96] Studying the pattern of women's output, Turner concludes that there was an upsurge in publications by women in the last decades of the century. These were the decades in which women were increasingly challenging male assumptions about female behaviour. Wollstonecraft's *Vindication of the rights of Woman* (1792), Mary Hays's *Appeal to the Men of Great Britain on Behalf of the Women* (1798) and Priscilla Wakefield's *Reflections on the Present Condition of the Female Sex* (1794) demanded that women be allowed both to contribute to the economy and to earn a living. It is not surprising to find that a number of women writers linked women's role in society to education, and, finding that female education was inadequate, criticised contemporary society through their novels. It is proposed to examine the treatment of the heroine's education in a sample of popular novelists of the late eighteenth and nineteenth centuries, and to comment on the eventual emergence of formal higher education in fiction in the late nineteenth century.

One of the most popular of the late eighteenth-century novelists was Fanny Burney (1752-1840). Her novels *Evelina* (1778), *Cecilia* (1782), *Camilla* (1796), and *The Wanderer, or, Female Difficulties* (1814) are all concerned with the first encounters of a young heroine with society, and her struggle to gain social recognition. They also treat of filial duty, problems of inheritance, and the limitations of female education to equip women to deal with life and economic realities. In addition, they are of interest here because of their portrayals of both educated and uneducated female characters. The heroines of Burney's novels are all without a mother's guidance, and are therefore thrown onto their own resources. They are precisely the kind of daughters to whom so many eighteenth-century conduct books and books of advice were directed. Doubtless Burney was influenced by her own circumstances: her mother died when Fanny was ten. Fanny's father remarried five years later, but Fanny's closest confidant was always her sister, Susan. Fanny was the quiet member of a lively and clever family. Her father, Charles Burney, was a respected musician and well known teacher, who moved in the most fashionable and cultured London circles. He encouraged all his children to excel intellectually, but Fanny was shy and liked long periods of solitude. Self-educated in her father's library, she quickly turned to writing, although she kept this pleasure a secret from her family. When her first novel, *Evelina*, was published anonymously to considerable acclaim, her family did not know that Fanny was the author. In *Evelina* Burney used the epistolary form, but moved away from the episodic style which preceded her and maintained a close focus on the experiences of the central character. Thus, in her first novel Burney is considered to have made a new departure in the tradition of the novel, creating 'a mode which presents her readers with the very texture of women's lives',[97] and moving away from the male techniques, such as the inclusions of adventure, unusual exploits and panoramic scenes, which many of her female predecessors had adopted. As Simons (1987) has pointed out, while novelists such as Eliza Haywood and Mary de la Rivière Manley 'employed a largely masculine tenor in recounting their histories',[98] Burney focussed on the complexities of personality and the nature of woman's experience. Because such experience included negotiating the web of social *mores* that defined female life, it is not surprising that Burney explored female anxieties about behavioural codes.

Evelina, which adapts the techniques of the personal diary, tells the story of the initiation of a motherless country girl into polite London society, and of her shame about vulgar relatives on the maternal side of her family. She eventually secures a marriage to an aristocratic gentleman, Lord Orville, whose family had originally rejected her. To complete this romantic tale she is reunited with the father, Sir John Belmont, who had abandoned her mother because his family had disapproved of his marriage. Evelina's letters capture the fears and excitements of a young girl's awakening to social conventions, and Burney uses the novel to ridicule snobbery and to win sympathy for her heroine's naivety. Evelina, who is an innocent when she comes to London, must learn to play roles: as Simons (1987) notes, she learns 'to conform to the masculine ideal of womanhood, . . . [to become a] pallid courtesy book figure'.[99] Consequently, while she is astute, 'her intelligence and wit are allowed to function only within prescribed limits'.[100] In *Evelina*, we see a young woman subvert her natural wisdom in order to conform, yet in conforming she can attain exactly what she desires. Burney thus raises a question about the expense at which she attains social rank and security, but she does not explicitly challenge convention. Nonetheless, the theme of the pursuit of both female identity and social approval continues to interest her.

In *Cecilia*, Burney abandoned the epistolary form in favour of a detached narrative voice. Her central character is a twenty year-old heiress who has been completely orphaned. She is to inherit her uncle's estate on her twenty-first birthday, provided that when she marries her husband will agree to take her name. The novel examines female independence and the economic issues which were increasingly to concern women. Men are presented as duplicitous, and her various guardians prove unreliable. Cecilia, who is intelligent, begins to rely on her own judgements in order to protect herself. If Evelina has to learn to conform, Cecilia's education is one in the shallowness and selfishness of people, and in the importance of good judgement and independence. In *Cecilia*, Burney suggests the importance of female education. She condemns men such as Mr Delvile, who express the opinion that scholarship is inappropriate for women, while presenting intelligent female characters in a favourable light. Cecilia, who is educated, appears as resourceful and wise, while the thoughtful and literate Mrs Delvile, though caught up in an unstimulating marriage, is presented as a good friend to the heroine.

In *Camilla*, Burney focuses more explicitly on female education and development. She was herself familiar with the conduct literature of the day, (Gregory, Gisborne, More, Chapone and Lord Halifax were all best-selling writers of conduct literature in between 1770 and 1800), and she had even recommended Chapone's *Letters on the Improvement of the Mind* to her great nieces.[101] She had also read Rousseau's *Émile,* and, as the mother of a son, was interested in the contemporary debate about the importance of childhood in the development of the personality. *Camilla*, subtitled *A Picture of Youth*, contributes to this debate, as it centres on the effects of different types of upbringing on a group of children. The development of the heroine, Camilla Tyrold, is singled out for particular attention. She is high-spirited and impulsive, and her greatest lessons must be those in social awareness and self-control. Essentially, however, she is likeable and genuine. Against Camilla, Burney also presents the coquettish and ignorant Indiana, whose governess, Miss Margland, is a mouthpiece for conduct literature such as Lady Pennington's *Advice to a Daughter*. She advises that Indiana will damage her good looks by too much reading, and that scholarship will prevent success in the marriage market. Burney ridicules Indiana for her mediocre cultivation of the traditional female accomplishments, and forces a comparison between Indiana and her cousin, Eugenia. The portrayals of Eugenia and Indiana 'form an illustration of Burney's thesis on women and education'.[102] Eugenia, who has been handicapped by a childhood accident, turns enthusiastically to reading.

She enjoys a classical curriculum, and progresses rapidly to outstrip her brother.

However, though Eugenia is no pedant, she is ridiculed for her learning. In society she develops a reputation as an eccentric, as people imagine that her studies somehow stunted her growth. The idea that women could be physically damaged by mental stimulation was to gain currency in the next century even as the first colleges of higher education for women were being founded. Just as female learning could be perceived as eccentric, so was it perceived as unfeminine. Burney explores this in her creation of Mrs Selwyn (*Camilla*), who, though forceful and intelligent, is 'masculine' and has 'lost all the softness' of her sex.[103] The other clever women in Burney's novels, Mrs Delvile (*Cecilia*), and Mrs Arlbery (*Camilla*) have become cynical about romance and marriage, while in *The Wanderer* (1814) Elinor Joddrel, a character based on Mary Wollstonecraft, is portrayed as radical and rash. A champion of women's liberation, Elinor eventually tries to commit suicide twice, as Wollstonecraft had done, when suffering the pain of unrequited love. Burney contrasts her to the more moderate and rational Juliet, who accepts that a conventional pose of delicacy and restraint are necessary for female survival.

Burney's novels offer an early, sustained examination of the effects of education and upbringing on women. Her own position is hidden within the fabric of the novels. On the one hand she admired clever women and was an advocate of economic independence for women. On the other had, she accepted the guidance and control of her father even when a mature and successful writer, and tensions emerge in the novels where she seeks to balance a positive portrayal of female independence with observations of contemporary social roles and customs. As Simons has noted, Burney's ambiguous position on the public role of women was evident in her work. She recognised that in fiction one could express subversive attitudes in a climate that was hostile to radical ideas.[104]

Like Burney's fiction, the novels of Jane Austen may also be seen to express an argument for female education, though not for female independence. While Austen's women are improved by education, their destiny is marriage and not public life. Austen also recognises that pedantry is unattractive in young women, and balances this with the recognition that silliness is just as deplorable. Without overtly challenging the contemporary ideology of femininity, Austen presents a sustained argument for female education on precisely the grounds on which Astell had based her argument: it is the pursuit of truth. Like Astell's, Austen's view of education is essentially Platonic: education brings the heroine to the point at which she can distinguish reality from appearance. As David Devlin (1975) has noted:

> All Jane Austen's novels, and many of her minor works, unfinished pieces and juvenilia, are about education. It is the imprudences and

education of her heroines that chiefly interest us. . . . Education, for the heroines, is a process through which they come to see clearly themselves and their conduct, and by this new vision or insight become better people.[105]

Austen's heroines are blinded from truth by personal failings, such as sensibility, pride or prejudice, and must come both to self-knowledge (seeing themselves clearly) and knowledge of the world through education. Such 'blindness' in Austen's work has been examined by Devlin. It is seen to cause unhappiness and confusion. In *Northanger Abbey*, Catherine must come to distinguish reality from the world of fiction, and in describing her metaphorical awakening to truth Austen writes:

> Catherine was completely awakened. Henry's address had . . . thoroughly opened her eyes to the extravagance of her late fancies.[106]

In *Pride and Prejudice*, it is Elizabeth Bennet's prejudice that blinds her to Darcy's merits. Far from courting truth, Elizabeth reflects in chapter thirty six that she has 'courted prepossession and ignorance, and driven reason away'.[107] In *Sense and Sensibility*, both heroines, Marianne and Elinor, gain new insights into the characters of Colonel Brandon and Willoughby, while in *Emma* the protagonist overcomes 'the blunders, the blindness of her own head and heart' and attains happiness only having learned to see what *is*, as opposed to what she imagined to be the case. If, as Devlin has argued, Austen's novels are concerned with coming to 'see clearly . . . to gaze on what is real',[108] then the process by which this happens is Austen's lesson in female education.

Austen's novels were doubtless influenced by personal experience. The seventh of eight children born to the Revd George Austen and his wife Cassandra, she was educated at home. Her father, who tutored her, introduced her to contemporary fiction and poetry, and encouraged her writing. In her fiction she concerned herself with family life, within a country village setting. It is the world into which she was born: 'the provincial gentry, socially confident in the hereditary possession of land, allied by marriage to the lower reaches of the aristocracy and to the upper levels of trade and providing for its younger sons a respectable independence in the church or armed services'.[109] In such a society, marriage is a woman's guarantee of social consequence, and female education is designed to render a girl marriageable. Even in *Emma* and in *Persuasion*, the spirited Emma and the wise and kindly Anne are ultimately rewarded not with independence but with a suitable husband. However, in Austen's fiction, marriage is presented as an institution which can provide for a woman's happiness and fulfilment, insofar as the match is made prudently. Austen's heroines, therefore, are educated in the prudence necessary to secure happiness within the social conventions of the time.

Austen thus recognises the importance of cultivating female wisdom, and highlights this by creating a number of female characters whose idleness has made them foolish and even dangerous. For example, motherhood alone is seen to reduce women to silliness: Isabella Knightley in *Emma* is obsessed with her children's health, while Mrs Bennet's nerves, in *Pride and Prejudice*, and the idle meddling of the protagonist in *Emma*, 'are all symptoms of a corrosive ennui'.[110]

Austen privileges home education over school or college education for girls and women. It is at home that character is formed, and good character is formed in an environment of love. Writing on Austen in the *North British Review* (1870), Richard Simpson observed:

> Miss Austen seems to be saturated with the platonic idea that the giving and receiving of knowledge, the active formation of another's character, or the more passive growth under another's guidance, is the true and strongest foundation of love.[111]

In her exploration of the importance of parental guidance, she was also influenced by Locke whom, as Devlin noted, she had read. She certainly had known Locke's *Some Thoughts Concerning Education* (1693) which had reached its twenty-fifth edition by 1777. It stressed the importance of childhood education, and the importance of a private tutor. Austen extended the notion of a private tutor to include a wise older person, such as Mr Knightley in *Emma*. She also emphasised, most particularly in *Mansfield Park*, the Lockean position that errors in early education are manifest in adult life.

Her preference for home education over school education is evident in *Emma*. Mrs Goddard's old-fashioned boarding school is described as an establishment where 'a reasonable quantity of accomplishments were sold at a reasonable price . . . [and where] girls might be sent to be out of the way and scramble themselves into a little education, without any danger of coming back prodigies'.[112] Significantly, it provided Harriet Smith with her education. Mr Knightley, the voice of authority and wisdom in *Emma*, remarks of Harriet that 'she is not a sensible girl, nor a girl of any information. She has been taught nothing useful'.[113] Similarly, the inadequate education of the plain and impoverished Miss Bates has left her in a 'predicament' no doubt familiar to eighteenth-century women readers: '. . . she had no intellectual superiority to make atonement to herself, or frighten those who might hate her, into outward respect'.[114]

A superficial education in 'accomplishments' is also criticised by Austen. In *Pride and Prejudice* Mr Darcy observes that in fact 'the word [accomplishments] is applied to many a woman who deserves it no otherwise than by netting a purse, or covering a skreen'.[115] With similar cynicism, Austen describes Charlotte's room, in *Sense and Sensibility*, in which their hung 'a landscape in coloured silks . . . proof of her having spent seven years at a great school in town to some effect'.[116]

In addition to a reliable tutor, good home education for Austen's women is provided through well chosen reading material. Nonetheless, Austen also recognised the dull aridity of contemporary conduct literature for women. In *Pride and Prejudice*, when Mr Collins is asked to read to the Bennet family, they present him with a novel:

> On beholding it (for everything announced it to be from a circulating library,) he started back, and begging pardon, protested that he never read novels. . . .Other books were produced, and, after some deliberation he chose Fordyce's *Sermons*.[117]

His choice of Fordyce's popular contemporary conduct book for young ladies is met with horror by the lively Lydia who quickly tries to interrupt him. The offended Mr Collins remarks:

> I have often observed how little young ladies are interested by books of a serious stamp, though written solely for their benefit. It amazes me, I confess; – for certainly their can be nothing so advantageous to them as instruction.[118]

While the foolish Lydia could most benefit from the guidance of a good home education, the lessons of Fordyce, in the mouth of Mr Collins, are clearly unlikely to be of any lasting worth. Austen's female characters learn the lessons of life through the guidance of a worthy mentor or tutor, or by harsh experience. Her novels suggest that information gleaned from books alone is not true wisdom. Mary Bennet, the least colourful of the sisters, is the bookish member of the family. At crucial moments in her sisters' lives, she is 'deep in the study of thorough bass and human nature' and she obliges them to listen to 'some new observations of thread-bare morality'.[119] She is called upon by Mr Bennet for her opinions on family matters because she is 'a young lady of deep reflection . . . and [has] read great books', yet she cannot think of 'something very sensible' to say in response. So removed is she from the social pastimes in which her sisters engage, that the reader is not surprised to find her unmarried at the end of the novel. Nonetheless, Mary is not ridiculed for her erudition and the 'solidity of her reflections':[120] it merely places her at a remove from her family. Indeed it is to Mary that Austen gives one of the most significant observations on human nature in the novel, when she comments to Elizabeth:

> Pride . . . is a very common failing I believe. By all that I have
> ever read, I am convinced that . . . human nature is particularly prone to
> it. . . . Vanity and pride are different things, though the words are often
> used synonymously. A person may be proud without being vain. Pride
> relates more to our opinion of ourselves, vanity to what we would have
> others think of us.[121]

While Mary's lessons in life are learned second-hand, she has the ability
to translate them to real life. She contrasts with Mr Collins, who, despite his
diet of sensible books, has not attained self-knowledge: concerned deeply
with the opinions of others, he is truly vain. Austen tells the reader that
Collins, 'though he belonged to one of the universities', has not been improved by education:

> Mr Collins was not a sensible man, and the deficiency of nature had
> been but little assisted by education or society.[122]

For Austen, 'theoretical' instruction is not adequate: the importance of all
learning is that it can be put into practice. She develops this theme in *Mansfield
Park*, causing Sir Thomas Bertram to reflect, at the end of the novel, on his
'plan of education' for his daughters:

> He feared that principle, active principle, had been wanting, that they
> had never been properly taught to govern their inclinations and tem-
> pers. . . . They had been instructed theoretically in their religion, but
> never required to bring it into daily practice. To be distinguished for
> elegance and accomplishments – the authorised object of their youth –
> could have no useful influence that way, no moral effect on the mind.[123]

Sir Thomas's daughters are the products of flawed female education, and
through them Austen criticises the contemporary neglect of the development
of female reason. Sir Thomas begins to see 'a deficiency' in them which,
despite 'the cost and care of . . . [their] education', he recognises as undevel-
oped 'character'.[124]

Austen's novels may be seen as a development from the tradition of
conduct literature examined in Chapter Two (*supra*). In suggesting the deficiencies in the education of her heriones, she educates her readers. Her messages, while woven into the fabric of entertaining fiction, are clear: good
character, prudence, good humour and humility are rewarded with happy
marriages and stability; vanity, pride and foolishness can only bring misery.

The novels of Burney and Austen are seen to develop from the tradition
of conduct literature, in so far as they treat of the character development of
the heroine, and they are underpinned by a moral code. By the middle of the

nineteenth century, however, references to female education reflect actual developments in the schooling and college education of women, and offer perspectives on the social role of educated women. Among the most popular mid-Victorian novelists to address the theme of female education was George Eliot, while the poet Lord Tennyson, in *The Princess* (1847), created one of the most enduring literary images of the 'sweet girl graduate'. Significantly, both Eliot and Tennyson were aware of the movement for the higher education of women. George Eliot (1819-80), published her major works between 1858 and 1876. Writing in the middle of the nineteenth century, she was influenced by the contemporary debate about higher education for women, and took an interest in the founding of Girton College, Cambridge.[125] Tennyson, a member of the Cambridge Apostles, a circle of men which had included F.D. Maurice, one of the founders of Queen's College, was doubtless influenced by what John Killham (1958) has described as nineteenth century 'feminism at Cambridge'.[126]

George Eliot's fiction suggests tensions between the recognition of the need for the intellectual liberation of women, and the reactions of society to intellectual women. In *Middlemarch* (1872), she 'delineates the disastrous effects of the narrow scope permitted to women in the nineteenth century'.[127] Rosamond Vincy's superficiality is a consequence of her genteel education in the accomplishments. While a model young lady, she is selfish and vain, and brings misery to herself and her husband, Tertius Lydgate. Dorothea Brooke, on the other hand, is hungry for learning, but her intellectual needs are stifled within her role of wife to Casaubon. Like Rosamond, she suffers the consequences of a faulty education, for she is initially unable to judge Casaubon's true intellectual worth and his suitability as her husband and mentor. For Dorothea, after the 'toy-box history of the world adopted to young ladies which made the chief part of her education, Mr Casaubon's talk of his great book was full of new vistas'.[128] As her marriage approaches, she looks forward 'to higher initiation in his ideas'.[129] But, as Evans (1980) has argued, Casaubon cannot educate Dorothea because he is, himself, uneducated: his knowledge is not applied to benefit himself or society.[130] In describing the ideal marriage he articulates a contemporary view, shared by those who subscribed to female education in accomplishments, that the woman should be educated for marriage rather than for independent thought. It signals to the reader that Dorothea, with her vision of a union based on mutual interests and respect, is fated to a sterile marriage:

> A man of good position should expect and carefully choose a blooming young lady – the younger the better because more educable and submissive – of equal rank . . . , of religious principles, virtuous disposition and good understanding . . . a modest young lady, with the purely

appreciative unambitious abilities of her sex . . . sure to think her husband's mind is powerful.[131]

Dorothea, though she fills many of the above requirements for Casaubon, is intellectually curious. Her intellectual poverty is partly a result of her own insufficient education and partly a result of marriage to a man who imagines that she has the 'appreciative unambitious abilities of her sex'. In *The Mill on the Floss* (1860), Maggie's superficial education has also contributed to her feeling of intellectual emptiness:

> . . . of all her school life there was nothing left her now but her little collection of school books which she turned over with a sickening sense that she knew them all, and they were of barren comfort. Even at school she had often wished for books with *more* in them: everything she learned there seemed like the ends of long threads that snapped immediately.[132]

While critical of the type of education that left women with little self-esteem or resources for intellectual development, Eliot did not propose formal higher education for women as a desirable option. She carried out a lengthy correspondence with Emily Davies, founder of Girton College, in which she encouraged Davies to be ambitious in seeking financial support for her college for women, but she did not articulate support for such a venture in her novels. In fact her novels indicate a certain cynicism about university education *per se*. In *Daniel Deronda* (1876), Sir Hugo advises Daniel against a life of scholarship, arguing that unless a man is to get 'the prestige and income of a Don . . . its hardly worthwhile for him to make a Greek and Latin machine of himself'.[133] In *Middlemarch*, Casaubon has become just such a machine, and his service to scholarship destroys his health, his marriage, and any possibility of self-knowledge. However, as Carol A. Martin (1980) has argued, in her creation of the self-centred Rosamond (*Middlemarch*), Esther (*Felix Holt*) and Gwendoline (*Daniel Deronda*), Eliot criticises 'the whole of English society in the 1860s' without 'offering a definite plan' for the education of Englishwomen.[134]

Tennyson's *The Princess*, which he began in 1839 and published in 1847, does, however, present a plan for female education in a university created expressly to separate women from men, and with a central female character who does not, at first, believe that a woman can be both a scholar and a wife. Exactly what inspired Tennyson to write *The Princess* remains a subject of conjecture, but it can reasonably be assumed that he was very familiar with contemporary discussions about female education, from popular periodicals, and within his circle, the Cambridge Apostles. Within Cambridge generally, feminist debate was growing. Tennyson, who entered Cambridge in 1827, was a contemporary of J.S. Mill and Charles Buller, both of whom spoke in support of female suffrage. It is possible that Tennyson had been influenced by an article by Frederick Dennison Maurice, a founder member of Queen's College and a Cambridge Apostle, which appeared in the *Metropolitan Quarterly Magazine* in 1825. This magazine was the publication of the Cambridge Apostles. Discussion of the article among the Apostles is a possible source of inspiration. It is equally possible that Tennyson may have read Maurice's novel, *Eustace Conway* (1834), in which a young lady, responding to her brother's grumbles about university life, suggests that the universities should be given over to women.

Tennyson probably drafted his earliest ideas for *The Princess* in 1838 or 1839. His *Memoirs* suggest that he discussed the writing of it with his mother in 1839, at a time when 'the project of a Women's College . . . was in the air'.[135] However, as the first women's colleges of higher education, Queen's College and Bedford College, were founded in 1848 and 1849 respectively, it is unlikely that any specific college inspired the writing of *The Princess*, although Tennyson certainly equated the college in *The Princess* with a university college rather than a small private seminary for ladies. The manuscript bore the title 'The New University',[136] and in 1845 Aubrey de Vere listened to a reading of Tennyson's 'University of Women'.[137] Additionally, in 1846 Elizabeth Barret Browning wrote to Robert Browning that Tennyson had finished the second book of a blank verse fairy tale 'called the university, the uni-members being all females'.[138]

It is likely, then, that the idea for *The Princess* developed from ideas and discussions rather than a concrete contemporary college proposal. This is hinted at within the Prologue to the poem. The Prologue suggests that it was supposedly related by a group of young men to entertain guests at a house-party. They were, as Killham has pointed out, playing a game enjoyed by Tennyson and the Cambridge Apostles: 'Taking up a topic of conversation – the aspiration that women should be allowed to enjoy a university education – they one after another fitted to it a story made up as they went along'.[139] The Prologue tells us that the theme was inspired by the hosts' sister, Lilia, who was jealous of the college life of her brother, Walter, and his friends.

In the Prologue, Walter dismisses women as the weaker sex, but Lilia defends her sex with the familiar argument that they are weaker because of their defective education, and she dreams of founding a college for women:

> It is but bringing up, no more than that:
>   . . . Oh I wish
> That I were some great princess, I would build
> Far off from men a college like a man's,
> And I would teach them all that men are taught. . . .[140]

The young men are amused at Lilia's proposal, and one of them, reflecting with amusement on the image of a female college, replies:

> . . . Pretty were the sight
> If our old hall could change their sex, and flaunt
> With prudes for proctors, dowagers for deans,
> And sweet girl-graduates in their golden hair.[141]

The men, for the entertainment of the party, begin the game of inventing this female college in a story which forms the text of *The Princess*. It concerns the Princess Ida who founds a university for women, imposing a death penalty on male intruders. However, the princess, while a baby, was betrothed in marriage to a prince who pursues her to the university and enters disguised as a woman. When he meets with the princess, she explains that the purpose of the university is 'to lift the woman's fallen divinity/upon an even pedestal with men', but he argues that this is not woman's destiny:

> . . . you
> With only Fame for spouse and your great deeds
> For issue, yet may live in vain, and miss,
> Meanwhile, what every woman counts her due,
> Love, children, happiness.[142]

She responds passionately that motherhood is not every woman's desire: many women desire the posterity brought by great deeds which is reserved for men: 'Children . . . we like them well, but children die; and let me tell you, girl, howe'er you babble, great deeds cannot die'.[143] The prince ultimately wins his princess, but only because she learns that he has come to understand and share her views on the emancipation of her sex, and because she realises the importance of motherhood.

The university for women, founded by the Princess Ida, recalls the almost conventual life for women envisaged by Mary Astell in the *Proposal* (1694) and Sarah Scott in *Millenium Hall* (1762). The university gates carry the bold inscription 'LET NO MAN ENTER IN ON PAIN OF DEATH'[144] and the university statutes demand the following of the students:

> Not for three years to correspond with home;
> Not for three years to cross the liberties;
> Not for three years to speak with any men. . . .[145]

The students follow the traditionally male curriculum:

> The morals, something of the frame, the rock,
> The star, the bird, the fish, the shell, the flower,
> Electric, chemic laws, and all the rest. . . .[146]

Yet while the aim of the university is to establish the equality of the sexes, and to lift woman onto 'an even pedestal with man', some of the students articulate the contemporary fears engendered by those hostile to female education:

> . . . [they] murmured that their May
> Was passing: what was learning unto them?
> They wished to marry; they could rule a house;
> Men hated learned women.[147]

As John Killham (1958) has noted in his study of *The Princess*, it does not deal directly with the question of woman's academic or remunerative work at all, rather it deals with the issue of the marriage relationship after women have been allowed to exploit their intellectual capacity. The poem does not, ultimately, challenge the contemporary ideology of femininity: the princess marries the prince and comes to recognise the importance of motherhood. What Tennyson failed to address in *The Princess* was the possibility that female communities or colleges might be founded as a positive alternative to – rather than a negative reaction to- marriage. Certainly there was a groundswell of popular opinion, articulated by Tennyson's contemporaries in books, periodicals and magazines, that proposals to found colleges for women were conceived in a spirit of indifference – or even hostility – to the female duties of marriage and motherhood.

The Princess may have done something to allay fears that women would forfeit marriage for education in giving to popular literature a new stereotype, that of the 'sweet girl graduate'. It was an acceptable and anodyne image, and one which served the pioneers of women's education well. With her 'golden hair', the sweet girl graduate provided a popular alternative to the stereotypical learned woman who was invariably a masculine or pedantic figure. *The Princess* was referred to in a number of contemporary articles on female education. It was discussed in the *Quarterly Review* (1848),[148] and was quoted in the *Englishwoman's Journal* (1859, 1863).[149] In 1892, the popular novelist L.T. Meade adopted the image for one of her most popular novels for girls, *A Sweet Girl Graduate*. Set in a college modelled on Newnham, it offered a 'non-threatening picture of an early women's college, one that served to enhance the respectability of real women's colleges'.[150] She followed it with a novel based loosely on Girton College in *The Girls of Merton College*.

Similarly, Angela Brazil's fiction which reflected developments in schooling at the start of the twentieth century, suggested to readers the distinct possibility that the graduates of such schools could challenge the Victorian concepts of femininity. In her novel *St. Catherine's College* the school boasts of the success of three sisters: 'Joyce was studying for her degree at Northcliff University, Jean attending a college of Domestic Science, and Dora was . . . to devote herself entirely to Art'.[151] Brazil presented her readers not with limits but with goals. Girls could identify with those fictional sisters who attended university and colleges of domestic science, and widen their vision of the opportunities that life might bring them, and a career became a viable alternative to marriage.

Literature continued to reflect developments in female education in the late nineteenth century and indeed it is noteworthy that the Renaissance stereotype of the masculine learned woman re-emerged in such literature as the 'New Woman'. David Rubenstein (1986)[152] and Elaine Showalter (1982)[153] have provided comprehensive studies of late nineteenth-century New Woman fiction, penned by writers such as Sarah Grand, Louise Ram ('Ouida'), George Meredith, George Gissing, George Moore and Thomas Hardy, which would have been read by the women who had graduated from the first colleges for women. They have also noted the reaction of the 'anti-feminists' to such literature, and the characterisation of the New Woman as 'mannish, dowdy, flighty, incompetent and insistent'.[154] Intellectual women, especially those who went to college, were lampooned in popular periodicals and magazines such as *Punch* which carried the following verse in 1894, at a time when women were pursuing full membership of the University of Cambridge:

> There is a New Woman, and what do you think?
> She lives upon nothing but Foolscap and Ink!
> But, though Foolscap and Ink form the whole of her diet,
> This nagging New Woman can never be quiet.[155]

At the end of the century the caricature of the learned woman, re-named the New Woman because of her formal education, differed little from the caricature of the learned woman in literature since the Renaissance.

Literary texts, then, can be said to occupy a particularly important place in the history of the education of women in English writing. They treated of many of the issues which were of concern to those debating the question of higher education for women: the curriculum, the purpose and the governance of a female university were all subjects for writers. These works also anticipated the problems which would beset those women who pioneered the opening of university education to women: Emily Davies at Girton College and Mrs Reid at Bedford College would negotiate the dangerous area of defining a new curriculum for women, and of establishing college rules that would temporarily separate women from men without calling into question the ultimate status of marriage and motherhood.

4

Anatomizing Female Reason: Medical Literature and Popular Print Culture

MEDICAL OPINION AND SCIENTIFIC EXPERIMENT

In the seventeenth century, arguments put forth by women in support of the higher education of their sex emphasised that such an education would make women more pious, chaste and obedient.[1] In the eighteenth century, the basis of the argument shifted and the development of female reason became the focus of much educational writing. This shift was consonant with the contemporary intellectual climate: the Lockean concept of the human mind as a *tabula rasa* at birth gave substance to the argument that there was no sex characteristic in the human intellect, hence, with the same education, men and women could develop similar intellectual abilities.[2] Emphasis on female piety gave way to the notion of female virtue, arrived at by the exercise of female reason: a woman who grasped the tenets of Christianity through reason would better aspire towards virtue and would not simply 'learn' to be good.

By the nineteenth century, a third fundamental shift in the ideological basis of the argument for the education of women may be traced in contemporary writing. Women increasingly associated female education with intellectual equality, vocational preparation and financial independence. As a *raison d'être* for female education, the salvation of the soul was supplanted by the development of the self. This shift reflected not only change in the intellectual climate of the time, but the impact of transforming movements within the church, the economy, science, and the dynamics of family life. The spread of Evangelicalism gave women important vocational roles both in the spiritual education of their children and in the organisation of charitable societies. The burgeoning economy and growth of industrialisation rendered women of the middle classes virtually redundant as agents of domestic economy, allowing them leisure time in which to develop intellectual interests. Against these changes, the middle of the nineteenth century saw medical science and evolutionary theory providing new evidence in support of arguments for the physical and mental unsuitability of women for education.[3] By the end of the century, however, women themselves had entered the fields of medicine and scholarship and furnished the debate with authoritative accounts of the suitability of women for higher education. Additionally, economic necessity, together with a gradual change in attitude towards the role of women, rendered it possible – even desirable – that women of the middle and upper-middle classes should attend colleges of higher education.

It is not a coincidence, however, that women began to enjoy greater physical and intellectual liberty at the end of the nineteenth century, when it had finally become clear that menstruation was not a disease (Ryan: 1841) or an illness (Waller: 1839), rather it was linked causally to ovulation and reproduction (Hitchmann & Adler: 1908).[4] The intellectual stimulation of the female mind became an acceptable concept only when it was widely agreed that it could not damage the female mind. It was widely agreed that excessive mental stimulation could result in hysteria, a term which covered 'the entire range of the emotions, including depression, nervous fits and psychosomatic illness'.[5] Hysteria (Laycock: 1840; Ryan: 1841; Tilt: 1852; Carter: 1855; Skey: 1867; and Barnes: 1873), a female syndrome which the great body of medical knowledge accepted as gender-specific and somehow related to the uterus, was not dismissed until the early twentieth century, and chlorosis, a widespread female complaint blamed upon a variety of causes including mental and physical exertion, and sometimes occasioning the cessation of the menses, was not recognised as anaemia until the end of the nineteenth century. It had been defined as 'an obstruction from the womb-vessels of females' (Solomon: 1817) and a disease resulting from 'grief, sadness, jealousy, disappointment in love, and privation of sexual enjoyment' (Ryan: 1841). In 1893, Alfred Lewis Galabin MD recognised it as a 'disease largely dependent upon congenital predisposition, and frequently associated with imperfect development of the heart', explaining the poor skin colour of afflicted females by concluding that 'chlorosis differs from other forms of anaemia chiefly in the fact that the deficiency in haemoglobin is far more than proportionate to the deficiency in number of the red corpuscles'.[6]

As Jalland and Hooper (1986) have noted, the nature of woman in nineteenth-century England 'was conceived by contemporaries primarily in biological terms',[7] and 'views of the biological destiny of women often included a biological devaluation of women's capacity outside the domestic world of reproduction'.[8] It seems that medical opinion throughout most of the nineteenth century concurred with the general notion that the female mind and body were directly and somewhat mysteriously influenced by the uterus, and it was widely agreed that there was 'sex in mind', that is, essentially different male and female mental capabilities.[9] Much scientific writing supported the theory that there were 'radical, natural, permanent distinctions in the mental and moral conformation, corresponding with those in the physical organisation of the sex' (Allan: 1868).[10] Webster's argument that there was 'no more important relation in the human organism than that existing between the brain and the reproductive system' (Webster: 1892)[11] exercised sufficient contemporary credence that the over-exertion of the female mind through education was arguably a very real fear for parents.

Excessive stimulation of the brain could lead to nervous hysteria, a female illness much discussed in the nineteenth century. Burstyn (1980) argues that in utilizing such theories the nineteenth century 'discussion of higher education for women bore a different stamp from earlier ones'.[12] This is not the case. As noted earlier, Renaissance scholars frequently cited the 'etymological association of hysteria with the uterus'[13] as a reason for the inferior mental powers of the female sex, and their unsuitability for education. Such theories were commonplace from the early sixteenth century at least. Tiraqueau's *De legibus connubialibus* (1513) established woman's inferiority to man in part on medical evidence, and indeed Renaissance medical scholarship frequently referred to Aristotle's *Historia animalium* (IX.I) which supported the idea that the effect of the uterus on the mind was to weaken rationality.[14]

That the close association of hysteria with the uterus should have survived intact into the nineteenth century is of major significance to a comprehensive understanding of women's history: it is a clear indication that a great weight of authority supported notions of biological determinism which kept women from strenuous physical and mental activity. Laycock (1840) argued:

> The relations of hysteria to the present modes of education are of great importance. The anxiety to render a young lady accomplished, at all hazards, has originated a system of forced mental training, which greatly increases the irritability of the brain.[15]

Laycock's 'cure' for such a disposition was marriage. In support of his position he cited the 'father of medicine' Hippocrates (460-375 BC), again suggesting centuries of continuity in the theoretical basis of medical knowledge of women. Marriage was suggested as a cure for hysteria, since the 'robust unmarried female' had fully developed reproductive organs thus 'strong passions, indolence, and luxury, fail[ed] not to produce their effects on the system, and to develop the sthenic form of hysteria'.[16] Once married, and 'the ovaria being excited to the performance of their proper function',[17] women, it was argued, were much less likely to suffer from nervous hysteria.

It is evident from contemporary medical essays that motherhood was viewed as the primary function of women:

> The character of a woman's mind is chiefly determined by the part she

bears in relation to generation. Her destiny [is] to be united to a husband and to become a mother.[18]

Marriage not only fulfilled female destiny through motherhood, but it legitimised female sexual activity which was seen, at least by some writers, as
necessary to their health:

> It is a fact . . . that women who have never had sexual commerce begin
> to droop when about twenty-five years of age, that they become pale
> and languid . . . their forms degenerate, their features sink, and the
> peculiar character of the old maid becomes apparent.[19]

The life of the single woman, on the other hand, was likely to be confined
and unhealthy, and hysteria was considered to be 'most prevalent in the young
female members of the higher and middle classes, of such as live[d] a life of
ease and luxury' (Skey: 1864), while 'young ladies who subscribe[d] to the
circulating library . . . [were] most superlatively affected' (Johnson: 1850).

In addition to fearing the possible strain of overwork on women's brains,
medical opinion was sufficiently unsure of the nature of reproduction and
menstruation to fear the damage an active life might do to potential mothers.
Mason (1845) and Allan (1869) articulated a view of woman that reduced
her to 'an admirably constructed apparatus for the most mysterious and sublime of nature's mysteries – the reproductive process' (Allan:1869). The exact
workings of this apparatus were, for most of the nineteenth century, still a
subject of speculation, and ignorance bred enough fear to warrant the protection of women by limiting their activities. In particular, the nature and origins of menstruation confused doctors, and caused them to advise that 'during
the performance of this function all strong mental and corporeal exertions
ought to be carefully avoided'. (Ryan:1841).

The onset of menstruation marked puberty. Puberty was a widely accepted 'phase' of the female life-cycle,[20] following childhood, in which a girl
became ready for marriage and childbirth. In the light of contemporary su-
perstition and confusion about the female reproductive process, adolescent
girls were considered particularly sensitive and over-stimulation (both physical and mental) was criticised in medical literature:

> . . . we must insist, as we have the good of the nation at heart, that no
> woman shall enter upon . . . absorbing intellectual pursuits in the criti-
> cal, formative period between the advent and the full establishment of
> womanhood.[21]

(Webster: 1892)

During the crisis of puberty, and until puberty is fully confirmed, there should be a general relaxation from study, which might otherwise too forcibly engross the mind, and the energies required by the constitution to work out nature's ends.[22]

(Tilt: 1852)

A great weight of evidence shaped nineteenth-century middle-class parents' understanding of what their daughters should and could do. It is difficult to argue that such evidence was gathered with the explicit intention of using it to exclude women from education and from public life, although the dissemination of such ideas into the public sphere *via* popular periodicals doubtless influenced many parents and educationalists. Anne Digby (1989) has, however, argued that in the second half of the nineteenth century the 'hostile pronouncements' of several leading medical men 'were precisely correlated with specific developments in women's education so as to achieve maximum impact'.[23] Digby focuses on the work of Drs Clouston, Maudsley, Playfair and Thorburn.[24] Maudsley's views on women and education were derived from the ideas of Dr Clarke of Harvard University who had published, in his book *Sex in Education*, evidence that advanced education for women had pathological effects. Maudsley's 'Sex in Mind and Education', published in the *Fortnightly Review* in 1874,[25] quickly brought the main arguments of Clarke's book to the British scene. Digby (1989) suggests that the *Fortnightly Review* gave his ideas a much wider readership that a specialist medical journal might have done. Left unchallenged, Maudsley's allegations could have seriously damaged the newly created Girls Public Day School Company, and weakened establishments such as Queen's College and Girton College. As seen below, Elizabeth Garrett Anderson found it necessary to counter his claims in a subsequent edition of the *Fortnightly Review*.[26]

T.S. Clouston's *Female Education from a Medical Point of View* appeared in 1882, in the midst of a heated debate as to the dangers of overwork and strain on school children. His enquiries into 'advanced schools for ladies' revealed that the competitive spirit and the stress of public examinations was 'alien to their mental constitution'.[27] Clouston viewed the body as a machine and considered that the female body was less capable of 'the regular grind that the man can keep up':

The [female] machine is less tough, and breaks down at slighter causes. It has more calls on it. It needs more careful management . . . Having beauty and harmony as two of its greatest aims, its strength is not so great. Having to lay up more strength for the future, it can't expend so much in the present. Sensitiveness always implies delicacy, and in many cases instability in nature.[28]

Clouston's message was very clear: the female was, by definition, fragile. It is noteworthy, however, that frailty was presented as a desirable female characteristic. Clouston became part of the tradition of writers who bolstered their arguments with references to the somewhat unscientific premise of sexual attraction when he notes that 'men certainly don't, in their hearts, like to see girls competing keenly with each other for anything'.[29] This appeal to women's sense of what renders them attractive to men greatly weakened the essential argument that women are incapable of keen competition and rigourous study. Similarly, when Clouston argued that study might cause young women to lose weight and damage their health, the veneer of medical objectivity was underscored with the observation that 'fat, the most essential concomitant of female adolescence . . . gives roundness, plumpness, and beauty'.[30] Clouston provided readers with a terrifying account of the dangers of female education:

> I have seen girls, the daughters of well-grown parents, who simply stopped growing too soon. They are more or less dwarfish specimens of their kind; this being caused, as I believe, by the vital and nervous force being appropriated by the mental part of the brain in learning its tasks; and the conditions of life in the schoolrooms not being good . . . I have seen other girls who grew tall enough, but wouldn't fatten. They remained thin and scrawny. Now, this is not what a woman should be at any age if it can be helped.[31]

The many diseases and afflictions which Clouston believed could afflict studious girls included 'anaemia . . . stunted growth . . . nervousness . . . undue excitability, bodily restlessness . . . ungrounded fears, deficient power of self-control, [and] over-sensitiveness in all directions'.[32] Clouston, like many of his contemporaries, then turned to the question of female duty, and rested his 'scientific' conclusion that girls should not pursue learning on the conventional perception of true womanhood:

> No intellectual results, no culture, no mental elevation can make up to the world for the loss of any perceptible degree of motherhood.[33]

His paper, a discourse based on his observations as a medical man, reflects personal opinions and makes an appeal to sentiment and tradition as it concludes with a reflection on learned women:

> The unceasing grind at book-knowledge, from thirteen to twenty, has actually warped the woman's nature, and stunted some of her most characteristic qualities. She is no doubt cultured, but then she is unsym-

pathetic; learned, but not self-denying. . . . Softness is deficient. It takes too much to alter the female type of mind, but a few generations of masculine education will go far to make some change. If the main aims and ambitions of many women are other than to be loved, admired, helped, and helpful, to be good wives and mothers with quiverfuls of children, to be self-sacrificing, and to be the centres of home-life, then those women will have undergone a change from the present feminine type of mind.[34]

Clouston's paper doubtless had much influence: it was presented at the Philosophical Institute, Edinburgh, in November 1882, published as a pamphlet in the same year, and was reprinted in the *Popular Science Monthly* in 1883 and 1884. Digby (1989) notes that John Thorburn, Professor of Obstetrics at Manchester, 'extended Clouston's argument to the realm of higher education in 1884, in a lecture delivered only a week after the University of Oxford had recognized women there'.[35]

Thorburn argued that in pursuing higher education, women entered upon one of the most dangerous occupations in life. Hard mental strain during a menstrual period, he argued, could cause permanent mental damage. Much of his argument against higher education for women was predicated on references to the negative effects of such education on the female periodic function, and little other substantial negative evidence was produced. However, when Thorburn repeated much of the material a year later in *A Practical Treatise on the Diseases of Women*, he drew on the potent image of the masculine woman when he suggested that study could result in 'the unsexing of the girl'.[36]

Elizabeth Garret Anderson MD, in letters to the *Times* in 1880 and 1881,[37] argued that parents had a responsibility to see that girls did not overwork, but stated that between the ages of sixteen and eighteen girls were quite capable of taking local examinations, and, from the age of eighteen, young women could pursue university education without damage to their health. Sophie Bryant, the experienced high-school teacher, and later headmistress of North London Collegiate School, concurred with Garret Anderson's point that schoolgirls were capable of certain amounts of study. In *Overwork: From the Teacher's Point of View, with special reference to Work in Schools for Girls*, a lecture delivered at the College of Preceptors in 1884 and later published by Frances Hodgson in 1885, Bryant suggested that doctors quickly diagnosed 'overwork' as the usual cause of headaches and emotional excitement in girls, and then prescribed 'rest' as the cure. Bryant continued:

Doctors scarcely ever say: 'Your daughter is too much given to emotional excitement . . . you must put a stop to everything that feeds this

tendency – no novels, no dissipating amusements, no excitement . . .
give her some definite steady work which will keep her mind fully
occupied. When she gets stronger . . . increase the work, and take every
means to promote the development of her intellectual way. Send her to
a school where the hard-headed classical and mathematical subjects are
taught, as these are the best-known cures for soft-headedness.[38]

Both Anne Digby (1989) and Carol Dyhouse (1976)[39] suggest that, in the
closing decades of the nineteenth century, attacks on girls' education written
form a medical point of view, often reflected the pervasive ideas of 'Social
Darwinism, with its stress on motherhood and the reproduction of the human race'.[40] Dyhouse's research supports the fundamental perspective of this
thesis when she writes:

> . . . narrative accounts which attempt to chronicle 'setbacks' on the one
> hand, to chalk up 'progress' on the other, tend equally toward oversim-
> plification where insufficiently related to changing ideologies and val-
> ues, to the broader themes of social history in any period.[41]

Dyhouse provides scholars with a social context against which to read changing attitudes towards female education in the late nineteenth century, namely
a developing set of 'social Darwinistic ideas about national efficiency and
social progress'.[42] Much of Dyhouse's study focuses on evidence from academics and medical men writing at the turn of the century, and does not fall
into the period under examination in this study. For example, a number of
influential treatises on motherhood, eugenics and the birth-rate were published between 1900-14.[43] However, Dyhouse notes the pervasive influence
of Herbert Spencer who, in *The Principles of Biology* (1867), expressed reservations about the effects of mental strain on women:

> That absolute or relative infertility is generally produced in woman by
> mental labour carried to excess is more clearly shown. Though the
> regimen of upper-class girls is not what it should be yet . . . the defi-
> ciency of reproductive power among them may be reasonably attrib-
> uted to the overtaxing of their brains, an overtaxing which produces a
> serious reaction on the physique. . . . In its full sense the reproductive
> power means the power to bear a well-developed infant, and to supply
> that infant with the natural food for the natural period. Most of the flat-
> chested girls who survive their high pressure education are unable to do
> this.[44]

Earlier, in a treatise written on education in 1861, Spencer had expressed a commonplace opinion when he wrote that 'Men care little for erudition in women, but very much for physical beauty. . . . How many conquests does the blue stocking make through her extensive knowledge of history?'[45] As Dyhouse illustrates, his work reveals a disinclination to distinguish between social arrangement and natural law, a disinclination which, as seen above, he shared by many of his contemporaries in medicine and intellectual life. Dr Whithers-Moore, chairman of the British Medical Association, argued in his address to a meeting at Brighton in 1887:

> I think that it is not good for the human race, considered as progressive, that women should be freed from the restraints which law and custom have imposed upon them, and should receive an education intended to prepare them for the exercise of brain-power in competition with men. And I think this because I am persuaded that neither the preliminary training for such competitive work, nor the subsequent practice of it in the actual life and struggle for existence, can fail to have upon women the effect more or less (and rather more than less) of indisposing them towards, or incapacitating them from their own proper function – for performing the part, I mean which . . . nature has assigned to them in the maintenance and progressive improvement of the human race.[46]

Such historical sources as those cited above indicate that during the last decades of the nineteenth century, in an atmosphere of medical enquiry and of increased awareness of the significance of heredity to the race and nation, we see a shift in emphasis from God (through the word of the Bible) as the source of ordination of woman's role, to nature as having determined her function. Both God and the natural law prescribed the female role as motherhood. It was not difficult, then, for new knowledge in medicine and the principles of Darwinism to become an instrument in the education debate. Digby (1989) has gone so far as to suggest that medical pronouncements concerning women and education 'could be conditioned by their social context'.[47] She concludes:

> The character of much of this medical discourse reflected specialists' investment in it – in both social and economic terms. Investment in . . . social conservatism . . . meant that there was reluctance to subject to critical scrutiny the 'self-evident' truths of received wisdom, as, for example in cases of female hysteria or of nervous diseases. Equally significant was an associated failure to correlate quantitive evidence on the incidence of such illnesses with qualitative rhetoric on its social significance.[48]

While it was outside the scope of Digby's paper to develop this theory, it is here hoped to illustrate clearly the means by which the 'medical' perceptions of female educability achieved plausibility and gained further currency through the medium of popular print culture.

To further develop Digby's position, it may be argued that, while much nineteenth-century medical literature put forward a view that female education could produce a 'crisis' in young women, there is not enough evidence to determine the accuracy of contemporary doctors in their diagnosis of cases of hysteria, or diseases of the uterus, and certainly methods of examination and medical treatments were still crude.[49] There is some suggestion that examinations of ailing women were conducted more in the spirit of gynaecological research that ethical treatment. For example, the 'constant and general use of the speculum' (F.R.C.S.: 1857) caused some alarm among mid-Victorian doctors, while the practice of clitoridectomy came under severe scrutiny following the Barker-Brown controversy which resulted in the expulsion of Isaac Barker Brown from the Obstetrical Society of London in 1867.[50]

What did emerge from the vast *corpus* of Victorian medical writing was a synthetic view of woman as essentially weak, and prone to physical and medical illness. Indeed the constant reiteration of this point of view leads the historian to suspect that ideas were simply regurgitated by doctors in successive publications without the support of new or substantial research. From this view they concluded that women, unlike men, were sensitive, emotional and intuitive (Ryan:1841; Allan:1869). In short, women were in need of protection and were best suited to domestic life. It is not difficult to see why this view of biological determinism will be seized and used by those who sought to oppose the higher education of women. It is important, however, to understand the context in which such a view emerged.

DIDACTIC NON-FICTION: PARADIGMS OF FEMININITY

Just as the sphere of the nineteenth-century woman was limited by the contemporary understanding of her physical and mental capabilities, so too was it curtailed by essentially 'feminine' social, spiritual and sexual constructs. Nineteenth-century representations of appropriate female behaviour have clear indicators as to what was perceived as feminine and masculine. As already noted, marriage followed by childbirth was widely viewed as the most appropriate female behaviour, *ergo*, it was feminine behaviour. Contemporary literature and historical fact combine to give a picture of the freedom women were allowed in defining their social, spiritual and sexual worlds, and provide a key to understanding the terms of the debate about higher education for women.

The public sphere of women in the early decades of the nineteenth century became increasingly limited for a number of reasons. Women's waged work was negatively affected by increased industrialisation. It took them away from traditional occupations in agricultural work and home industry and moved them into 'sweated' industries and domestic work.[51] By 1851, 'two-fifths of working women were in service, and a further two-fifths in textiles and clothing'.[52] Some 600,000 women worked in needlework, millinery and dressmaking by 1861. Much of this labour was accomplished in sweatshops, as employers sought to avoid the legislation which protected women factory workers. Other sources of employment included laundry work, which employed 175,000 women by the 1890s,[53] and retailing. The second half of the nineteenth century saw the number of women shop assistants grow from some 87,000 in 1861 to 250,000 by 1901. These occupations, however, were not deemed suitable for the women with which this study is concerned: women who, like their brothers, sought access to higher education and some of the professions. The presence of women working in industries and homes owned by middle and upper-class men did not seem to suggest to such men that *all* women were capable of work. The division within the female labour force was clearly one of class and not of gender; at no point was it considered that the maid-of-all-work found her daily regime as physically punishing as her mistress would have found Latin and Greek.

It was not until the middle of the nineteenth century that systematic efforts were made to make teaching a viable occupation for gentlewomen. They had always worked as tutors and governesses, but had often suffered abuse at the hands of ungenerous employers. As M. Jeanne Peterson (1980) has noted, this was partly due to their 'status incongruence': the governess 'was a lady, and therefore not a servant, but she was an employee and therefore not of equal status with the wife or daughters of the house'.[54] Additionally, governessing was a sorry reminder to their employers of the economic uncertainties of the time. As Emily Davies pithily observed: 'It is a platform on which middle and upper-classes meet, the one struggling up, the other drifting down'.[55]

If governessing was an acceptable occupation for a 'distressed gentlewoman', this was only so because it imitated motherly duties: those of rearing young children and teaching older daughters the ladylike accomplishments. It was essentially a 'private' sphere and did not threaten the femininity of the governess by involving her in any open or public display. The strong antipathy of many Victorians towards women in public life is reflected in contemporary literature and in the law. Between 1813 and 1815, the *Female Preceptor* reflected the widely-held view that women had no place in professional public life:

> Women . . . are not designed to govern the state, or to command armies; to plead in Westminster Hall, or to preach in the church; and therefore need not study the several sciences leading to those professions.[56]

It was a view which reflected the teachings of St Paul and the educational writings of Vives,[57] and it percolated down to the writers of the popular works on female duties which replaced the eighteenth-century conduct book. Mrs John Sandford reminded readers that 'domestic comfort is the greatest benefit [woman] confers upon society',[58] while the very widely read Sara Ellis advised:

> As women, then, the first thing of importance is to be content to be inferior to men . . . [your] highest duty is so often to suffer and be still . . . [your] deepest enjoyments are all relative.[59]

Sara Stickney Ellis (1799-1872) was a prolific writer of conduct books and fiction, who established a school based on the principles she expounded. Born a Quaker, she rejected the Society of Friends and joined the Congregationalists. In 1837 she married William Ellis, a missionary. She was actively involved in the temperance movement, and took a morally uncompromising stance in her books.[60] Three of her most popular works, each of which ran to several editions, were standard conduct reading for mid-nineteenth-century girls: *The Women of England* (1838), *The Daughters of England* (1842), and *The Wives of England* (1843). Ellis articulated a common concept: that woman's life is 'relative' to man, and that woman 'has nothing, and is nothing, of herself'.[61] If this position was, as already indicated, substantiated by the limited vocational and professional female spheres, it was firmly corroborated by contemporary legislation which denied an independent legal existence to wives. The great eighteenth-century jurist Sir William Blackstone had, in 1765, illustrated that in marriage the legal existence of woman was incorporated into that of her husband, and that the earnings and property of a married woman belonged to her husband, as did the children of the marriage.

The year 1851 saw the publication of a short work by a prominent feminist to educate women about their position under the law: this was Barbara Bodichon's *Brief Summary of the Laws Concerning Women*, and it was printed as part of the campaign for a Married Women's Property Act. Barbara Leigh Smith Bodichon (1827-91), the daughter of a Radical MP for Norwich, had an unconventional upbringing in the home of her liberal parents who never married. She studied law, political economy and art at the Ladies' College, Bedford Square, and founded and taught at the innovative Portman Hall School where children from different classes and religious backgrounds were educated together. In 1857, she travelled to Algiers where she met and married Eugene Bodichon, and they embarked on a tour of America where they met leading abolitionists and prominent figures in the Women's Rights Movement. Barbara was, all this time, a prolific artist who studied at Corot's studio and frequently exhibited her work, but having become involved in the nineteenth-century women's movement in England, following the publication of her provocative *Brief Summary of the Laws*, she elected to divide her time between Algeirs and England. When in England she wrote for the *English Woman's Journal*, and was instrumental in founding Girton College Cambridge to which she left £10,000, the proceeds of the sale of her paintings, upon her death. Bodichon's *Brief Summary of the Laws* drew attention to the 'Legal Condition of Unmarried Women or Spinsters':[62] the common practice of primogeniture deprived daughters of a share in the family estate equal to that of the eldest son, and the possibility of such daughters earning a living was limited:

> The Church and nearly all offices under Government are closed to women. . . . The professions of law and medicine, whether or not closed by law, are in England closed in fact.[63]

It would seem then that just as the contemporary understanding of gynaecology and psychology limited women's public life, so too did economic change and contemporary legislation. The 'sphere' of middle and upper-class women, for seemingly well-founded reasons, was domestic. As early as 1797, Thomas Gisborne had articulated this position clearly when he listed the following as the ways by which a woman may contribute 'to the welfare of mankind':

> In contributing daily and hourly to the comfort of husbands, of brothers and sisters, and of other relations, connections and friends, in the intercourse of domestic life, under every vicissitude of sickness and health, of joy and affliction. . . . In forming, and improving the general manners, dispositions, and conduct of the other sex, by society and example. . . . In modelling the human mind during the early stages of its growth.[64]

Gisborne argued that God gave to women 'qualities . . . particularly suited to the sphere in which women were intended to move'.[65] These included 'modesty . . . delicacy . . . [and] sympathising sensibility'[66] and they combined to create a popular paradigm of 'female excellence'. The ideology of female excellence, which had been firmly established in eighteenth-century conduct literature, precluded intellectual ability. Intelligent women were 'variations from the general course of things',[67] thus in the early decades of the nine-teenth-century education for women was desirable only 'to enrich the mind with useful and interesting knowledge suitable to their sex'.[68]

It would seem that from the start of the nineteenth century there was some hostility to the idea that such an education should take place in female boarding schools and colleges. Again, the contemporary inclination towards confining the 'public' social world of women is evident, and the idea of a learned female community is largely rejected. Gisborne recommended 'small and select parties, to which a virtuous character shall be a necessary introduc-tion, and in which virtuous friendship and rational entertainment may be enjoyed',[69] anticipating the strong Victorian reaction to the eighteenth-cen-tury salons which he dismissed as 'vast and promiscuous assemblages'. Allega-tions of unseemly behaviour within boarding schools equally fuelled a small fire of hostility towards communities of schoolgirls:

> Thrown together in schools, into one common reservoir, at a danger-ous age, when nature bids an unusual fervour rise in their blood . . . they insensibly convey an infection to each other by tales of sentiment, sympathy and friendship. . . . Hence private correspondencies [sic], as-signations, and intrigue . . . Boarding schools . . . give a forwardness to fruits, but deprive them of their natural healthiness.[70]

More directly, the anonymous author of *The Cherub or Guardian of Female Innocence* (1792) had advised:

> From negligence in some boarding schools, the pupils are permitted to indulge a libidinous curiosity; and excite even a premature inclination, by the perusal of obscene books, which are conveyed privately by the servants.[71]

Such texts suggested a dangerous underside to formal education for girls and women. They also reinforced the point that education did not necessar-ily prepare women for marriage. The Revd John Bennet had argued, in *Stric-tures on Female Education* (1787), that the boarding school did not give women the 'qualities which every man of real taste and sense wishes, particularly, to find in a woman . . . innocence, simplicity, and domestick worth'.[72] A similar argument is used against female colleges in the late nineteenth century:

> The practical question is . . . whether . . . this 'university education' would produce the kind of woman that we should wish as the repre-sentative of the nineteenth-century English lady.[73]

'The welfare of mankind' (Gisborne: 1797) and the 'fundamental notions and instincts of our social life' (*Quarterly Review*, 1869) were notions which shaped nineteenth-century literature on the social role of woman. They were challenged in the mid-nineteenth century, when the image of women as dependent and protected was threatened by the findings of the 1851 census. It clearly indicated a 'surplus' of single women in the population. The higher child mortality rate among boys, together with the loss of men through war and emigration, resulted in fewer men available for marriage. Additionally, towards the middle of the century, fewer men married under the age of thirty. By 1871, two-thirds of all women between the ages of 20 and 24 were single, as were 30% of those aged between 24 and 35. Taking widows into account, it was estimated that for every three women over 20 who were wives, there were two who were widows or spinsters. The implications of these figures for the 'female education' question cannot be overstated. The pioneers of higher education for women built much of their case around the need to provide occupation and training for 'surplus' women. The harsh reality which emerged in the later decades of the nineteenth century was that the female 'sphere' was a luxury which, increasingly, could not be afforded.

The pioneers of higher education for women were also faced with the problem that the contemporary view that just as there was 'sex in mind' (Maudsley: 1874), there was also 'sex in souls'.[74] This perspective gave further weight to the argument that there were separate spheres for men and women, the boundaries of which should not be crossed by education. As already noted, in the seventeenth-century women had laid a claim to education on the very grounds that they had souls, for it had long been disputed that they shared the spiritual dimension of men's lives. The eighteenth-century spirit of Enlightenment, with its increased emphasis on reason and intellectual inquiry, affected a shift in women's conceptions of why they should pursue learning. As already seen, it was increasingly sought as an end in itself. But the female soul as a subject of debate did not vanish. In the nineteenth century, in an atmosphere of industry and family values, the spiritual dimension of women's lives came under renewed scrutiny. It was argued that women were more naturally virtuous than men, and that on women must rest the responsibility for setting the high moral tone that would shape Victorian England. This stand-point became bound up with the contemporary ideology of femininity. Chastity and modesty were desired and necessary virtues for the Victorian girl who aspired towards marriage. On her continued virtuous behaviour following marriage depended the purity of family lineage. Women who flew in the face of such deep-rooted beliefs were not truly 'women' – their femininity was called into question on the grounds of spiritual wantonness.

To no small degree, women's relationship to God was evinced by their social behaviour, and was subject to public scrutiny and censure. God, it was often reminded, had endowed woman with specific female attributes and had equipped her to carry out her female duties. As 'the Giver of all good . . . [God gave] to females . . . qualities particularly suited to the sphere in which women were intended to move',[75] one contemporary writer concluded. Her duties included 'forming and improving the general manners, dispositions, and conduct of the other sex, by society and example'.[76] Taking up this charge, women participated in the social purity movements and philanthropic societies which increased in number in the nineteenth century. These legitimised a role for women in public life.

Between the seventeenth and nineteenth centuries there was a change in the concerns of women guided or motivated by religion. There was a move outward from the 'private' world of the female soul, to the 'public' world of female philanthropy. Movements within the Church doubtless influenced this change. While it is outside the scope of this study to analyse such movements, some important observations can be made. As noted earlier, the spread of the Evangelical movement in the late eighteenth century had been characterized by the zeal of reformers such as William Wilberforce and Hannah More, whose ideas 'helped to reinforce the social hierarchy, which was threatened by the increasingly restive lower classes'.[77] Evangelicalism was particularly well adapted to the expanding middle ranks, men and women who, as Asa Briggs (1979) has noted, found it easier and more advantageous to be good and serious than to be wicked and flippant.[78] The movement enjoyed the renewed energies of the Victorian middle classes, whose watchword was respectability. Its methods of indoctrination included the expanding Sunday school movement, and it is here that the nineteenth-century ideologies of femininity which shaped female education may be located.

Pious periodicals and Sunday school tracts, directed largely at working-class and lower middle-class audiences, reflected a desire among reformers to inculcate in girls 'a two-fold sense of subservience . . . based on social inferiority as well as on the inferiority of gender'.[79] Middle and upper-class girls received signals about appropriate female behaviour from fiction and advice books.[80] The fiction was largely concerned with home and family life,[81] while didactic writings continued to relegate women to a private sphere, and emphasised the synonimity of such a sphere with the salvation of the female soul. 'Who can find a virtuous woman?' asked the *Female Preceptor* (1813), quoting Proverbs (xxxi.10-13). It went on to conclude that 'the Chief excellencies of the female character [were] chastity and piety: on these depend[ed] her success and happiness, not only here but hereafter'.[82]

As seen in earlier literature, the Pauline representation of the man in authority over the woman, and the evidence from Genesis that woman was created as man's 'helpmeet', are commonplace references in contemporary texts:

> Woman . . . is at this hour what 'in the beginning' the great Creator designed her to be – namely Man's help . . . accustomed from the first to ministrations of domestic kindness and the sweet charities of home . . . she is, what she was intended to be, the one great solace of Man's life, his chiefest earthly joy.[83]

Nor were politicians above citing Divine providence in support of a point. The Tory opposition to the Women's Disabilities Bill (1871) included the following in support of 'separate spheres':

> Was the head of the family to be the master of the family or was he not? Was it nature's intention, and was it our Maker's intention, that when society was founded on the family, the man should be at the head of the family and should rule? . . . (Cheers)[84]

Female education, then, was desired insofar as it taught girls ways of virtue, while 'charity' and 'obedience' were considered to be 'moral properties'.[85] In addition to this, Judith Rowbotham (1989) indicates that 'authors writing for the middle class adolescent girls' market were very consciously using their work to convey messages of contemporary . . . concern'.[86] Charlotte Yonge, for example, viewed fiction as 'a sort of instrument for popularising church views'. [87]

The popular view of the spiritually virtuous woman as pious, modest and chaste had, then, remained in tact since the Renaissance. In the nineteenth century, however, it found public expression. Anti-vice agitation, which had enjoyed a brief period of visibility in the 1690s through the Societies for the Reformation of Manners, became the focus for much female energy in the early nineteenth century, and again in the 1880s.[88] Organisations from the later period were particularly vocal, and challenged sexual double standards. The Social Purity Alliance, the Moral Reform Union, the National Vigilance Association, and the Association for the Improvement of Public Morals, all emphasized a 'single moral standard applicable to both sexes and fashioned on the principles of a Christian ethics'.[89] In this respect, they pushed for a vision of virtue that negated the concept of 'sex in souls'.

Many Victorian men rejected the idea that their morality should be policed by women. The fraught debates which surrounded the Contagious Diseases Acts (1864)[90] indicated that there were in operation separate male and female codes of sexual behaviour, which many men were loath to jettison. Many, perhaps, salved their consciences by supporting charitable causes, and by encouraging women to engage in philanthropic work. F.K Prochaska (1990) in a study on nineteenth–century philanthropy, found evidence that in the 1890s middle-class households on average 'spent a larger share of their income on charity that on any item in their budget except food'.[91] Historians increasingly interpret charity 'as a means by which the dominant professional and commercial classes confirmed their power and status'.[92] In a sense, therefore, philanthropic women colluded with men in reinforcing hierarchical values. At the same time, however, many of them learned administrative and organisational skills, and philanthropic work was to 'propel some women into pubic service on local government boards'.[93] The 'spiritual' dimension of female life, which for so long had been identified with piety and chastity, was, by the end of the nineteenth century, identified with a purposeful and moral life to be lived, if not in the service of husbands and children, then in the service of mankind. This shift will be seen to have had a subtle but significant effect on the public perception of the role of higher education in women's lives.

As noted, the social and spiritual dimensions of nineteenth-century women's lives have received some attention in recent scholarship. The study of nineteenth-century women as sexual beings, however, remains relatively unexamined. This is possibly because historians find nineteenth-century sexuality to be a particularly invisible phenomenon. Contemporary sexual problems have been discussed with reference to contemporary medical literature, and some research has been done on marriage patterns, family planning, abortion, and childbirth.[94] But this type of research has centred on women in relation to their biological destiny: motherhood. These are valid areas of research, given that the contemporary ideology of womanhood was so firmly rooted in defining physical and mental limits. But they fail to address a more subtle concept of woman as defined by outward signals of her sexuality, and the challenge to contemporary ideology that unfamiliar or new signals might pose.

Women indicated their femininity by 'looking fresh and pretty'[95] and by exhibiting feminine virtues such as 'patience, self-sacrifice, tenderness, [and] quietness'.[96] How they dressed and behaved gave out clear signals. These signals indicated their suitability, even availability, to live out their biological destiny through marriage and childbirth. In other words, the signals identified the signifier as a (hetero)sexual being. What has not been examined is the tension that emerged when women gave out signals which were not consonant with the general perception of female/feminine behaviour. In fact, reseearch reveals that there was considerable hostility expressed towards women who crossed the perceived borders between male and female spheres, and that this hostility provided the pioneers of higher education for women with yet another challenge: to disassociate the image of intellectual women from the accusation of freakishness.

The hostility was directed at three types of woman: the spinster, who in failing to marry was not fully a woman,[97] the woman of masculine appearance/dress, and the intellectual woman, who was also often attacked for being both masculine and a spinster. This, it will be argued, was one of the most powerful weapons in the armoury of those who opposed women's education. It attacked a vulnerable aspect of the human personality: self-image. Aware of such attacks, Emily Davies and Elizabeth Garrett, two of the pioneers of higher education for women, were acutely aware of the importance of the 'feminine' image of college women.

From the many discussions of womanhood which were printed in nineteenth-century periodicals, there emerged a vision of the woman as defined by her husband. William R. Gregg (1809-81), industrialist, social critic and prolific journalist, in his influential and controversial article in the *National Review* (1862) argued that the 'essentials of woman's being' are that 'they are supported by, and they minister to men'.[98] Dr Maudsley's equally controversial essay 'Sex in Mind and in Education' (1874), which prompted a lengthy response from Dr Elizabeth Garrett Anderson (1874),[99] reminded readers of the *Fortnightly Review* that woman was particularly designed 'to be the helpmate and companion of man in mental and bodily union'.[100] Grant Allen (1848-99), a journalist and populariser of Herbert Spencer's theories of social evolution, discussing the reproduction of the race in the same journal in February 1889, added that 'her emancipation must not be of a sort that interferes in any way with [her] primal natural necessity'.[101] Allen argued that it was 'mathematically demonstrable that most women must become mothers of at least four children, or else the race must cease to exist'.[102] From this point he continued:

> What is the ideal that most of these modern women agitators set before them? Is it not the ideal of an unsexed woman? Are they not always talking to us as though it was not the fact that most women must be wives and mothers? . . . Women ought to glory in their femininity.[103]

The equation of femininity with motherhood, and 'agitation' with 'unsexed women' created potent stereotypes. So too did descriptions of the mannish woman, and it was a woman writer, Eliza Lynn Linton (1822-98), who penned some of the most vitriolic attacks on masculine, and later on intellectual, women. Linton was the youngest of twelve children born to the Revd James Linn, a scholarly man who gave no formal education to his daughters. She became extraordinarily self-reliant and ambitious and taught herself French, Italian, German, and Spanish, and in 1845 she moved to London to become a writer. Writing reviews and articles, she earned an impressive £250 a year and she gradually made a name for herself as a novelist. She had a short and unsuccessful marriage, yet despite this and the fact that she had a lucrative career and a very public life, her writing increasingly circumscribed the female sphere. In 1868, she caused a sensation with a series of essays titled 'The Girl of the Period', which appeared in the *Saturday Review*. They caused enormous controversy, and the expression 'Girl of the Period' became both a generic term and the title of a new magazine.[104] Linton described the Girl of the Period thus:

> She knows that part of her mission is to please and be charming . . . and being womanly she likes the praise of men . . . She has no newfangled notions . . . She does not want to ape the manliness she can never possess. She has always been taught, as there are certain manly virtues, so there are certain feminine ones.[105]

To contrast with the image of the Girl of the Period, Linton sketched out 'the illogical creature who professes to hate men, and who nevertheless imitates them as closely as possible'.[106] Clothing added to the stereotype as she described women 'with cropped hair mostly parted at the side; turned-down linen collars and small black ties' who 'abjured the natural beauties and allurement'.[107] These 'unsexed' females were 'sturdy' and 'stout',[108] in contrast to the 'elegance and grace'[109] which fiction and conduct literature attributed to the female sex. Thomas Gisborne had argued that the female form 'in countries where the progress of civilisation is far advanced . . . [was] cast in a smaller mould, and bound together by looser texture'.[110] The active, robust and capable female was thus unfeminine. *Punch,* a valuable indicator of contemporary attitudes, depicted college women as unattractive and lampooned lady cyclists for de-sexing themselves by graceless exercise:

> When lovely lady takes to wheeling,
> And finds too late that bikes betray,
> Beauty, grace and finer feeling
> She'll see her sex has chucked away.[111]

Even more vitriolic was the contemporary attack on spinsters who were also considered to have 'chucked away' their sex. Maria Rye (1829-1903), the daughter of a London solicitor and an active participant in charity work, had attempted to solve the problem of surplus single women through the Female Middle Class Emigration Society which she organised in 1861. Additionally, the growing women's movement was a reminder that not all women wanted to marry: many would rather an education and paid work. However, it would seem that the spinster was not easily accommodated by the contemporary ideology of womanhood. Grant Allen (1889) argued thatt he self-supporting spinster was 'a deplorable accident of the passing moment', concluding that society 'ought not to erect into and ideal what is in reality a painful necessity . . . the vast majority of women must be wives and mothers, . . . and if either class must be sacrificed to the other, it is the spinsters whose type perishes with them that should be sacrificed'.[112] Allen continued to argue that 'literary women, schoolmistresses, hospital nurses . . . are not of the centre. They are side-lines off the main stream of feminine life',[113] while Linton concluded that it was the 'large dead-weight of spiritless spinsters' who clung to the emancipation movement like 'parasites'.[114]

Linton, with her allegations of 'bastard manliness', stirred up some concern that association with branches of the women's movement called into question a lady's reputation. Equally she, and contemporaries who shared her point of view, argued that such women were 'modern man-haters' and that their educational and vocational ambitions caused them to hold 'home duties in disdain'.[115] Intellectual pursuits were widely considered unnatural for women on the grounds that they 'unsexed' them:

> Women who have cultivated their powers have been branded as 'blue-stockings', or 'petticoated' philosophers', and have been shunned as a species of female monsters.[116]

To reinforce the point that female learning was 'not to be looked for', authors reminded women, much as Hannah More and Dr Gregory had advised a century earlier, that learned women were not attractive to men. Commenting on the notion of university-educated women, the *Quarterly Review* (1869) argued that 'this sort of woman will not be popular with men. The half-educated very naturally do not like it; the highly educated, as a rule, prefer a less intellectual type'.[117] In a similar vein, the diarist, political writer and social reformer Beatrice Webb (1858-1943) recorded in her diary that she had been advised by her friend Professor Marshall 'that marriage was a sacrifice to masculine freedom, and would only be tolerated by male creatures as long as it meant the devotion, body and soul, of the female to the male. Hence the woman must not develop her faculties in a way unpleasant to the man . . . Hence masculine strength and masculine ability in women must be firmly trampled on and boycotted by men'.[118]

The whole dynamic of female sexuality is seen then to be central to any understanding of the education debate. Women, defined by their relationship to men in marriage, fulfilled their biological destiny in childbirth. Deviations from this pattern could be — and were — viewed with suspicion, and allegations of masculinity were made with the clear intention that it was insulting term when applied to a woman. The possibility of being unattractive to men must have alarmed and dismayed some intellectual women. Certainly Beatrice Webb was struck by the way in which Professor Marshall summed up: 'If you compete with us we shan't marry you'.[119] Among the many pre-

conceptions about women with which the pioneers of female education would
have to wrestle was the age-old one that learned women, quite simply, were
unattractive to men. A wealth of contemporary material in Victorian popular
periodicals suggests that the question of women's suitability for education
was discussed in an increasingly public sphere from the middle of the nineteenth century. It is noteworthy that the concerns of journalists, reviewers
and feature writers were couched in language and images which echoed
Renaissance pamphlets and the eighteenth-century conduct books. The *Quarterly Review* (1869), reverting to a Renaissance image, hinted at a widespread
concern:

> The one thing men do not like is the man-woman, and they will never
> believe the College, or University, woman is not that type.[120]

THE EDUCATION OF WOMEN IN POPULAR PERIODICALS

Two landmarks in the history of higher education for women in nineteenth-
century England were the founding of Queen's College, London, in 1848,
and the founding of Girton College (as the College for Women) in 1869.
Queen's offered lectures to governesses and trainee teachers, and lessons to
girls over twelve. It was to produce some of the pioneers of female education.
Among its early students were Sophia Jex Blake who would later 'win the
battle for entry of women into the medical profession and found the London
School of Medicine',[121] Dorothea Beale who would become Principal of
Cheltenham Ladies College, and Frances Mary Buss, Principal of the North
London Collegiate School, and founder of Camden School. Buss, like
Dorothea Beale, would give evidence to the Taunton Commission (1864–
1647). Girton College, founded later and with different aims, was the first
English college founded exclusively for the higher education of women. It
was also the first residential women's college of higher education, and was
eventually to become a member college of the University of Cambridge. A
number of early Girtonians were to become the first women academics in
England, while others became school principals and teachers. In the decades
in which Queen's and Girton opened their doors, interest in the debate about
the education of women was heightened in London and Cambridge.

It is not surprising then to find that the 1840s and the 1860s were years
in which the question of higher education for women came to public attention through popular print culture. It is, however, important to examine the
treatment of this issue by various journals, and to account for shifts in attitude
and perspective. Equally important, though considerably more difficult a task,
is to suggest the impact on society of attitudes expressed in popular periodicals. To gain some insight into the general influence of periodicals on the

mass reading public, it is necessary to examine publishers output and sales figures. In the case of most nineteenth-century periodicals, such figures do not exist in any complete and reliable form. *The Wellesley Index to Victorian Periodicals* notes this with some regret, while pointing scholars to Richard Altick's study of the nineteenth-century mass reading public for an overview in which available figures have been reproduced.[122]

Altick's research clearly indicated that with the rapid growth in population during the nineteenth century there came a huge increase in the mass reading public. In particular, he noted an increase 'in the amorphous stratum between the old established middle class . . . and the working class proper'[123] which was to provide a new mass audience for printed matter during the first half of the nineteenth century. He noted that the evangelicals, who 'stressed the act of reading as part of the program of the truly enlightened life',[124] and the utilitarians, whose faith in the power of printing to disseminate knowledge, widened the reading public. Equally, 'the upper class and especially the older portion of the middle class' bent on 'preserving the hallowed structures'[125] supplied specific reading audiences for journals which were ideologically consonant with their beliefs.

Alvar Ellegard's short study, 'The Readership of the Periodical Press in Mid-Victorian Britain'(1957),[126] collected all available data on sales figures and print runs of the great reviews and magazines. Ellegard, like Altick, noted that the 1860s were 'characterised by a very great expansion in the field of periodical publishing'.[127] This was influenced by the abolition of the compulsory newspaper stamp duty as from July 1st, 1855. Newspapers and reviews could, after this date, be stamped with the 1*d*. impression which allowed them to be sent free of extra charge through the post, thus the stamp returns, which were recorded in the Postmaster General's statistics of newspaper stamps published each year in the House of Commons papers, can be used to estimate circulation. Not all copies were sold through the post, however, and in order to use stamp returns to estimate the total circulation, it is necessary to estimate first that total circulation of each publication.[128] After 1855, selling through a newsagent implied a saving of 1*d*. per copy, thus an ever-increasing number of readers bought unstamped newspapers and magazines. Additionally, stamp returns for the 'pure' Reviews, (that is, those not classed as newspapers) were not recorded, and Ellegard, commenting that information about their circulation is remarkably scarce noted that 'it was apparently not considered good form to reveal circulation figures to the outside world'.[129] The great Reviews, sold through bookshops and by private subscription, were also obtainable through the circulating libraries, and by the end of the nineteenth century, periodicals were cheaply produced, quickly read, and each edition sometimes passed between two or three readers.

Denominational magazines, such as the *Evangelical*, the *Gospel*, and the

General Baptist, had the highest output. Of the periodicals in this study, the *Quarterly Review* and the *Edinburgh Review* each sold about 12,000-13,000 copies per edition, in their early nineteenth-century heyday, while sales of *Blackwood's* peaked in 1831 at 8,000. The *Cornhill's* readership was impressive at about 84,000 between 1860-2, while *Punch's* circulation reached 40,000 in 1854. Altick concurs with the editors of the *Wellesley Index* who illustrate that there was a sizeable readership for magazines and journals of an educational or 'higher class' (see Table 2). These were the journals which addressed the question of women's education with some regularity, and theirs was the educated middle-class readership which engaged in the debate and which provided the first women's colleges with students.

As noted, the denominational periodicals had the largest readership. These publications, throughout the century, reinforced the traditional idea of Christian womanhood, frequently citing the Bible as the source of authority on the divine ordination of male and female spheres. As early as 1832, the *Christian Observer,* a monthly which appealed chiefly to Clergymen of Evangelical opinions,[130] published its 'Review of Works on Female Duties'[131] and by 1866, even as higher education for women was becoming something of a reality following the foundation of Queen's and the inauguration of public lectures for ladies in London, it advised that 'to know something of herself, to love her Bible, and to Love God, are worth all the languages of Babel: which in after-life often serve no better purpose than to make girls useless'.[132]

TABLE 2 Sale of Monthly Periodicals: 1851-1900

Description	No.	Price	Copies per Month
Religious	84	½d.-5d.	1,500,000
Religious Mags.	22	6d. up	400,000
Temperance	20	1s.-2s.3d.	800,000
Entertaining/Educational	19	1d.-6d.	350,000
Magazines and Serials of a Higher Class	54	1s.-2s.6d.	250,000
Serials Issued by the Great Publishing Houses	—	1s.-3s.6d.	350,000

Source: Richard Altick, *The Common Reader* (1957).

Other denominational publications offer an indication of the anti-intellectual attitude of contributors (many of whom were clergy) and a sustained interest in outlining female duties. In the decades of heated public debate about women's education, the *Christian Miscellany* carried 'Woman's Mission'(1862), and 'The Good Wife' (1864), while the *Christian Witness* included 'Obedience of Wives' (1848), and 'The Sphere of Woman' (1860). The nature of female duty was also frequently discussed in the *Christian Penny Magazine*, the *Church of England Magazine*, the *Church of England Quarterly Review* and the *Church of England Monthly Review*. [133] Denominational publications occasionally extended this discussion to embrace a vision of the possible 'use' to women of education. For example, the *Christian Remembrancer*, a quarterly exponent of conservatively orthodox High Church views which was available at Mudies Circulating Library, carried 'Uneducated Women' (1847) and the evangelical *Christian Observer* included 'The Education of Women'(1865), while both the *Christian Teacher* (1835) and the Christian *Remembrancer* (1866) carried articles titled 'Female Education'. The topic was also aired by the *Christian Penny Magazine* in 'Importance of Female Education' (1837) and by the *Christian Witness* in 'Education of Daughters' (1858).

In addition to denominational publications, there were a number of popular journals and magazines with a wide general readership which gave considerable space to the question of women's education and which are a reminder of its contemporary topicality. These articles reflect aspects of the debate as outlined earlier: that is, women's suitability for higher education on biological, social, and sexual terms. The question of suitability on physical/mental grounds was addressed in *Bow Bells*, a light-weight journal popular with women, in 'Female Intelligence' (1862), 'Woman's Intellect and Nature' (1865), and 'Amiableness and Intellect' (1865), and in the *British Controversialist* in 'Is Woman Mentally Inferior to Man?' (1852). *Bow Bells* also carried 'Female Physicians' (1862), 'Female Education' (1863), 'Male and Female Education' (1865), 'Female Education' (1866) 'Woman's Education' (1867) and 'A Few More Words on Woman's Education' (1867). There was also a number of articles in popular journals which stressed the importance of femininity, such as 'Female Clothing' (1864) in the *London Reader*, and 'Advice to the Ladies upon Costume' (1852), 'Be as Beautiful as you Can' (1858), 'How Ladies Should Dress' (1863) and 'Catching a Husband' (1865) in *Reynold's Miscellany*. The latter publication also treated of woman's role in 'A Wife's Duty' (1863), and 'Duties of Wives' (1865), while the *Monthly Review* had included 'Woman and her Master' (1840), 'Female Character' (1842) and 'Women in England' (1843).

The image of the old maid was a powerful one with which to dissuade young women from intellectual pursuits. At the time of increasing interest among women in opening up access to college education, a number of essays on spinsters appeared, including 'Old Maids' (*Belgravia*: 1866), 'What is an Old Maid?' (*Bow Bells*: 1866), 'Old Maids' (*Reynolds' Miscellany*: 1860), and 'What is an Old Maid?' (*Reynolds' Miscellany*: 1862). Articles such as 'Strong-Minded Women' (1863) in *Fraser's Magazine*, and 'The Husband of the Strong Minded Woman' (1853) in the *British Journal* reinforced the image of the intellectual woman as less attractive than her uneducated sisters.

A number of professional journals with a smaller circulation also gave space to the question of women's education. In 1856, the *Association Medical Journal* debated 'Shall We Have Female Graduates in Medicine?' while the *Lancet* gave this question much attention throughout the 1860s in 'Shall Women be Doctors?' (1861), 'Female Physicians' (1862), 'The Female Students' Question' (1862), 'Female Medical Colleges' (1863), 'Female Physicians' (1863), 'Admission of Women to Academical Degrees' (1863), 'The Female Medical College' (1865) and 'Female Education' (1867). The *English Journal of Education* also treated of the female education question, following the founding of Queen's College. Various numbers included 'Queen's College, London, for Female Education' (1849), 'Female Education' (1855), 'Female Education' (1856), 'Women as Educators' (1856) 'The Governesses Benevolent Association [*sic*]' (1859), and 'City of London College for Ladies' (1859).

As suggested, the founding of Queen's College may be seen as a landmark not only in the history of women's education but also in the debate about such an education in contemporary journals. *Fraser's*, like the *English Journal of Education*, marked this pioneering venture with a review article, 'Queen's College, London' (1849), and the *Quarterly Review* carried 'Queen's College, London' in 1850. As already noted, the *Quarterly*, together with *Blackwood's*, the *Edinburgh Review*, the *Contemporary Review*, and *Macmillan's*, demand some closer attention because they both reflected and influenced the thinking of their educated middle-class readerships. Some idea of the average circulation of these periodicals has been compiled from Ellegard (1957), and is represented in Table 3. The table indicates the years in which these publications were established and discontinued, and estimates the circulation over one decade, the decade in which interest in the question of higher education for women reached a peak.

The *Quarterly Review*
The *Quarterly Review* was founded in 1809, as an organ of Tory opinion, and appealed to the 'educated upper and upper middle class'.[134] It was intended by its founders, including Sir Walter Scott and the publisher John Murray, that the *Quarterly* would challenge the Whiggish *Edinburgh Review*, founded in 1802. Scott had outlined in its program that the *Quarterly* would be of 'liberal and enlarged nature'[135] and while it 'supported the privileges of the

TABLE 3 Circulation details of five contemporary periodicals

	Estab.d	Disct.d	Price 1860	Price 1865	Price 1870	Estimated circul. 1860	Estimated circul. 1865	Estimated circul. 1870
Edinburgh Review	1803	1929	6s.	6s.	6s.	7000	7000	7000
Quarterly Review	1809	—	6s.	6s.	6s.	8000	8000	8000
Contemp. Review	1866	—	—	—	2s.6d.	—	—	4000
Blackwood's	1817	—	2s.6d.	2s.6d.	2s.6d.	10,000	8000	7000
Macmillans	1859	1907	1s.	1s.	1s.	20,000	20,000	8000

Source: Compiled from Alvar Ellegard, 'The Readership of the Periodical Press in Mid-Victorian Britain', *Gšteborgs Universiets Årsskrift*, vol. LXVIII, 1957.

Church of England and of the landed aristocracy, [it] insisted upon the responsibilities of both'.[136] It is considered that its underlying habit of mind remained unchanged for some one hundred years. Arguably the most esteemed of the Reviews, 'it was usually mentioned before all other quarterlies in the contemporary press notices'.[137] It was available through the well-known Mudie's Circulating Library and, while its sales were outstripped by *Macmillan's* for a brief spell (see Table 3), it was probably the most widely read of the mid-Victorian periodicals.

During this time, it carried articles by and about women, though it never represented radical or ground-breaking ideas. Lady Eastlake (1809-93), the prolific journalist and art critic, was a regular contributor from the 1840s to the late 1870s, though it was not until 1878 that she wrote specifically on female education in 'The Englishwoman at School'.[138] Frances Power Cobbe, who published a study of Mary Somerville in the *Quarterly* in 1874, was the only mid-Victorian feminist to contribute to this journal, and once again, the article was not directly concerned with the higher education of women. However, of the periodicals examined in this study, it was the *Quarterly* which first treated of the issue of women's education in a serious fashion when it documented the opening of Queen's College in the March edition of 1850. This article, unsigned, described without comment the founding of the Governesses Benevolent Institution and its early recognition of the need to provide training for governesses. It reported that some two hundred and fifty pupils, from twelve years upwards, had enroled at Queen's, while free lectures to over seventy employed governesses were being made available in the evenings. The article concluded that such an education met the 'enlarged requirements of the present day',[139] but contributors to the *Quarterly* did not continue to reflect tolerance or openness to developments in education for women.

It next treated of this issue in April 1866, in a piece by the classical scholar James Davies (1820-82) who was a regular contributor. Davies, like many writers for 'review' periodicals, structured his article around two publications: *Principles of Education*, (2 vols.) by Elizabeth Sewell, and the tenth edition of *Women's Mission* (anon.) The article indicates that Davies concurred wholly with the opinions of Sewell (1815-1909), whose work is paraphrased and who is praised without reservation. Hers was an important publication, written as it was by a popular and very successful author. Writing between 1840 and 1880, Sewell had a considerable following in Great Britain and the USA, principally among her self-chosen audience of girls and women 'of the educated class',[140] though she is now remembered as a minor novelist of the Anglican revival and the Oxford Movement, and as a friend of Charlotte Yonge. Citing Sewell, Davies argued that girls were unsuited to the gregarious lifestyle of boys' schools, and concluded that 'seminaries for young ladies involve . . . all the jealousies, heart-burnings, and contentions of the public examination system without its good results'.[141] His article reflected contemporary concern with a number of issues including the limits of the female brain and physique, the need to educate women for the duty of motherhood, and the danger of education rendering women unfeminine. It expressed a distaste for the 'unfeminineness of rivalries and competitions among meek-eyed maidens, and deem[ed] the fervid emulation of honours and classes more suited to the "palaestra" than the "gynaeceum",'[142] while waving the spectre of spinsterhood at girls in a style characteristic of a number of contemporary writers. It solemnly advised that 'the opinion of sensible men on these matters may be gathered from the significant fact that they rarely take a wife from the ranks of those ladies who have courted the appellation of *blues*'.[143]

Davies did not completely dismiss the question of education for women. He argued that they were suited to 'light literature and music', commenting that such subjects were 'most attractive to the male sex [and] most fitted for reproduction in small talk . . . '[144] and he suggested that older women 'of thought and tact' were best suited to educating younger women. Like Sewell, he believed that ladies could learn little from lectures given by male professors, concluding: 'Either they will be afraid of them, or they will quiz them, or they will make romances about them'.[145] Davies's article was a lengthy one, written at a time when public lectures for women were gaining popularity and proposals for a women's college at Cambridge were under way. It reflected hostility to the idea of a college for women, appealing to the reserve of parents among its readers in a subtle yet potent paragraph, in which he quoted from Tennyson's *The Princess*:

> Of late years some attempt
> > 'To life the woman's fall'n divinity
> > Upon a pedestal with man'
> has proceeded from the promoters of 'ladies Colleges', to be officered by eminent professors of the stronger sex; and a kindred scheme is that which proposes to admit to public examinations and degrees young ladies, school or home-bred. Such schemes proceed on the assumption that
> > 'With equal husbandry
> > The woman were an equal of the man'
> but probably such Utopian dreams will influence few parents or guardians until at least it is ascertained that all milder and less revolutionary means of improving the class of female educators are fruitless.[146]

The *Quarterly Review* next treated of women and education in 1869, in 'Female Education' by Montagu Burrows.[147] Much of the article represented a deeply conservative view of woman's destiny, and her unsuitability for college education. The article was based on reviews of publications which had added much fuel to the female education debate. Among the books being reviewed were the *Reports, Minutes and Evidence, &c of the Schools Inquiry Commission* (1864-66), the *Memorandum of the Principal Points in the Constitution and Management of Alexandra College, Dublin*, and an anonymous American publication, *The Coming Woman* (1868). While Burrows was rigid in his condemnation of the 'man-woman' produced by over-education, and while he argued emphatically that the sphere of women was the home, he found in both the S.I.C. *Reports* and the *Memorandum* of Alexandra College some guidelines for the development of a viable model of higher education for women. He quickly pointed out the flawed logic in pursuing Local Examinations for girls at a time when 'the system [was] condemned wholesale for boys',[148] believing that the best option was to provide lectures for young ladies where ever there were sufficient numbers of students and good lecturers. The article was unstinting in its praise of Archbishop Trench, described as 'a cultivated and high-minded man', [149] who, as a founder of Alexandra College, had infused 'a religious tone into the merely intellectual character of the system'.[150] It was to this that Burrows attributed the success of Alexandra College, noting that it had 'received perhaps a greater amount of approval from competent judges than any other of the modern experiments'.[151] Contemporary ideologies informed his opinion of the success of Alexandra College:

'The young ladies do not seem to be turned into 'blues', nor to have lost that charming bloom of simplicity and modesty which would be ill exchanged for any amount of male degrees and honours'.[152] Burrows concluded that lectures for ladies could offer a little 'higher polish', or some teacher training, but he stressed a distaste for highly educated women in his conclusion:

> For one woman who will beat the man out of the sphere he now occupies, there will be two or more who will frighten him out of matrimony . . . Improve [female] education systematically, and train the teachers, but keep the male and female types essentially distinct.[153]

Burrows, then, accepted suggestions from the *Reports* of the S.I.C. which argued for a 'systematic' female education and the improved training of women teachers, but he was hostile to the prospect of women invading the traditionally male sphere. Again, spinsterhood was presented as a threat to aspiring female scholars, and at no point did either Davies or Burrows allow that marriage was not the only vocation for women. The *Quarterly* did not show a sustained interest in the question of women's education and, until 'Women at Oxford and Cambridge' (1897), it neglected the opening of colleges for women completely.

The *Edinburgh Review*

The *Edinburgh Review* drew attention to the question of female education as early as 1841, in an article titled 'Rights and Conditions of Women' by T.H. Lister.[154] The *Edinburgh* had been founded in 1802, with the aim of reviewing outstanding books, and allowing writers to express their opinions on issues such as slavery, the economy and Ireland. Regular contributors included William Wilberforce, Sir Walter Scott, Carlyle, and Hazlitt, and 'its moderation . . . enabled the *Edinburgh Review* to exert . . . a powerful influence upon nineteenth-century opinion'.[155] It was considered to be second only to the *Quarterly* as a great Review, and articles were paid for handsomely. Its readers were 'the educated upper and upper-middle classes'[156] and it was available at Mudie's. The *Edinburgh* treated of women's education with neither outright hostility nor uniform support. On the one hand it published Lister's 'The Rights and Conditions of Women' (1841), in which Lister concluded that women were inferior to men 'in the power of close and logical reasoning',[157] yet it also published Harriet Martineau's 'Female Industry' (1859)[158] which insisted that the need and the supply of female industry had increased to the extent that the contemporary social organization needed to be restructured.

Lister's article reviewed a number of influential contemporary publications which, as noted earlier, shaped the Victorian ideology of femininity. The review included Lady Morgan's *Woman and her Master* (1840), Mrs

Sandford's *Woman in her Social and Domestic Character* (1839) and *Female Improvements* (2nd edn., 1839), Sarah Stickney Ellis's *The Women of England* (13th edn.,1839), and two anonymously published works, *Woman's Mission* (8th Edn, 1840) and *Woman's Rights and Duties* (1840). Lister accurately observed: 'the number of works recently published on the education, rights, and conditions of women, sufficiently proves that increased attention has been directed to that subject'.[159] None of the above books suggested a radical redefinition of women's role, nor did they promote the idea of a college for women. Lister observed that Sandford's books were 'of a pure and sound tone of moral and religious feeling', while Ellis's book was 'well intentioned'.[160] Lister's own views on women's sphere suggest that these books reinforced his opinions. The article concluded with a directive to the readership which drew on an array of styles of stereotypical female behaviour and, with the use of the word 'we' clearly established that his voice was intended to represent the opinion of civilized English gentlemen:

> But let it be granted, for argument's sake, that it is substantial power, and no mere shadow of additional influence, which a woman would gain by such as change . . . and we then ask will the consequent result be an improvement in their position? We decidedly think that it would not. In all modern civilised communities, and especially in the most refined and cultivated portion of those communities, women are treated with peculiar deference, tenderness, and courtesy. Do they owe this treatment to their strength or to their weakness? Undoubtedly to the latter . . . but let a sense of competition be introduced, let a man be made to feel that he must stand on the defensive – and the spirit of chivalry . . . will speedily cease.[161]

Lister's article stands in marked contrast to that of Martineau, which was published some eighteen years later. While Lister appealed to sentiment, with references to female tenderness and male courtesy, Martineau's article was rooted solidly in economic fact. This signals a pattern which emerged in nineteenth-century articles on women's education: women and men who opposed higher education for women wrote in a language ridden with nostalgic images, clichés, and even vitriol, while those who supported this cause buttressed their arguments with references to economic and demographic change, and to the ever-increasing wealth of medical knowledge which indicated the suitability of women for advanced study.

Martineau's article included reviews of four publications which provided solid theoretical and statistical evidence that higher education for women was both desirable and necessary. She reviewed the *Results of the Census of Great Britain in 1851* (1853), *Reports of the Governesses Benevolent Institution* (1858),

Barbara Bodichon's *Women and Work* (1857), and *The Laws of Life with Special Reference to the Physical Education of Girls*, by Elizabeth Blackwell, MD (1858). The article brought some of the most thoughtful and thought-provoking literature on women's lives before the readership of the *Edinburgh Review*. As noted earlier, the 1851 census returns showed a population surplus of single women, who, not expecting to marry, would have to earn a living. While Lister (1841) had argued that 'the deference, the tenderness, the courtesy of man towards the other sex [was] founded principally on the feeling that they need[ed] his protection',[162] the 1851 census supported Martineau's harshly realistic appraisal of the social structure:

> We go on talking as if it were still true that every woman is, or ought to be, supported by father, brother or husband. A social organization framed for a community of which half stayed at home, while the other half went out to work, cannot answer the purposes of a society, of which a quarter remain at home, while three-quarters go out to work.[163]

The *Edinburgh Review* had noted in an 1856 article[164] that some attempt to educate women had been undertaken by the Revd Denison Maurice in 1855. This article referred to the inauguration of a college for working men at 31, Red Lion Square, London, in 1854, which had since chosen to extend its services to ladies with a series of 'Lectures on Practical Subjects'. The London Lectures were given by men who generally supported the move towards college education, and included the Revd R.C. Trench and Maurice himself. The author recognised that 'ladies who [had] no immediate family duties, who [were] not particularly fitted to be teachers . . . who [were] neither gifted, clever, nor independent'[165] might wish to put their time to good use through study and charitable works. The *Edinburgh Review* did not continue to discuss women's education through the years of feminist activity and pioneering ventures. It next discussed women's education in 1887, in 'The Education of Women' by B.G. Johns, but by this time there was a number of women's colleges, and women at Cambridge were heavily involved in moves to gain access to the University.

The *Contemporary Review*

The *Contemporary Review* showed a sustained interest in women's issues from its first volume in 1866 until the end of the century. Published by Alexander Strahan, it was founded to represent the views of the Established Church,[166] and was influenced by the success of the early Liberal *Fortnightly Review* founded one year earlier. The *Contemporary Review* was the first journal of its day to devote extensive space to art and music. Contributors included Gladstone, Arnold, Stanley, Huxley, and Ruskin, while Herbert Spencer contributed throughout his life. The *Contemporary Review* had the distinction among non-denominational Victorian periodicals of giving eminent Catholic writers an opportunity to address non-Catholic fellow countrymen. Available at Mudies, its readers were 'upper to middle class, highly educated tending to Evangelicalism in religion, and predominantly Liberal in politics'.[167]

Throughout the nineteenth century, the *Contemporary Review* published on educational issues, and carried a number of articles on female education. Its first volume included 'The Education of Women' by the clergyman Thomas Markby (1824-70).[168] This was a scholarly piece, giving a detailed history of women's intellectual pursuits from antiquity to contemporary England, and it included an enthusiastic response to the successful endeavours of nineteenth-century pioneers in opening the Cambridge Local Examinations to girls in 1863. The article opened with reference to the huge increase in interest, in recent years, in the question of female education, and reminded readers that 'from the very earliest times the bringing up of girls must have been a subject of anxious care, not only to the matrons, but to the men of every civilized nation'.[169] Subsequent references which linked civilized behaviour with female education, supported a persuasive argument that a nation which ignored the intellectual development of its women was essentially backward. Additionally, Markby reversed the usual pattern of citing the Bible as a source of authority on the subservient status of women, and argued:

> To go no further than the Bible for examples, the pages of both Old and New Testament exhibit many a bright portrait of a maiden armed with all the graces of her sex.[170]

Sources from history were also cited: 'Our annals teem with the names of royal and noble dames renowned for every feminine accomplishment . . . the era of Tudors was fruitful of graceful and accomplished women'.[171] Markby was, however, scathing towards the Bluestocking salons in which was to be found 'the heartless gaiety and cold sparkle of the witty woman of the world'.[172] He argued that the Victorian era would herald great change in attitude toward the intellectual status of women, believing that this was 'due not merely to the fact of there being a woman on the throne',[173] but to there being an increased awareness of 'the work of wise and self-denying women, which had been quietly going forward all the time . . . [the] mothers' meetings, cottage flower shows, parish sewing-societies, well-organised schemes of emigration, and . . . refuges and penitentiaries'.[174] He suggested that increasingly such women understood that the root of the problems of the female sex 'lay in ignorance', hence the women's movement grew out of a desire to voice the appeal for female education 'in a more clear and united voice'.[175] He concluded the article with a note of praise for the success of girls in the recently opened Cambridge Locals and, while he lamented the contemporary necessity to have women taught by men, he was supportive of the idea that colleges for women should be founded.

Two years later, Markby published another lengthy paper in the *Contemporary Review*.[176] 'On the Education of Women' (1868) continued the history of women and education which he had begun in the earlier piece, and focussed in particular on the contemporary attitudes towards women's education. Of the Cambridge Locals he wrote: 'Many of the strongest adversaries to the scheme have come round, and now give it effective support',[177] and added: 'in the course of the last two or three years public opinion has so far gone in the right direction that the claims of women to consideration are everywhere listened to with respect'.[178] He was evidently aware, and disapproving, of the proliferation of articles and pamphlets treating of the female education question, commenting 'the monstrous rubbish which has been written about the position and education as well as the social and political dependence of women, forms one of the greatest difficulties which those who would fain improve their condition have to encounter'.[179] He considered that the 'wild discourses of some lady writers', and the 'talk equally foolish and much more abounding on the part of men, concerning what they conceive to be women's duties' had confused the issue and jeopardised the claims of women such as Emily Davies. He applauded Davies's *Higher Education of Women* (1866), and the idea of building a female college 'within a convenient distance of London', concluding with a plea to 'let the ladies have their professors'.[180]

The following year, the *Contemporary Review* published 'Some account of a proposed new College for women', by Emily Davies.[181] The article, based on a paper read at the annual general meeting of National Association for the Promotion of Social Sciences (1868), drew on the findings of the Schools Inquiry Commission[182] to argue that a systematic education for girls and women was urgently required. Like Martineau in the *Edinburgh Review* (1859), Davies structured her paper around empirical data, and made no appeal to sentiment or chivalric generosity. Davies argued that opening Local Examinations to girls was not in itself enough, pointing to the fact that 'the deficiency . . . is that of a superior education, and examinations, however valuable and necessary in their place, are not education'.[183] She emphasised that the *Report* of the S.I.C. had illustrated the commissioners approval of her 'proposal for the establishment of a new college'[184] to raise the intellectual aspirations and abilities of women. Like Martineau, she pointed to the fact that many 'unmarried women . . . [were] not called upon to take an active part in household work'[185] and could better use their time in academic pursuits. Ever cautious about appearing too radical, Davies concluded:

The object of the new College is not to enable women to make money, though that may be among the results attained. It has a wider scope. . . . It will not be specifically directed towards changing the occupations of women, but rather towards securing that whatever they do shall be done well.[186]

The *Contemporary Review* continued to pay close attention to the question of higher education for women, and carried a number of articles by leading nineteenth-century feminists, including Lydia Becker's 'On the study of science by women' (1869), Josephine Butler's 'The Lovers of the Lost: Refuges for Penitent Women' (1870), Emily Shirreff's 'College Education for Women' (1870), Frances Power Cobbe's 'The Little Health of Ladies' (1878) and her controversial 'Wife-torture in England' (1878), and two articles by Millicent Garrett Fawcett: 'Holes in the Education Net' (1887) and 'Degrees for Women at Oxford' (1896). A number of other articles on women's lives appeared throughout the century. It is impossible to know the editorial policy of the *Contemporary Review* on women's issues but it is noteworthy that, next to the *Englishwoman's Journal*, it gave more space both to the writing of the mid-Victorian feminists, and to the theme of women's education generally, than any other periodical of its time which appealed to the educated middle-class reader.

Blackwood's Magazine and Macmillan's Magazine

The sales of the *Quarterly*, the *Edinburgh*, and the *Contemporary* were outstripped by those of *Blackwood's Magazine* and *Macmillan's Magazine* (Table 3, *supra*). An examination of the contents of both was undertaken for this reason. It was found, however, that neither played a major part in publicising the contemporary debate about female education. *Blackwood's* was founded in 1824 and represented Tory ideas. Its readers were 'upper middle to upper class, of good education [and] politically conservative'.[187] Available at Mudie's, it was a somewhat waspish, often entertaining review in its early years, but it became quite staid by the middle of the century. Many of its articles on women were published anonymously or under pseudonyms, and in its early years it toyed with popular 'female' issues in articles such as 'Men and Women; a brief hypothesis concerning the difference in their genius' (1824), 'Letter to Mrs M. on the Equality of the Sexes' (1826), and 'Characteristics of Women' (1833).[188] One of its long-standing contributors was Mrs Oliphant, whose novels were serialised in *Blackwood's* from the 1850s to the late 1880s. Oliphant turned her hand to women's issues from time to time, [189] and *Blackwood's* also included among its articles on women such pieces as W.E. Aytoun's 'The Rights of Women' (1862), William Hamley's 'Women in the Middle Ages' (1964), and his 'Old Maids' (1872), but it did not cover the higher education question or the opening of colleges for women.

While *Macmillan's* would certainly have brought the ideas of these writers to a wide educated audience (*Macmillan's* sold 10,000 of its first edition), it only published occasional articles on female education in the 1860s and it did not sustain an interest in the topic in the later decades of the century. This may reflect the fact the *Macmillan's*, founded as late as 1859, elected to cover women's issues at the period when they were both novel and controversial, in an attempt to court a wide readership. *Macmillan's,* designed to combine political and religious articles with travel sketches, fiction, and poetry, was considered to be a magazine of high quality which rivalled the popular *Blackwood's*. One of its attractions was its serialised fiction. It carried Trollope, R.L. Stevenson, Hardy, and James, although its editors would have considered the serialised fiction of Katherine Cooper, Anne Keary, and Frances Burnett to have drawn a huge audience. Of the Victorians concerned with women's education, Frances Power Cobbe, Millicent Garret Fawcett and the Revd J. Lewellyn Davies published in *Macmillan's*. Cobbe's 'Social Science Congresses and Women's part in them' appeared in 1861; Fawcett's 'The Education of Women of the Middle and Upper Class' appeared in 1868, and the Revd Davies's short piece on Hitchin College, 'A New College for Women', appeared in 1868.

The 1860s also saw the publication of articles on women's education in a number of other periodicals not surveyed in this study, and saw the publication of pamphlets and essays which disseminated ideas among a smaller reading public. *Fraser's Magazine* included Frances Power Cobbe's 'What shall we do with our old Maids?' (1862), in which she attacked the idea of exporting surplus females to the colonies and argued that full and worthwhile lives were possible for single women. A year later, the *Victoria Magazine* carried 'The Influence of University Degrees on the education of Women' by Emily Davies, an article which addressed the thorny issue of the compromised femininity of educated women:

> . . . [it is] an unproven assertion that women ought not to pursue the same education as men; and that they would become unwomanly if they did. A woman so educated would, we are assured, make a very poor wife or mother. Much learning would make her mad, and would wholly unfit her for those quiet domestic offices for which providence had intended her. . . . She would become cold, masculine, fast, strong-minded, and . . . generally unpleasing.[190]

The attack on femininity gained a new potency here, as it was articulated – albeit with derision – by a woman. It indicated a willingness on the part of pioneers of women's education to recognise the fears and prejudices of their contemporaries, and to isolate each fear and provide a response. Davies agreed that it *would* be wholly undesirable to un-sex women, but explained that higher education had not the power to do so, arguing that 'the differences between a man and a woman are either essential or conventional, or both. In any case, it is difficult to understand how they affect the right of a women to pass an examination and to take a degree'.[191]

Davies could also cite scripture for her purpose, as she continued, 'do we not read that God created man in his own image, in the image of God he created he him, male and female he created He them? Should not a man's thoughts of god be a woman's thoughts also?'[192] And finally, to dispel fears that college life might make women wanton or wild she concluded 'that the fast women and the masculine women are not those who sit down to their books and devote themselves to an orderly course of study'.[193]

The 1860s also saw the publication of Maria Rye's *Emigration of Educated Gentlewomen* (1861), Mrs Craik's *A Woman's Thoughts about Women* (1862), Frances Power Cobbe's 'The Education of Women and how it would be Affected by University Examinations' (1862), and Josephine Butler's *The Education and Employment of Women* (1868), all of which provided the debate with carefully argued and logical grounds for extending higher education to women. On occasion, women used periodicals to engage in public debate with a writer who opposed women's education. Cobbe's 'What shall we do with our old Maids?' (*Fraser's*, 1862) was written in direct response to W.R. Greg's suggestion in the *National Review* (1862) that surplus women should be exported to the colonies, rather than educated for employment. In a more controversial exchange of ideas, Dr Henry Maudsley and Elizabeth Garret Anderson MD, used the pages of the *Fortnightly Review* to debate the question of women's suitability for education in 1874. These articles demand some attention, for together they may be said to sum up all of the contemporary grounds on which women's education was both promoted and opposed. Maudsley's paper, 'Sex in Mind and in Education' (1874)[194] argued that women were physically and mentally unsuited to higher education, and that those who advocated educational reform ignored 'the fact that there are significant differences between the sexes'.[195] His argument was substantiated by his opinion, as a medical man, that 'the development of puberty . . . [drew] heavily on the vital resources of the female constitution'[196] and rendered strenuous mental and physical activity dangerous to developing girls, while young women fulfilled their destiny in childbirth and thus could not endanger their health with excessive stimulation. The physiological sex differences between men and women suggested to Maudsley that there was equally 'sex in mind':

Whether [women] care to be mothers or not, they cannot dispense with those physiological functions of their nature that have reference to that aim. . . . They cannot choose but to be women; cannot rebel successfully against the tyranny of their organization. . . . There is sex in mind as distinctly as there is sex in body; and if the mind is to receive the best culture of which its nature is capable, regard must be had to the mental qualities which correlate differences of sex.[197]

Maudsley cited American opinion that the American practice of 'training the sexes in mixed classes' entailed 'lifelong suffering, and even incapacities'[198] for young women. He concluded that this was because female 'nerve centres . . . being in a state of greater instability, by reason of the development of their reproductive organs', rendered girls 'more easily and . . . more seriously deranged'.[199]

One month later a reply by Elizabeth Garrett Anderson MD, was published in the *Fortnightly Review*.[200] It was a particularly lucid and well-argued paper, which quickly suggested that Maudsley's arguments were misleading and inaccurate. Garrett Anderson noted that Maudsley's essay was 'a reproduction of a lecture on the same subject by Dr Clarke, formerly a Professor at Harvard College, United States'.[201] She also quickly suggested that 'there [was] grave reason for doubting whether such a subject [could] be fully and with propriety discussed except in a professional journal', and questioned the motives of Dr Maudsley in 'placing medical and physiological views before the readers of a literary periodical'.[202] However, finding inaccuracies throughout Maudsley's essay, Garrett Anderson elected to reply. She pointed out that there were no groups of women in England, of which she was aware, who were attempting either to 'rebel against the tyranny of their organization', or to assimilate the two sexes, as he had suggested. Then she turned quickly to his speculation that formal education would be detrimental to the well-being of women:

> If girls were less like boys that the anthropomorphic apes, nothing but experience would prove that they would not benefit by having the best methods and the best tests applied to their mental training. And if the course of study which Dr Maudsley is criticising be one as likely to strengthen the best powers of the mind as good food is to strengthen the body . . . there would seem to be no good reason why the special physiological functions of women should prevent them from running it, and more than these same functions prevent them from eating beef and bread with as much benefit as men . . . Nature in the long run protects herself from our mistakes: and when we are in doubt, we may be guided by general principles of equity and common sense, while waiting for the light of a larger experience.[203]

The *Englishwoman's Review*

In addition to the mainstream periodicals examined above, there was a number of nineteenth-century journals for women which discussed female education and employment. Some of these journals were short-lived: from 1874 to 1876, Emily Faithful published a weekly guide to female employment, *Women and Work*; Louisa M. Hubbard edited the *Woman's Gazette* which, from 1875 to 1879, provided a monthly guide to work for genteel women; and the *Women's Penny Paper*, a lively feminist publication in newspaper format, appeared weekly from 27 October 1888 to 27 December 1890. Other publications enjoyed a longer run: the *Englishwomen's Year Book*, an annual directory of women's opportunities, societies and clubs, appeared from 1875 to 1916, and is a useful source for historians. The *Women's Union Journal* appeared quarterly from February 1876 to October 1890, representing socialist principles, while the first British feminist temperance paper, the *British Women's Temperance Journal*, appeared monthly from January 1886 to September 1892. Other feminist publications included the *Shield* (1870-1970) and the *Women's Suffrage Journal* (1870-90).

The *Journal of the Women's Education Union* (1873-82) provided a platform for information on female education, and covered the opening of higher education to women. It was the official organ of the National Union for Improving the Education of Women of all Classes, an organisation out of which the Girls' Public Day School Company developed in 1872.[204] In an early edition, it printed an appeal for public support for the building debt of Girton College, proposed by Emily Davies at a meeting of the Union. Davies began by describing Girton College:

> The college . . . aims at giving to women what the universities give to men. It is a college in the Oxford and Cambridge sense of the word. It does not follow that it is a servile copy of the old colleges. Men and women were not exactly alike, either by nature or by practice . . . We have to ask what women want, and as far as possible provide it.[205]

Davies allayed any fears that a women's college would make women masculine, by disassociating intellectual pursuits from an exclusively masculine sphere. The pursuit of learning at a female college was presented as a logical step in the fulfilment of womanhood, rather than a desire to imitate men. Davies briskly concluded that 'for women to do this or that merely because men do it would be childish'.[206] Girton could offer women what Davies believed to be 'the essential requisites' of a good education: 'the best teaching, the best tests, and the best circumstances . . . for moral and physical as well as intellectual development'.[207] This article also drew attention to the wider capacity of a female college to give young women room to develop, as she explained that 'college life supplies what may perhaps be regarded as the two great needs for moral, intellectual, and physical development – the need of solitude, the need of sympathy and companionship'.[208]

Davies, writing from the perspective of one who had founded the pioneering residential college for women, added dimensions to the debate that had not, heretofore, appeared in print. As one who had no formal education, she was aware of the limitations this posed in public life. She was aware, too, of the constraints that home life presented to most women of her class. She continued:

> It can scarcely be necessary to urge the importance of being able to go alone, and uninterrupted, in order to produce the best work. It is not merely that more work can be done in the time, but it is of a different sort. To be able to sit down quietly and think out a difficult point, without fear of being broken in upon and called of to do something else, gives a different quality to the thought, a steadiness of tone in the habitual manner of thinking, and is, perhaps, the best antidote to the flightiness which is the snare of women and other uneducated classes.[209]

Davies also pointed out a wider value for college life, one in which she, as a woman who made her closest friendships late in life when she became involved in the women's movement, placed much faith:

> College life also gives the opportunity of forming congenial friendships and of working in sympathy with others. I am tempted to lay special stress on this feature, because it is one which is most highly valued by the students themselves. As a rule, women have little opportunity of choosing congenial friends. They are obliged to make friends of those with whom they have family links, or who are neighbours, or whom they meet in society. But a college life brings them within range of persons of different antecedents, living in widely different circles, and friendships formed under these circumstances may be based on real sympathy, on caring for the same things.[210]

Davies's resolution in favour of Girton College was seconded by the Revd C. Beard, who added that, considering 'the enormous revenues which existed in the universities, both in England and Scotland, for the higher education of women', it was 'a very little thing to ask that there should be one modest home provided near the university of Cambridge for women'.[211] The *Journal* notes that the resolution in favour of Girton College was carried unanimously, and one thousand pounds was subscribed in the room towards the liquidation of its building debt.

The same edition of the *Journal* drew attention to the public lectures for ladies that had been going on at Merton Hall, Cambridge, since 1871, under the supervision of Miss A.J. Clough. This would late develop into Newnham College. The *Journal* continued to provide information on developments in women's education. In June, 1874, it noted the decision of the Convocation of the London University in favour of opening their degrees to women,[212] in April 1879 it outlined developments in women's education at Oxford,[213] in August 1879 it carried a piece titled 'Thirty Years Progress in Women's Education',[214] and it provided readers with regular listings of lectures for women. It was, however, the *Englishwoman's Review* that made the most sustained and important contribution to the discussion about higher education for women in the nineteenth century.

The *Englishwoman's Review* was the official organ of the nineteenth-century women's movement. It gave women a platform for the ideas which would shape higher education for women and it signalled an increasing awareness by women of the grounds on which the struggle for higher education might be won. It is noteworthy that articles by nineteenth-century feminists in the *Review* are substantially finer in style and content than those by their female predecessors writing on the same theme. In its examination of women's contribution to the debate in late-seventeenth-century and eighteenth-century print culture, this study has noted the limited frames of reference of women writers. From the mid-nineteenth century onwards, however, women writers evinced wide social awareness and wide reading. Their work increasingly drew its support from empirical, or 'hard' data, such as census returns and statistics from societies, rather than on conjecture and subjective passion. They challenged the Pauline interpretation of Scripture, the Rousseauesque idea of female education, contemporary medical literature, and even social Darwinism which suggested that women were the inferior species of the human race.

It is to be expected, then, that women who wrote about female education were themselves educated to some degree, and that they had launched themselves into public life. It is not surprising to find that, like the eighteenth-century Bluestocking circle, they formed something of a homogeneous group, but their interests were wider and less class-specific, and included female education, employment, legal rights, and the parliamentary franchise. The key figures of this circle are widely considered to have originated the nineteenth-century women's movement, and at various stages it included Emily Davies, Barbara Leigh Smith Bodichon, Bessie Rayner Parkes, Frances Power Cobbe, Josephine Butler, and Millicent Garret Fawcett. Their concern with women's access to the public sphere is well documented by historians in the last twenty years, and there are biographies of Emily Davies who gained access to university examinations for women and who founded Girton

College, Cambridge; of Josephine Butler who led the Contagious Diseases Campaign; of Barbara Bodichon who fought for married women's property rights, and of Millicent Garret Fawcett, president of the National Union of Women's Suffrage.[215]

The movement developed from the work of a small group of women who, in the late 1850s, worked from an office in London which housed an employment bureau, a library and a meeting place, and from which was produced the *Englishwoman's Review*. The women were concerned with expanding education and employment for women, and with the married women's property acts. During the 1860s the movement grew and diversified. New publications, the *Victoria Magazine* and the *Englishwoman's Review*, began. New concerns were placed on the agenda: the question of women entering the medical profession, the suffrage question, and the Contagious Diseases Agitation were major concerns, and resulted in the movement establishing a number of separate organisations and societies at various provincial centres. While these societies were not formally linked, they had some overlapping memberships, and those names best remembered for activity in the Victorian women's movement are to be found in minute books and membership lists of a number of women's organisations.

Throughout the second half of the nineteenth century, female education remained a pressing question. Bessie Rayner Parkes, Barbara Bodichon, Frances Power Cobbe and Emily Davies contributed to the debate, although it was Davies who elected to give it her undivided attention and it was she who opened the doors of Cambridge University to women when she founded Girton College, Cambridge.[216] Their work shows evidence of methodical research and logical argument. Emily Davies grounded her proposal for a women's College in statistical evidence that increasing numbers of women were remaining unmarried and needed education and training, and she gave evidence to a major education Commission (S.I.C., 1864-66). Barbara Bodichon, who concerned herself with the legal status of women, published *A Brief Summary in Plain Language of the Most Important Laws Concerning Women* (1854), a pamphlet which was a powerful stimulus to legal reform. It indicated clearly that most married and divorced women had virtually no legal rights whatsoever, and her campaign for a Married Women's Property Bill was supported by Frances Power Cobbe who, like Bodichon, gathered considerable amounts of empirical information on women and the law. Barbara Bodichon, together with Millicent Garret Fawcett, was also actively involved in the suffrage campaign of the 1860s, while minute books and journal articles indicate that Frances Power Cobbe lent her support, and in a speech made before the Recorder of London on 13 May 1876 Cobbe advocated women's suffrage as the means of gaining protection for the rights of the weaker half of the nation.

The *Englishwoman's Review* was a successor to the *English Woman's Journal*, which ran from March 1858 to August 1864. These journals were regarded, by the women who wrote for them, as one publication and where this study includes generalisations about their content they will be referred to as the *Englishwoman's Review*. The *English Woman's Journal* was founded by Bessie Rayner Parkes and Barbara Leigh Smith Bodichon, as a company with shares, to publish on women's education, employment, suffrage, and social and legal status. It reflected the interests of its contributors: Parkes and Bodichon organised petitions to amend the laws concerning the property of married women and organised the first female suffrage petitions; Emily Davies, who edited the *English Woman's Journal* for a brief period, was founder of Girton College, Cambridge; and Elizabeth Garret Anderson, England's first woman doctor, wrote on women's health and medicine as a profession for women. The offices of the *English Woman's Journal*, at 19 Langham Place, London, were soon to be shared by Jessie Boucherett's Society for Promoting the Employment of Women, and by the Ladies Institute which provided women with a reading room and a lunch room, and a Registry for Women's Work

Between August 1864 and August 1865, the *English Woman's Journal* was incorporated with the *Alexandra Magazine*, edited by Parkes. In 1866, Jessie Boucherett revived the journal as a quarterly, the *Englishwoman's Review of Social and Industrial Questions*, but by January 1870 a new quarterly series, edited by Boucherett and titled the *Englishwoman's Review*, was begun and was set to enjoy forty years of successful publication. The *Englishwoman's Review* had a number of editors over the next four decades. Boucherett, who resigned due to ill health in 1871, was succeeded by the active suffragist Caroline Ashurst Biggs (1841-89) who brought great energy and some personal money to the *Englishwoman's Review* and turned it into a monthly publication from January 1875. Upon Biggs's death, the editorship was taken up by the Irishwoman Helen Blackburn (1842-1903). Blackburn, also a suffragist, was a competent historian and her book *Women's Suffrage: a Record of the Movement in the British Isles* (1902) remains a key text in this field. She also collected a superb library of books on women's history and women's issues which she bequeathed to Girton College at her death in 1903. She was succeeded by her friend and collaborator Antoinette Mackenzie, but by 1910 the magazine was suffering financial loss and it ceased publication in the spring of 1910.

As Murray and Stark (1980) have noted, the *Englishwoman's Review* drew its readership 'from those with aspirations toward new opportunities for women in several areas',[217] and its clear aim 'to record what women were doing in education, in politics, in industry'[218] make it a valuable source of contemporary history. That it recorded events so meticulously had much to do with Boucherett's foresight. In 1867 she explained that since magazines are 'generally kept, and are sometimes bound in volumes', the *Englishwoman's Review* should 'represent a durable history of those events, as they occur, which form a part of the great social reformation'.[219] The *Review* continued to adopt a policy of record-keeping: it regularly recorded changes in legislation, anniversaries of reforms concerning women, and obituaries of interest to its readers, and in 1889 and 1900 it published a bibliography covering English feminism under headings which included Medicine, Education and Law. The *Review* also attempted to 'form opinion and promote change'[220] and to rediscover women's history. It carried biographies of women such as Mary Astell, and it regularly celebrated extraordinary achievements by women, such as distinctions at university examinations.

The *Englishwoman's Review* supported educational opportunities for women from its inception. Its articles therefore provide both a chronology of developments in the education debate, and a *corpus* of information on women and education. The 1850s and 1860s saw many articles on female education and educational opportunities appear, representing all facets of the debate. Elizabeth Blackwell MD (1812-1910) contributed 'Extracts from the Laws of Life, with special reference to the Physical Education of Girls' (1858), 'Letters to Young Ladies Desirous of Studying Medicine' (1860), and 'Medicine as a Profession for Women' (1860). In 'Letters', written at a time when there was no school of medicine open to women in England, she acknowledged some of the obstacles to be overcome by women who wished to become doctors, as she illustrated that 'society has not yet recognised this study as fit woman's work. Gossip and slander may annoy the student, and want of confidence'.[221] Blackwell argued that women were particularly suited to treat female patients, and dismissed suggestions that pursuing a medical degree would have an injurious effect on women students. In addition, she offered a uniquely altruistic view on the wider significance of women pursuing knowledge, as she concluded that 'what is done or learned by one class of women becomes, by virtue of their common womanhood, the property of all women'.[222]

Throughout the late 1850s and the 1860s, the *Journal* and later the *Review*, attempted to deal with prejudices towards female education. In 'Female Education in the English Middle Class' (1858), an attempt was made to assess 'in what commensurate proportion [had] female education kept pace with male'.[223] The article provided the debate with a new perspective on the dangers of neglecting the educating of women. It harnessed facts gleaned from the work of leading medical men such as Fletcher's *Rudiments of Physiology*, and Webster's *Observations on the Admission of Medical Pupils to the Wards of Bethlem Hospital*, and argued that the high proportion of women patients in mental asylums was related to the paucity of female education. Webster's *Observations* had indicated that 'the Registers of Lunatic Asylums show the number of female patients to exceed that of male by nearly one-third',[224] yet among the female patients there were few who had 'a judiciously cultivated mind'.[225] The article continued:

> We need not ask what woman's destiny is – nature has written it in characters too clear to be mistaken; the large development of the intellectual organs, and the feeble muscular power, mark her for the high-minded purifier of society – her strength must be that of knowledge; yet, we refuse the kind of culture which such an organization requires, hide the victim of mismanagement in a madhouse, and then talk proudly about an enlightened age.[226]

Far from suggesting that female education was the cause of insanity, this article proposed that lack of female education weakened the mental fibre of the nation. It also cited evidence of the population 'surplus of females' above the age of twenty from the Returns of the 1851 Census, concluding that education for women was linked to economic necessity:

> ... it is no longer a question whether woman ought to or ought not to leave the sphere of home duties, and take her part in industrial and other occupations. What, in this respect, was speculation and theory fifty years ago, has become practice and necessity now. . . . No man of the middle-classes, be he engaged in professional, mercantile, or other pursuits, be he prosperous as he may, can assure to his daughters pecuniary independence.[227]

In 'Why boys are cleverer than girls' (1858),[228] the *Journal* argued that the poor education afforded to girls was the sole reason as to why they failed to compete successfully against boys. The argument was developed in 'Are men cleverer than women?' (1859)[229] which asserted that 'men are superior to women because they know more, and they have this knowledge because they have three times the opportunities of acquiring it than women possess'.[230]

The article further suggested that, in addition to music and languages, a practical education should be made widely available to women in order that they might be able to better look after their own financial situation:

> They should learn also things of practical use, – how to get a post-office order, to write a cheque on a banker, etc., and should be taught the meaning of various business terms such as 'discount', 'above and below par', and what funds and securities are, for at present young ladies know far more about the course of the planets than they do of these useful mundane institutions. This elementary instruction would enable those scholars who had any natural intelligence to learn more hereafter, and

thus give them the power of protecting their own interests, while even
the stupid ones would be made capable of understanding the conversations of men.[231]

In 'Colleges for Girls' (1859),[232] an attempt was made to justify the participation of women in university life on the basis that many of the great
university colleges at Cambridge and Oxford had been endowed or founded
by women. The munificence of a number of women was noted: Lady
Dervorgille, widow to John de Balliol, had appointed statutes under her seal
in 1282 and founded a college in her husbands name at Oxford. Also at Oxford, Exeter College benefitted from Lady Shiers; Queen Anne contributed
to Oriel; Queen's was aided by Queen Phillippa and two queens of the house
of Hanover; the plans for the founding of Wadham were executed by Dorothy
Wadham, widow of Nicholas Wadham, and Mrs Sarah Eaton endowed seven
fellowships and five scholarships at Worcester.[233] At Cambridge, Clare Hall
was built in 1344 by Elizabeth de Burg; Pembroke Hall was founded by
Mary, Countess of Pembroke in 1343; Queen's was founded in 1448 by
Margaret of Anjou; Christ's, while founded by Henry VI, was completely
endowed in 1506 by Margaret, Countess of Richmond and Derby who also
endowed St John's College, and Sidney Sussex College was founded with the
bequests of Frances Sidney, Countess of Sussex.[234] The article argued:

> These scanty details will show our readers how largely the colleges of
> Oxford and Cambridge have been indebted to women, in some in-
> stances for their actual foundation, in many more for the increase of
> their efficiency. Is it not time that the ancient debt were as liberally
> met, and that men in their turn should contribute largely to the better-
> ment of the female sex?[235]

The article then gave a succinct account of developments which had been
made to secure higher education for women, pointing out that a university
education proper was not yet available to women. The opening of Queen's
College and of Bedford College were noted, as were 'colleges possessing
more or less of corporate constitution . . . in various parts of London and in
the provincial towns, varying in their character between the chartered dignity of Queen's College, and the classes of a superior day school'.[236] However, it suggested that 'until parents aim differently in educating their daughters,
and until daughters themselves pursue their own education with a different
ultimate purpose, collegiate advantages are, for the majority, offered completely in vain, and . . . colleges will be chiefly sought as offering cheap classes
and cheap masters for young girls, instead of a solid and progressive education
for young women'.[237]

In the late 1850s and throughout the next decade, articles in the *English Woman's Journal* linked the need for female education with demographic changes and to female employment. Bessie Rayner Parkes contributed 'The Market for Educated Female Labour' (1859), 'What can Educated Women Do?' (Part I: 1859), and 'What can Educated Women Do?' (Part II: 1860). In 'The Market for Educated Female Labour' (1859), Parkes quickly dismissed the popular notion that governessing could provide a source of income for all genteel women who had to support themselves. She cited the Reports of the Governesses' Benevolent Institution which estimated that there were fifteen thousand governesses in England in 1859: '. . . fifteen thousand educated women, chiefly single or widowed, unsupported by their male relations, and in innumerable cases obliged to support *them*',[238] Parkes observed. That there was not sufficient employment for these women was further evinced by the G.B.I. Reports. Parkes noted that in 1858, 838 governesses had applied for temporary assistance to the G.B.I., while a total of 10,334 applications for assistance had been made to the G.B.I. since it was founded in 1843.[239] In 'What can Educated Women Do?' (Part I: 1859), Parkes suggested a widening of female employment opportunities to include work in hospitals, prisons, reformatories, workhouses, factories and educational institutions. 'We have no women competent to instruct other women in the highest branches of knowledge',[240] she stated, adding that women were particularly suited to 'the office of inspector in girls' schools', and asking: 'Why should a distinguished poet, who also holds the office of school-inspector, be seen (as I have seen him) minutely examining the stitches in pocket-handkerchiefs and dusters?'[241]

A number of other feminists contributed to the discussion about women's education in the *English Woman's Journal*. Often their articles challenged contemporary knowledge about the suitability of women for higher education as outlined in IV(i). For example, Isa Craig promoted learning as a cure for, rather than a cause of, insanity among women in 'Insanity: its Cause and Cure' (1859):

> . . . the nurture and education of most women are as enervating as possible. Their physical development is uncared for, if not positively retarded. A species of hot-house culture is forced upon the mind . . . What wonder if the course of training and the mode of life we reprobate should sow and cherish the seeds of insanity. Over-excitement and aimlessness are two of the most unsanitary conditions to which the human mind can be subjected, and it is easy to trace to them restlessness, melancholy, and tendency to the painful class of hysterical affections.[242]

In a similar fashion, Jessie Boucherett linked the lack of female education and employment to the distress and poverty of the 39,073 female inhabitants of workhouses, as revealed by the 1861 census, in 'On the Cause of the Distress Prevalent among Single Women' (1864).

The early 1860s also saw some reports on early efforts at opening higher education to women, in 'The University of London and the Graduation of Women' (1863), and 'The University of Cambridge and the Education of Women' (1863). These articles provide historians not only with evidence of a crucial period in this debate, but also with some idea of the language and tone in which the debate was argued. The background to the former article merits some explanation. The article refers to an early application by Emily Davies to the University of London for the admission of women to its degrees. She had been prompted to this through her desire to help Elizabeth Garrett to be awarded a medical degree. She and Garrett applied for leave for Garrett to enter for the University of London matriculation examinations, but the application was rejected by one vote at a meeting of the Senate on 9 April 1862. A Memorial was then sent to the University of London asking that the new Charter, which was then being drawn up, should include a clause providing for the extension to women of the privileges of the University.[243] Emily Davies enlisted the support of many influential figures, and sent their names to the Senate. On 7 May 1862, the Vice-Chancellor moved that the Senate should endeavour to obtain a modification of the Charter providing for the admission of women to degrees but not to Convocation. The motion was lost by one vote, and when in the following year the Annual Committee of Convocation passed a resolution in favour of provision being made for the examination of women, this too was thrown out. In 'The University of London and the Graduation of Women' (1863), the specious arguments put forward against admitting women to examinations and certification are recorded and refuted:

> We were told that this was a cry got up by 'a few amazons;' and on the other hand it was assumed without question that, the doors of the University once opened, the daughters of England would one and all be prepared for taking a degree. One gentleman drew so lively a picture of the sacrifices and hardships which a regular education enjoined – the loss of rest and recreation – the ceaseless struggle from the age of nine to the age of twenty-one, that we only wonder he had survived to tell the tale, and that his audience had been spared to hear it. One orator protested that it would be an insult to the women of England to suppose that they could be better educated than they already are, while doctors threatened the gravest cerebral complications, and a blight upon all future generations, if the possible wives and

mothers of Englishmen were allowed to study Algebra or read Greek plays.[244]

The article indicated that the memorialists had familiarised themselves with the Charter of the University of London. It noted:

> The objects of the University of London, as declared by its charter, are to hold forth to all classes and denominations of Her Majesty's subjects, without any distinction whatsoever, an encouragement for pursuing a regular and liberal course of education, and to ascertain, by means of an examination, the persons who have acquired proficiency in Literature, Science, Art, and other departments of knowledge . . . and of rewarding them by Academical Degrees and Certificates of Proficiency as evidence of their respective attainments, and marks of honour proportioned thereunto.[245]

The article indicated, then, that the reasons offered by convocation were inadequate and insubstantial. While it disassociated women who pursued higher education from the 'amazons' mentioned by several speakers, it acknowledged the frustration that could give rise to 'strong-mindedness':

> No one can regret more than we do the abnormal self-assertion and rebellious eccentricity of some of our sisters, which serve to hinder, instead of to promote, their real freedom and progress. But we would remind our readers that this eccentricity and defiance of public opinion is more often than not the result of an ardent longing for the blessings of liberty . . . and a larger measure of justice. The strong-minded woman is the result and the complement of the narrow-minded man.[246]

Shortly after this defeat, Davies opted to request that the Local Examinations,[247] designed as an external test and standard administered by Cambridge and Oxford to middle-class boys' schools, should be opened to girls. By October 1863, the Cambridge Syndicate had agreed to allow girls to be examined on an experimental basis. Copies of the boys' examination papers were to be made available to the Committee, which would have to organise their own centre for girls. The examination date was set for December 14th, and Davies's friends brought together a group of candidates representing the more prominent girls' schools. The *Journal* celebrated the opening of the Cambridge Locals to girls, in 'The University of Cambridge and the Education of Women' (1863)[248] published some fourteen days before the first cohort of female candidates was examined. The *Journal* was optimistic, as it commented: 'now that these examinations have begun, we have no fear of their being discontinued',[249] and it expressed a hope that girls throughout England would begin to enter for the examinations.

By the end of the decade the *Journal* had become the *Englishwoman's Review*. It noted the founding of Hitchin, printed Emily Davies's first appeals for students, and thereafter followed the development of Girton and of Merton Hall (later Newnham College) closely. It celebrated the successes of three outstanding students: Charlotte A. Scott in 1880, Agnata Ramsay in 1887, and Phillipa Garrett Fawcett, who was placed above the senior wrangler in 1890. As the question of university degrees for women was brought before the university senate in the 1880s and 1890s, the *Englishwoman's Review* followed its progress in detail. Neither Cambridge nor Oxford awarded full degrees to women before the *Review* ceased publication, but it marked the opening of the new universities and colleges to women, including the Victoria University. Ever interested in women's progress in medicine, the *Review* recorded key events such as the opening of the London Medical School for Women in 1874, supported and staffed by Elizabeth Blackwell, Elizabeth Garrett Anderson and Sophia Jex Blake. It 'heralded the passing of Mr Cowper Temple's bill in 1875', allowing women to obtain medical registration, and it also 'traced the removal of the last impediments from the Irish medical profession' in the closing years of the 1870s.[250]

In any study of popular literature such a periodicals, it is unknown how many of the subscribers read every article in the publication to which they subscribed, nor can it be estimated whether the opinions of the readers concurred with what they read. Nor, indeed, is reading about a controversial issue always an inducement to action. What can be said, however, is that the discussion about women's education proliferated in mid-Victorian periodicals. Had such articles been unpopular or irrelevant, they would have appeared with less frequency. Their proliferation doubtless reflected the fact that the higher education of women was, at very least, either an interest or a concern of the majority of the educated middle and upper-middle class readers of the periodicals under review. It was this sustained interest and concern, when put to practical ends, that influenced the opening of higher education to women. In addition, because it elected to record all the major events concerning women's progress in public life, the *Englishwoman's Review* is a fine example of a periodical which provides historians with valuable records of the history of women's education in Victorian England. It provides responses to, and alternative perspectives on, articles which appeared in mainstream journals of the time, and – most significantly – when mainstream journals elected not to treat of women and college education in the late nineteenth-century years of greatest triumph, the *Review* recorded and celebrated the opening of higher education to women. It may be argued that the *Englishwoman's Review*, which had a circulation of no more than five hundred readers with common aims and aspirations, did not bring its ideas to the mass reading public. However, what must be acknowledged is that the *English-woman's Review* is the most complete published primary source for the history of the nineteenth-century movement for the higher education of women.

5

'Bringing the Dream down from the Clouds': The Opening of Higher Education to Women

Throughout the nineteenth century, education was made available to middle-class women through scientific and cultural societies, the mechanics' institute movement and the working men's college movement.[1] As June Purvis has noted, this constituted a form of part-time 'adult' education, distinct from the full-time 'higher' education available to men, and later women, at the universities. Some of the main scientific and cultural societies, founded by an élite circle of men and operated like men's clubs, were closed to women. The Geological Society and the Ethnological Society of London were closed to women on the grounds that they were viewed by members as providing a place for initiated discussion rather than education.[2] Many literary and philosophical societies, however, admitted women to lectures, and some women gave lectures.[3] For example, in 1871, while campaigning for support to build a college for women near Cambridge, Emily Davies presented a paper at the Nottingham Literary and Philosophical Society. Davies, Frances Power Cobbe, and many other women associated with the mid-Victorian women's movement also attended, and participated in, meetings of the National Association for the Promotion of Social Sciences (N.A.P.S.S.). Thus while the possibility of attending a college had been impossible for women such as Davies and Frances Power Cobbe, they were not unfamiliar with the benefit to women of lectures and formal discussion groups.

The mechanics' institutes and the working men's colleges were sources of educational provision for working class men. From the 1830s onwards, middle-class women increasingly attended the lectures which they provided. The fees which were required from women rendered it unlikely that working-class women would attend. Student numbers indicate that women were interested in both academic and vocational education. As Purvis has noted, at Manchester and York in 1839, 'women formed nearly one fifth and one third, respectively, of the lecture audiences. At Sheffield in 1843, the lectures regularly attracted about 300 people, of whom about 100 were women'.[4] Purvis used the cost of lectures and library membership as an indicator of the social class background of the women who attended the institutes. At Manchester, for example, women paid 5s. a quarter for lectures and use of the library, or 6d. per single lecture, suggesting that the lectures were attended by 'women in the more affluent sections of society'.[5]

The working men's colleges were equally more likely to have attracted middle-class rather than working-class women. In 1859, at the London Working Men's College the termly fees for the women's day classes were '2s. for one day per week, 3s.6d. for two, 4s. for three and 5s. for four' while the South London Working men's College in Blackfriar's Road 'charged in 1868 a flat rate of 4s. per term for its day-time women's classes'.[6] These colleges offered classes to women in reading, writing, arithmetic, history, geography, book-keeping and the Bible, while men were offered a wider subject choice which included Latin, Greek, logic, algebra, chemistry and politics.

If the mechanics' institutes and the working men's colleges offered a somewhat limited range of classes to women, they were occasionally an outlet for the ideas of the organised women's movement. In 1870, Lady Kate Amberley spoke in favour of the suffrage at the Stroud mechanics' institute; Florence Fenwick Miller spoke on women's rights at both the Basingstoke and Chichester institutes in 1876 and 1877, and Dorothea Beale addressed a gathering at Cheltenham Working Men's College. At the London Working Men's College, a number of women read papers in the 1890s, including Millicent Garrett Fawcett (1895) and Emily Penrose, Principal of Bedford College (1897). Contemporary with the increased attendance at the lectures of the mechanics' institutes and the working men's' colleges was the founding of two London colleges for women: Queen's College and Bedford College. These colleges attracted middle-class girls and women, many of whom hoped to earn a living by teaching or governessing. Both Queen's College founded in 1848, and Bedford College founded in 1849, pre-date Girton College, Cambridge, in their offering of lectures to women. However, Girton College was a fully residential college founded with the aim of providing women with access to collegiate life and university privileges, and thus claims for itself the distinction of having lead the movement in England for education for women equal to that of men.

Queen's College, unlike Girton, was not founded by a woman, nor was it the intention of Queen's to extend the male sphere to women. Rather it emerged from the Governesses' Benevolent Institution, as a consequence of the endeavours of a group of men, and aimed to improve the position of indigent gentle-women, most especially unemployed governesses. The Governesses' Benevolent Institution (G.B.I.) was a society which, in 1844, developed out of the somewhat ineffectual Governesses' Benevolent and Provident

Institution (1841), and was directed by the Revd David Laing and the Revd Frederick Denison Maurice. Laing was the competent and active secretary of the G.B.I. His home, the Vicarage of Holy Trinity, St Pancras, was a meeting place for contemporary literary figures, and he was interested in a range of social and educational projects including the North London Collegiate School for Ladies, which was founded in 1850 by his young friend Frances Mary Buss. Maurice, Professor of English and Modern History at King's College, London, was an active member of the G.B.I. and was to play a key role in the founding of Queen's College and the establishing of its educational aims and objectives. The aim of the G.B.I. was to provide annuities to unemployed and retired governesses, but the committee quickly realised that the humiliation and degradation suffered by unemployed governesses required more than financial amelioration. Laing, corresponding with the National Society[7] and the Archbishop of Canterbury in 1844, suggested that examinations and certificates of qualification would raise the status of governesses and would also improve standards of female education. In 1846, the G.B.I. purchased 66 Harley Street (later re-numbered as 47), and established 'The Home' for governesses, and an agency for their employment. It also received the financial support of the Honourable Amelia Murray, a maid of honour to Queen Victoria, who held hopes that the College of Preceptors would devise a plan for aiding governesses.[8] Her interests were better matched by the work of the G.B.I., and it is assumed that it was she who secured Queen Victoria's support for the G.B.I. and for Queens' College.

By the spring of 1847, Laing had set about securing lectures and examinations for governesses. There were offers of help from a number of academics associated with King's College, and lectures were held at The Home in the summer and autumn of 1847. By this time, Queen Victoria had accorded the use of her name to Laing's college, and a Committee of education was formed comprising Laing and nine professors connected with King's College, including Maurice. The association of King's with Queen's will be seen to have had some significance, much as the association of Girton with Cambridge University would influence its direction, and the association of Bedford College with London University would result in its eventual acquiring of university status. King's had been founded in 1827, by supporters of the Church of England. Unlike the nonsectarian University College, London (later the University of London) in Gower Street, the atmosphere at King's was orthodox Anglican. It prepared young men of sixteen and seventeen for either a career in commerce or for further education at Oxford or Cambridge. Queen's College would operate in a similar way, accepting girls from the age of about thirteen and offering a general education (which might prepare a young woman to teach) rather than providing university education to women. King's had earlier admitted women to lectures, though it would seem that this was by default rather than design: some women attended lectures in Geology given by Charles Lyell in 1832. The Council of King's, alarmed by this occurrence, passed a resolution which thereafter closed college lectures to women.

It was, however, a group of King's men who, in September 1847, purchased the lease of the building adjoining The Home in Harley Street, and on 13 October 1847, Queen's College was launched. Young ladies were allowed to select the classes which they wished to attend. Compounders (taking a full-time course) paid nine guineas a term for any number of classes, and non-compounders (attending part-time) paid a guinea and a half per term for a subject with two classes per week. To facilitate the chaperoning of the students, a group of Lady Visitors was selected and these mature ladies were invited to attend the lectures on a rota basis. The Lady Visitors proved to be an influential group and their opinions were invited by the all-male committee. The examinations for certificates began in December 1847, with the awarding of certificates of proficiency in Italian to Isabella Merritt and Matilda Mary Williams, although the first Queen's College lectures did not begin until May 1848. Two hundred girls and women registered for the first term, demonstrating the need for female education. Among the first pupils was Dorothea Beale, later to become Principal of Cheltenham Ladies College. Evening lectures were available, free of charge, for working governesses, and it was here that Frances Buss took three certificates. She later wrote of her affection for Queen's to Dorothea Beale:

> Queen's College opened a new life to me, I mean intellectually. To come in contact with the minds of such men was indeed delightful, and it was a new experience to me and to most of the women who were fortunate to become students.[9]

Two of the most influential and admired lecturers at Queen's in the early years were Richard Chenevix Trench and Frederick Denison Maurice. Trench is now remembered as the Archbishop of Dublin who opposed the disestablishment of the Church of Ireland, and as the philologist who proposed the compilation of the Oxford English Dictionary. It was in 1846, while he was a Professor at King's College, that he was introduced to those interested in Queen's, and he was made a member of the newly forming Committee of Education. His lectures on Church History at Queen's were remembered with admiration and respect by early Queen's students. He appeared to have no difficulty with accepting women students and, in his preface to his *Lectures on Medieval Church History* (1877) he commented:

> I cannot think the antithesis of 'bonnets' and 'brains' to be a just

one . . . having regard to receptive capacity, to the power of taking in, assimilating, and intelligently reproducing, what is set before them, my conviction after some experience in lecturing to the young of both sexes is, that there is no need to break the bread of knowledge smaller for young women than for young men.[10]

Frederick Denison Maurice had demonstrated an interest in female education as early as 1825 when, as a Cambridge undergraduate, he contributed an article, 'Female Education,' to the *Metropolitan Quarterly Magazine*, the journal started by the Cambridge 'Apostles'. The Apostles, or the Cambridge Conversazione Society, met every Saturday evening to hear and then discuss an essay by one of the members. The group included Trench and Tennyson, and was the source of inspiration for Tennyson's 'The Princess'. In his essay, Maurice wrote:

> What is chiefly remarkable in the first division of female education is, the tenderness which is observed towards the pupil whenever any exertion is required of her intellect, and the corresponding hard measure which is dealt out to her when any exactions are to be laid on the memory . . . the books which are put into young ladies' hands are amongst the worst that have been written upon every subject; but to make up for this deficiency, they have to learn them by heart.[11]

Maurice, first Principal of Queen's, was also a much admired teacher at Queen's, and there are echoes of his 1825 essay in the description of Queen's which is found in his *Inaugural Lecture* (1848). In his 1848 lecture, Maurice sketched out the incidents which had brought Queen's into existence, and laid down its educational aims. Queen's, he wrote, had been founded not 'to realise some favourite theory', but 'to supply an acknowledged deficiency'.[12] The decision to call Queen's a college rather than a school was defended in his lecture, and the defence elucidates the underlying educational philosophy of Queen's:

> The teachers of a school may aim merely to impart information; the teachers of a college must lead their pupils to the apprehension of principles . . . When I speak of leading our pupils to the study of principles, I think I mean something as nearly as possible the opposite of introducing them to an encyclopaedia of knowledge.[13]

The early curriculum recalled those of both Mary Astell and Bathsua Makin in the late seventeenth century. While Maurice, like Astell and later Emily Davies, was critical of the wasting of time on ill-taught accomplishments, he concluded that drawing and music were more important to all students -male and female- than any other subjects. Drawing, he believed, cultivated a 'habit of observation, a clear living apprehension of form, a faculty of distinction, a real interest in nature and in the human countenance, a power of looking below the surface of things for the meaning which they express,'[14] while music was able to awaken a 'sense of order and harmony',[15] but he was critical of the tendency among parents and teachers to encourage girls merely to 'produce' and 'perform' in these subjects, rather than to understand their principles. Queens was to also offer mathematics, natural philosophy, language and grammar, Latin, English literature, pedagogy, practical mechanics, mathematical geography, history, and theology. His directive to teachers and pupils alike was that they should not 'make fashion, or public opinion, their rule; . . . Colleges for men and women in a great city exist to testify that opinion is not the God they ought to worship'.[16] The thorough nature of the learning to be undertaken, particularly by compounders, at Queen's was largely owing to Maurice's belief that a little learning was, indeed, a dangerous thing. The fragmentary nature of female learning was, he wrote, 'most dangerous':

> . . . it is most dangerous to have loose fragments of information clinging to our memories and understandings, a set of phrases untranslated, a nomenclature without and real equivalents. This learning checks the free play of the spirit; it imparts a sense of discontent, dreariness, self-conceit, unreality, to all that we think and do.[17]

As a lecturer in Theology and Mental and Moral Philosophy at Queen's, Maurice made 'no concessions to laziness and few to ignorance'.[18] The pioneer social worker Louisa Twining attended his lectures in 1849. Her lecture notebooks for this period suggest that he treated basic questions seriously and in depth, at the level at which an Oxford or Cambridge undergraduate might be taught in his first year.[19] Dorothea Beale, examined in English by Maurice in the first term, recalled 'his wonderful power of intellectual sympathy,' and his pleasure 'when a grammatical definition was enlarged beyond the scope of ordinary school-books'.[20]

If Maurice was a good teacher and a fine scholar, he was also a controversial figure in the 1840s and 1850s and this brought about his resignation from Queen's in 1853. Maurice was committed to Chartism by about 1848, and was also involved in the Christian Socialist Movement. In the *Quarterly Review* (1850) criticisms were levelled at the religious teaching at Queen's, and included in the article were quotations from Maurice's lectures. The article, cautioning readers against 'leanings that require to be watched' said that religious teaching at Queen's was 'a sort of modified pantheism and latitudinarianism – a system of not bringing religion into everything, but of considering everything as more or less inherently religious'.[21] The *Quarterly Review* (1851) also accused Maurice of a 'morbid craving for notoriety' which had lead him to preach the doctrines of Christian Socialism. In 1853, Maurice was dismissed from the Chair of Divinity at King's College, and in the same month he resigned from Queen's. His resignation was not sought by the majority of the Council of Queen's, but Maurice was aware that, as a minority favoured his resignation, he could not jeopardise the future of the college by lecturing while 'regarded with suspicion . . . by a number of those who [might] send their children to the College'.[22] Although Maurice returned to lecture at Queen's in 1856, his departure in 1853 was considered to mark the end of the first phase in the history of Queen's College. Camilla Croudace, student at Queen's from 1856-1862 and Lady Resident from 1881-1906, considered Maurice to have been the 'moving spirit' behind Queen's.

Most awe-inspiring for the early students was Dr Trench, who succeeded Maurice as Principal. Trench's principalship steered Queen's along a course that was to rule out any possibility that the college would become associated with a university. Trench, while holding the principalship of Queen's, was also a Professor at King's and, after 1856, dean of Westminster. He had little time to devote to making Queen's a pioneering venture in university education for women, and Queen's developed as an educational establishment within which there was school and college: that is, it provided education to students under fifteen and advanced lectures to students over fifteen. In this respect, Queen's provided the model for Alexandra College, Dublin, founded in 1866 by Anne Jellicoe and Trench, who was then archbishop of Dublin. At Alexandra, the long term aim had been to become a college of the University of Dublin.[23] At Queen's, the Committee would appear to have held more conservative aims which later drew Dorothea Beale to reflect:

> I have always regretted that my *Alma Mater*, which should have held the first rank, as it was the first in time, has not done so.[24]

Frances Buss similarly reflected, in a letter to Beale, 'Queen's College began the Women's Education Movement undoubtedly, but it grew conservative'.[25] This conservatism was one of the fundamental differences between Queen's College and Girton College, two colleges which eventually reflected the polarities in educational thought concerning women.

The management of Queen's, while under the Principalship of the very busy Dr Trench and later under the absent Dr Stanley, was left in the hands of Dr Plumptre. Plumptre, throughout his long association with Queen's, was a fine scholar and teacher, but he was not an innovator. It was during the period of his managing of Queen's, on behalf of Trench and later Stanley, that representations were made by women to move Queen's to the forefront of the movement for women's education, but such changes were resisted by Plumptre. In 1861, a Miss Drewry wrote to Queen's to urge the Committee to press for the opening of the Oxford and Cambridge Local Examinations to girls. The Committee 'decided that it was not . . . desirable for them to take any steps in the matter'.[26] In 1862, Emily Davies began her campaign for the admission of women and girls to the Locals, and received some encouragement from the Cambridge Board. In 1863, an experimental examination was arranged, and several students from Queen's were entered. The Committee at Queen's was, however, less than encouraging. At their meeting of 17 November 1863, the Dean reported that eighteenth or twenty pupils had indicated that they might enter for the examination and was requested 'to inform Miss Davies . . . that while the Committee had not thought it right to interpose any obstacle to the carrying into execution of the pupils' intentions in this matter they had left them to do so, at the discretion of their parents, without selecting any picked candidates or giving them any special training'.[27]

Davies had hoped that Queen's would lead the way to opening university education to women. In 1866, she wrote to Plumptre:

> It seems to me that [an] . . . affiliation to Cambridge would in the case of Queen's College be much more satisfactory than anything we are likely to get from the London University, and I am sure it would make the College much more popular with the schools and more looked up to in the country generally than it now is.[28]

Davies was, at this stage, aware that there was not a significant distinction between a Queen's education and an ordinary school education. With foresight, she predicted that the reputation of Queen's as a pioneering women's college rested on its development of a distinct programme of higher education. She drew Plumptre's attention to this:

> I find among the higher class of schoolmistresses in all parts of the country a strong disposition to put themselves into friendly relations with the London Colleges. They would like their schools to be to the Colleges what the Public Schools are to the Universities, but with that view they want the Colleges to be *really* places of higher education . . . I have heard of a case in which a girl was sent first to College, and then to school to finish. I do not see how this can be got over excepting by raising the age of the College students and giving them some higher kind of examination than is open to schools. I believe there would be no difficulty in getting these from Cambridge, if the Colleges are will-

ing to accept what the University has to give, that is, the examinations for ordinary Degrees.[29]

Plumptre was not enthusiastic about these suggestions, but in 1866, when the post of Assistant Secretary at Queen's became vacant, Davies applied. She recorded in her journal:

> My idea was that if I were inside the place, I might be able to help forward some plan for the affiliation of the College to the University of Cambridge.[30]

Her application was unsuccessful. Failing to rally the Committee of Education at Queen's to the pioneering task of opening university education to women, Emily Davies went on to found her own college, Girton, which would become attached to the University of Cambridge.

Quite aside from the limited aspirations of the governing body of Queen's, there are other reasons why this first college for women did not develop in the direction of university education. To establish these reasons, and to evaluate the exact contribution of Queen's to the higher education of women, it is necessary to examine the type of student and the type of teacher attracted to Queen's in its early days. Queen's College was frequently described as a college for the middle classes, and Elaine Kaye's examination of the register of pupils for the early years of the College 'shows that the students were largely confined to this section of society'.[31] When the G.B.I. Committee first discussed the possibility of founding a women's college, they had decided that it would be for 'the daughters of professional men, that term including clergymen, barristers, solicitors, physicians, surgeons and apothecaries, of officers in the army and navy, or of such other persons in the same rank of society as the Board may deem eligible'.[32] The occupation of the father appeared on all admission forms. The Reports of the Schools Inquiry Commission (1867/68) indicated that most of the pupils at Queen's were upper-middle class, but recognised that, as it was a non-residential college, it allowed for class mix. The S.I.C. also noted the high fees at Queen's and at Bedford College (between £22 and £28 per annum) which were considerably higher than the fees at established boys' schools (£9 per annum, on average). Of course, it has to be noted that, unlike the grammar schools and Public Schools for boys, neither Queen's nor Bedford were supported by educational endowments.

Many of the girls sent to Queen's were there to receive basic schooling and had no scholarly ambitions. Others, attending the College lectures, often did so having had little basic schooling, and they had little understanding of the lectures. Some, such as Dorothea Beale, had received a sound schooling and had a natural ability for academic work. Essentially, then, while the girls

and young women at Queen's were of similar social backgrounds, their academic backgrounds varied widely and their ambitions were far from uniform.
Such a variety of scholarly ability rendered it unlikely that Queen's could
develop as a constituent college of a university without undergoing much
modification.

Teaching at Queen's, while undertaken by some fine professors including Maurice, Trench, and the historian John de Soyres[33], was not of an even
standard, nor were all of the male professors equally comfortable teaching
girls and women. Because many of the students who attended lectures were
ill-equipped to judge of the teaching, or to seek extra help with their work,
College lecturing continued to improve only a small number of very capable
students, and was not uniformly suitable to preparation for university degrees. Despite this, the Principal who succeeded Stanley in 1873 made some
attempts to associate Queen's with university education. He was the Revd
John Llewellyn Davies, brother of Emily and a strong supporter of his sister's
attempts to open university examinations to women.

Llewellyn Davies had come under the influence of F.D. Maurice while
at Trinity College, Cambridge. He was ordained in 1881, and then came to
London where, for thirty-seven years, he was parish priest at Lisson Grove.
Like Maurice, he was a Christian Socialist, and he taught at the Working
Men's Colleges and supported the legalisation of Trade Unions. His sister
Emily had founded the College for Women at Hitchin in 1869, having failed
to persuade Queen's to affiliate itself to Cambridge, and when Llewelyn became Principal he renewed the endeavour to enable students at Queen's to
take degrees, this time those of London University. In 1874, Emily Davies
wrote to Barbara Bodichon:

> There is a prospect of reform at Queen's College. My brother has been
> made Principal, and he is aiming at getting it reconstituted on the model
> of University and King's, i.e. having a good school for girls under 18,
> and making them pass an Entrance Examination for admission to the
> College; which might then be a place of advanced teaching, preparing
> for London University Examinations.[34]

The Committee of Education postponed any serious discussion of the proposals made by Llewelyn Davies, and he resigned his Principalship. For the
next three years, Dr Plumptre was Principal, resigning in 1877 after forty
years' service to Queen's. The College under Plumptre was suffering from
declining numbers. By this time, the first schools of the Girls' Public Day
School Company had been founded, and Cheltenham Ladies College and
North London Collegiate School were established. All of these had women
staff, in many cases former students of Queen's, and were attracting large

numbers of students. Additionally, Girton College and Newnham Hall were established and offered higher education to women, in an exclusively adult environment. Although Llewellyn Davies returned to the Principalship of Queen's in 1877, and once again pursued his goal of establishing at Queen's two distinct types of education (school and college), by 1882 Queen's was overshadowed by many contemporary schools and colleges. In 1878, London University opened degree examinations to women, and in 1881 King's College admitted women to its newly formed department for the Higher Education of Women. While Queen's provided lectures to prepare women for matriculation and the London University B.A., only three students took the degree in 1882. The Queen's College Annual Report for 1882 noted:

> . . . the lectures at University College have been recently thrown open to women and largely attended by them. It would be impossible for Queen's College, except by an outlay quite beyond its means, to compete with the ample provision of teaching thus offered to students who seek the B.A. degree.[35]

Had Queen's been able to afford it, it is arguable that a complete separation of School and College at this time might have rendered it possible for Queen's College to have developed degree courses. By this time however, Cambridge, Oxford, and London University all offered higher education to women in the context of a university, and Bedford College, originally very similar to Queen's, made a successful transition to becoming a school of London University.

Bedford College was founded shortly after Queen's, in 1849, though from the outset it differed from Queen's College. This was largely because Bedford was essentially the vision of a foundress, Elizabeth Jesser Reid (1789-1866). 'A college for women, or something like it, has been my dream from childhood,'[36] Reid wrote to her friends Eliza Bostock and Jane Martineau in 1860. Elizabeth Jesser Reid was by then a wealthy and independent woman, who had inherited a considerable fortune following the deaths of her husband and her parents. Mrs Reid was sixty years of age when she found herself in a position to realise her wishes to found a college for women and, while she did not devote quite as much time to her task as Emily Davies did at Girton, she was undaunted by the prospect of engineering the whole project. She appointed three male trustees – Erasmus Darwin, Thomas Farrer and Hensleigh Wedgewood – to manage a trust fund of £1,500, and invited friends to form a committee and to teach. They leased a house on Bedford Square, from which the college took its name, and planned that the college would provide a liberal education, non-sectarian but not anti-religious, to females.

Like Queen's, and unlike the later Girton, Bedford College comprised a school and a college. Its first prospectus stated: 'Ladies are admitted over the age of twelve years,'[37] and indeed in the early years Bedford offered no advanced courses of study since the students were invariably either too young or too ill-prepared for serious study. By 1852, it was decided at a special meeting of the Lady Visitors, Professors and Council that a Junior School, accepting girls from the age of nine, should also be started in order to generate funds for the college, and it was opened at the beginning of the second term of 1853. That Bedford had both a school and a college caused much difficulty over the next two decades, and in 1860 when Mrs Reid drew up her educational trust (later the Reid Trust) she noted with concern:'My dread is that [the College will] merge in the School, and it is to avert this fatal retrogression that I make this bequest'.[38] Reid's vision was of a college for higher education for women, and in many respects she encouraged the development of the school only insofar as it supplied girls for the college, and it gave them the good education which she recognised as necessary for college work. In a 'Statement Respecting the Ladies' College, Bedford Square' drawn up in 1852, the emphasis was clearly on college education. It stated that the objectives of Bedford was 'to provide for ladies, at a moderate expense, a curriculum of liberal education . . . [to be] given on the same plan as in the public Universities, of combined lectures, examinations, and exercises'.[39] Certainly, however, the statement exaggerated somewhat when it suggested that the level of lecturing would be similar to that of the universities, and by 1891 the Council saw fit to demand an external examination of teaching at the college.

In the early days at Bedford, Reid's allies and co-workers included Francis William Newman, Professor of Latin at University College London, and the Revd James Booth F.R.S. Newman, the younger brother of the future Cardinal John Henry Newman, was considered to be among the more unorthodox and advanced people of his time, and he gave generously of his time in the early years of the College.[40] The first Council included Augustus de Morgan, Professor of Mathematics at University College, London, and William Sterndale Bennet who taught harmony and vocal music at Bedford from 1849 to 1856. At Bedford, as at Queen's, it was often difficult to find enough Lady Visitors to fulfil the duties of chaperoning girls at all lectures, and providing organisation and stability within a college which had, at first, virtually no administrative staff. Nevertheless, the practice of appointing Lady Visitors continued until 1889.

A number of eminent men and women were associated with Bedford, including Erasmus Darwin, one of the original Bedford trustees. Darwin, the older brother of Charles, was Chairman of Council from 1851 to 1869. However by the time of Mrs Reid's death in 1866, control of the finance and the property of Bedford College had been placed in the hands of women. In

1860, Reid decided to establish a small residence to accommodate some Bedford students. She invested £2000, to provide a fund for this project, and established Eliza Bostock, Jane Martineau and Eleanor Smith as Managers of the Boarding House. It was they, and not the College Council, who were to acquire the lease of a second house on Bedford Square, part of which was to be let to the Bedford College. Upon Reid's death, a further £16,400 was invested to provide an annual trust fund (the Reid Trust) of £800, and Bostock, Martineau and Smith were the trustees. At this time, these three women also became the owners of the leases to the two college houses on Bedford Square, and they continued to exercise considerable influence on the development of the college throughout the 1880s.

The terms of the Reid Trust, which become operable upon Mrs Reid's death in 1866, indicated Elizabeth Jesser Reid's desire to give both education and authority to members of her sex. Under the terms of the Trust, the trustees could only be unmarried women, and the fund was to be used for the higher education of women. In thus clarifying her wishes, Reid ensured that the fund could not be spent on the development of the school, and it suggested 'her distrust of men in their attitude to female education'.[41] The three trustees acted very much on what might have been Reid's own wishes, and Bedford steadily became a fine college of higher education while the school ceased to exist. This was achieved through a number of careful strategies. The trustees prioritised the awarding of scholarships and grants from the trust to individuals to attend Bedford College, using the Cambridge Senior Local Examination results and the College Entrance Examination results to select winners. They set about improving the standard of teaching at Bedford by adapting and building improved college premises, and they increased the salaries of lecturers.[42] The year 1874 had seen the college relocate to 8 and 9 York Place, London, when the leases expired at Bedford Square. The new properties were generously appointed and allowed for the opening of basement laboratories, a large lecture room, several classrooms, and a fine studio. Residence rooms were situated on the upper two storeys. A distinctly 'college' spirit was fostered by the availability of a large common room and a library, and by the organisation of societies and clubs. Finally, in 1878, the college decided to hold classes in preparation for the matriculation and degree examinations of the University of London. During the 1880s, the emphasis at Bedford was placed increasingly on preparation for these examinations, and Bedford attained University status. There was a decline in the intake of junior students, and the minimum age of entry was raised to sixteen.

In 1893, Emily Penrose was appointed as the first resident Principal. As Head of both the college and the residence, she stressed the importance of participation in the college community, and brought true collegiate spirit to Bedford. Students were also deeply influenced by Dr Catherine Raisin, who provided Bedford with a fine role model for young academic women. She had taken an honours degree in Geology from University College in 1884, coming to Bedford as a demonstrator in Botany in 1886. In 1890 she was appointed Head of the Geology Department, a position which she held until her retirement in 1920. Catherine Raisin attained her D.Sc. in 1898, was elected a Fellow of University College, London, in 1902, and at Bedford she also held the positions of Head of the Botany Department (1891-1908) and Resident Vice-Principal of the College (1898-1901).

Elizabeth Jesser Reid's foresight had allowed that, unlike Girton College, Bedford could award generous scholarships, exhibitions and prizes to encourage academic achievement and to raise student numbers. Additionally, in 1894-5 the Technical Education Board of the London County Council made a grant to Bedford College in exchange for free tuition to be made available to six scholars and a place for themselves on the College Council. The library benefited from not only Mrs Reid's own personal collection of books, but also from two gifts (comprising mahogany bookcases of some 300 books, and a set of stained glass windows), and Barbara Bodichon was a generous benefactress after whom the Bodichon Art Studio was named in 1895.

While it is beyond the scope of this study to supply a detailed study of the history of Bedford, it has to be noted that, unlike Queen's College which became a school for girls, Bedford went on to eventually become a college of higher education with university affiliation. In 1886, construction began on a new wing to accommodate science laboratories, and it was opened by the Empress Frederick, daughter of Queen Victoria, in 1891. The college enjoyed its jubilee celebrations in 1899, over three days in June, and in 1901 discussion began about a new constitution which would allow representation for employed lecturers of the college on Council and Board. In 1909, Bedford College was wound up, and everything was transferred to Bedford College for Women (University of London). In 1909 it developed new college premises at Regent's Park where it remained until 1985, when it merged with Royal Holloway College to become Royal Holloway and Bedford New College.

EMILY DAVIES AND GIRTON COLLEGE

In this study, Emily Davies emerges as the individual whose singularity of purpose brought to fruition the idea of university education for women equal to that of men, some years after she moved to Cambridge in 1873, to found a university college for women. Her associations with the University of Cambridge pre-date her arrival at Girton in 1873. Her father had been at Queen's College and received the degrees of B.D. and D.D. from the University of

Cambridge. He took orders, married Mary Hopkinson of Derby in 1823, and
then set up a boarding school for boys in Chichester. Between 1824 and
1832, three sons and two daughters were born: Sarah Emily Davies (1830)
was their fourth child. That anything at all is known about the early and
unremarkable years of family life in the Davies household is due to the existence of Emily's 'Family Chronicle,' an autobiographical journal which she
began at the age of seventy-five. Emily's earliest recollections of family life
date from about 1838. She recalled her own early education at home:

> . . . my father taught the two boys, and I did some lessons with my
> other or Jane . . . After tea, at 5 or 5.30 p.m. we had reading aloud, *en
> famille*.[43]

In 1839, Dr Davies accepted the living of Gateshead, and moved his family
into the Rectory. In 1841, Emily and her brother William began to write a
weekly newspaper and to compose extensive denunciations of Popery and
Tractarianism. In one edition Emily included the following advertisement
for a governess for herself:

> Wanted, a Governess in a gentleman's family. The lady who is to fill
> this station must be a person of great firmness and determination, as the
> young lady who is to be the object of her care is rather inclined to be
> self-willed. . . . The lady who is to fill this situation must be a person
> well skilled in the languages and sciences, as Miss Davies is ambitious to
> excel all her contemporaries in these departments of knowledge.[44]

Davies, however, was not to fulfil her early intellectual ambitions. Her
education was patchy: at nine years of age she spent a few months at a small
day school for girls, and later she had lessons in French, Italian and music
from a master. She later recalled that her education 'answered to the description of that of clergymen's daughters generally . . . they have lessons and get
on as they can'.[45] This education left her greatly lacking in confidence when
she founded Girton College: she refused to lecture or become involved in
the academic side of the college, believing herself to be severely handicapped
by a poor education, and her short spell as Mistress was accepted only under
duress and was concluded as swiftly as possible.

In 1848, the young Emily Davies made two important friendships: with
Jane Crow and Elizabeth Garrett. The three women would become lifelong
allies in the women's movement. Her other close friend was her brother
Llewelyn, who was ordained in 1851. When, in 1856, he was appointed to
the Rectory of Christ Church, Marlebone, he became an admirer and friend
of Frederick Dennison Maurice. Maurice was Principal and co-founder of

Queen's College, Harley Street from 1851 to 1853, and his interest in the education of women was soon shared by Llewellyn Davies who became Principal of Queen's College in 1873, a position which he held until 1886. While Emily was stimulated by her brother's work, she was not, at first, free to assist him in any way. Between 1855 and 1859 she nursed her sister, Jane, and brother, Henry, until their deaths in 1858 and 1859 respectively. In 1858 her brother William also died, while working in China. Following these bereavements, at this time of great personal sorrow, Emily Davies found occupation and purpose when she became involved with 'the first organized movement on behalf of women'.[46]

Emily Davies was introduced into the women's movement by Annie Leigh Smith and her sister, Barbara.[47] She had met Annie in 1858, while on a trip to Algiers to bring her ailing brother William home to England. Annie and Barbara corresponded with Emily Davies, and introduced her into the Langham Place circle in London.[48] Her introduction into this group occurred while on a trip to visit Llewelyn Davies in London in the spring of 1859, Emily and Elizabeth Garrett went to tea at the Leigh Smith's home, and there met Bessie Rayner Parkes.[49] Returning to Gateshead, Emily Davies attempted to introduce the ideas of the women's movement into her parish work. She established the Northumberland and Durham Branch of the Society for Promoting the Employment of Women, out of which developed a book-keeping class which prepared girls for the Examination of the Society of Arts, and a Register for Governesses was also opened. Among the committee members of this society was Mrs Anna Richardson, an educated and cultured woman whose continued friendship sustained Emily Davies through the years of hard work at Girton. Anna Richardson undertook to guide Emily's reading, and they attended a course of lectures in physiology.

Her lack of interest in physiology did not prevent Davies from being interested in seeing the medical profession open its doors to women, and her work for this cause effectively launched her into public life. It also introduced her to the broader question of higher education for women. Even as Davies approached this question, there was only one female physician legally registered in England. This was Elizabeth Blackwell MD, who had been obliged to take her degree in America in 1849. In 1850 and 1859 she spent time in London, and on both occasions Barbara Leigh Smith and Bessie Rayner Parkes made her work known to other women who were interested in medicine. Elizabeth Garrett attended the London lectures given by Blackwell in 1859 and, with the encouragement of Emily Davies, decided to pursue a career in medicine. Typical of young women of her time, Elizabeth Garrett was completely unprepared for a training in medicine. However, Garrett's letters which have been preserved in the 'Family Chronicle' indicate that Emily Davies began to deal systematically with the problem of educating Elizabeth Garrett.

Garrett took lessons in Latin, and improved her English composition by writing essays for Emily to read.

Davies also sought out doctors who might tutor Elizabeth Garrett, and eventually in 1860 Garrett was admitted to the Middlesex Hospital to begin her training. Her position eventually proved unsatisfactory as propriety forbade a lady to participate in all aspects of surgery and anatomy. Additionally, the Treasurer of the hospital much doubted the possibility of ever admitting her on a full-time basis, as he believed a female presence would distract the students. Hers was the position of an amateur, as she was not allowed to pay fees and was therefore denied student status.

Davies was familiar with the fact that Garrett was not the first woman to pursue unsuccessfully a medical education in England: in 1856, Jessie Merton White[50] had applied unsuccessfully to all the London Hospitals. To overcome her problem, Elizabeth Garrett decided to secure a promise from an examining body to examine her upon completion of her studies. Such a promise could then be used to persuade a medical school to admit her. Oxford, Cambridge, Glasgow, Edinburgh and Dundee all refused the application. Finally the Association of Apothecaries agreed to examine her, but much of her hospital practice had to be gained through the unsatisfactory arrangement of working as a nurse at the London Hospital. In 1865, she qualified to practice and her name was placed on the British Medical Register. In 1870, with no prospects of getting a medical degree from London University, she took her M.D. degree in Paris. She married J.G.S. Anderson in 1871, and in 1883 became Dean of the London School of Medicine for Women.

Garrett's example to other women had been thwarted considerably in 1868 when the Society of Apothecaries ruled that it would no longer examine students who had studied privately: all candidates thenceforth had to study in a regular medical school. This closed to women the only route to qualification, and added an impetus to Emily Davies's growing concern for the paucity of educational and professional opportunities for women.

Throughout 1860, as Elizabeth Garrett endeavoured to find a medical school which would prepare her for examination, she carried out a detailed and personal correspondence with Davies[51] which suggests early grounds for her eventual conservatism regarding the image of Girton women in Cambridge. The correspondence indicates that Elizabeth Garret knew she faced rejection from hospitals only on grounds of her sex. Fellow students and lecturers at Middlesex Hospital were courteous but she was obliged to receive her instruction under the guise of a nurse, and Garrett resented having to continue at the hospital in what she considered to be a false position. By 1861, Garrett's popularity among the more chivalrous students and lecturers had waned somewhat, in the light of her evident competence. Following a *viva voce* examination at which she gave better answers than her fellow class members, the students got up a memorial to the hospital authorities against her.[52] The memorialists succeeded in barring her from the lectures, and precipitated her departure to find an alternative route to qualification, via the Society of Apothecaries. It was clear that there was a grain of truth, then, in the advice of the writers in this study who recognised that many men did not like to be out-shone by clever women. This event was later to be replicated for Davies when Cambridge turned against successful Girton scholars who attained higher marks than Cambridge men in examinations.[53]

Garrett also wrote to Davies of the need to pander to her male colleagues, lest their masculinity should feel threatened by her presence. She resented using 'all kinds of little feminine dodges,'[54] but knew that she could not afford 'to appear too frigid and stiff with them'.[55] She also wrote to Davies the need to dress in a feminine way, and take pains to endorse feminine leisure activities. She complained to Davies that her reputation would be damaged by visits from a mutual friend who 'looked awfully strong-minded in walking dress . . . short petticoats and a close round hat, and several other dreadfully ugly arrangements,' while briskly concluding: '. . . this is most damaging to the cause. I will not have her visit me at the Hospital in it'.[56]

Garrett's dress style was dictated by her desire to be 'as much like a lady as lies in one's power,'[57] and she passed her leisure time with sewing and croquet when at home with relatives who disapproved of her studies. This endeavour to disarm prejudice, so evident in the strategies adopted by Astell in the seventeenth century, and by a number of eighteenth century intellectual women, was central to the success of Davies's campaign for the education of women at Cambridge. 'Masculine' dress, central to the controversy about femininity that raged in the Renaissance Pamphlet Wars, was to emerge as a critical determinant of the dangers of education to womanhood in the nineteenth century. The experience of Garrett at Middlesex Hospital was not lost on Davies: her relentless pursuit of educational equality of opportunity for women was, for many of her contemporaries, made acceptable only because of her emphatic refusal to allow that such education would compromise women's femininity.

Her close association with Garrett's pursuit of a medical degree also gave Davies valuable experience in writing. Composing letters, memorials and papers would occupy most of Davies's working life: it was for Garrett that she first took up her pen and wrote on the need for medical education for women.[58] That Davies had the freedom to commit herself to Garrett's cause was largely due to the fact that her father had died in October 1861, leaving her free to move her mother from Gateshead Rectory to London in January, 1862. They settled at No.17, Cunningham Place, close to Garrett and the activities of the Langham Place group. Here Emily Davies, supported by the increasing interest of her able and alert mother, began in earnest her work for the women's movement.

Davies's early work involved applying to the University of London for the Admission of women to its degrees. In 1857, in a letter to Barbara Bodichon, Jessie Merton White, who could not afford the legal battle that might have won her a medical degree from London, had advised Bodichon on how to penetrate the academy:

> Read the charter of the University carefully – take the clause in which 'Victoria, by the grace of God, of the United Kingdom of Great Britain and Ireland, Queen, Defender of the Faith . . . [deems] it to be the duty of our royal office, for the advancement of religion and morality, and the promotion of useful knowledge, *to hold forth to all classes and denominations of our faithful subjects without any distinction whatsoever* an encouragement for pursuing a regular and liberal course of education' – read this and I believe you will agree with me, in thinking that it will be difficult to exclude women legally from sharing in the benefits of said University.[59]

While Davies initially took up the challenge to facilitate Garrett, who could not gain admission to any medical school unless a University had agreed to allow her to sit the M.D. examinations, her aim from the outset was to open up university education per se to women. She and Garrett applied for leave for Garrett to enter for the University of London matriculation examinations, but the application was rejected by one vote at a meeting of the Senate on 9 April 1862. Davies recorded in the 'Family Chronicle' that 'it was decided that a memorial should be sent in, signed by Mr Garrett on behalf of himself and his daughter, asking for the insertion in the new Charter to be submitted to parliament of a clause expressly providing for the extension to women of the privileges of the University'.[60] Davies set about enlisting the support of influential friends and acquaintances, and it is from this incident that we can date her involvement in opening higher education to women.

While her own journal, the 'Family Chronicle,' records this period in some detail and there are copies of all relevant documents among the Davies Papers at Girton College with which to corroborate important material in her version, it is in her personal correspondence that a sense of the excitement surrounding this pioneering venture may be found. Davies wrote regularly, sometimes every day, to Barbara Bodichon, sparing her no detail of her new interests. Bodichon's papers[61] supplement the somewhat factual record of this period that Davies herself left behind, and illustrate Davies's political skills. To Bodichon she wrote:

17 Cunningham Place,
St John's Wood, N.W.
[1862]

Dear Mrs Bodichon,

Lizzie Garrett has asked me to write to you about a matter in which I am sure you will be interested. We are going to try to get the London University open to women. Lizzie is advised that she had better make sure of getting admitted to the M.D. examination before making any more attempts upon Medical Schools. The medical people make it an excuse for refusing her . . . [and] it would be as well to take it out of their mouths, and the object is besides quite worth struggling for in itself. We intend to try the question entirely on general grounds, carefully keeping medical schemes in the background, so as to avoid if possible, raising the hostility of the doctors. There are a good many of them on the Senate, and they seem to be the only people likely to resist the application. . . . Will you write to everyone you know, and get them to use their influence, either personally or thro' the press. It is important to get up some manifestation of public opinion, if possible, as the question will come before the general body of graduates. They have a right to discuss and make recommendations, tho' the ultimate decision rests with the Senate. . . . There seems to be a very good prospect of success. My brother, who is generally discouraging, thinks we can scarcely fail. He will bring a good deal of the Maurice interest to bear. Adelaide Procter is at work, and the Drewrys will do all they can in their circle, and I am going to stir up my Quaker friends. Don't you think it a point worth fighting for? . . . I should like to do something great! but I am afraid home claims and want of nervous strength will keep me to an insignificant part . . .

Yours aff.tly
E.D.[62]

Davies drew up a letter to send to 'persons of distinction and Members of the University of London'.[63] Her journal records her decision not to sign her Christian name in full, lest recipients would 'think it was some horrid woman in spectacles,' and as a consequence she received 'many letters addressed to S.E. Davies, Esq'.[64] Among these was a letter from Mary Somerville, the distinguished Mathematician after whom Somerville College, Oxford would later be named. She gave her unequivocal support to the petition, and to 'every plan for . . . intellectual improvement, that is consistent with the duties and refinement of our sex'.[65]

A Memorial was then sent to the University of London, asking that the new Charter, which was then being drawn up, should include a clause providing for the extension to women of the privileges of the University.[66] It read:

> A strong desire has for some time past been felt by many women, of the upper and middle classes, for some test of proficiency in the more solid branches of education, such as our Universities offer to young men.[67]

Her petition indicated that, from this early stage, she associated higher education for women with examinations and qualifications. She did not simply seek tuition as a worthwhile female pastime, she associated it with equality of opportunity. Unlike the founders of Queen's College and Bedford College, she was prepared to use University education for men as the key term of reference. The petition recalled central argument of Mary Astell's *Proposal* (1694) when it blamed the characteristic frailties of women on the inadequacy of their education, but Davies went a step further and insisted that University examinations were needed if women were to be motivated towards serious and well-directed study. If fact, she argued, the lack of such examinations tended to 'foster the inaccuracy and incompleteness which may perhaps be regarded as especially the faults of women'.[68]

Davies recognised that the Senate, comprised of senior members of the University who might be quite hostile to the idea of 'university women,' would have to have their fears assuaged somewhat. Her petition concluded with the mollifying assurance that women candidates for examinations would not upset the running of the University, while her closing line reminded the Senate that, strictly speaking, the Charter could be interpreted to allow women candidates as things stood:

> It is believed that this privilege might be accorded by the University of London, without risks of collateral evils. The University being simply an examining body, requiring no residence, and giving no course of instruction,the conditions of the examinations would not in any way interfere with a woman's ordinary domestic life. It is therefore hoped that the Senate may be willing to give the widest interpretation to the words of their Charter, and to 'hold forth to all classes and denominations' of her Majesty's subjects, not excluding women, 'an encouragement for pursuing a regular and liberal course of education'.[69]

The motion to obtain a modification of the Charter providing for the admission of women to degrees but not to Convocation was lost by one vote. When, the following year, the Annual Committee of Convocation passed a resolution in favour of provision being made for the examination of women, this too was thrown out.

Davies's battles on behalf of women and higher education at Cambridge continued to follow this pattern of drafting of memorials, enlisting of support, and facing failure (often marginal) time and again when the matter went to a vote. Her early experience seems to have hardened her against failure. It also brought home to her the importance of waging one's war on many fronts: she began to write, publish, and present papers on female education and to win widespread support for her ideas. Her name was quickly associated with gaining admission for women to medical education. In 1862 she received a number of letters from women who wished to know more about the possibility of studying medicine.[70] In come cases, they were from women who were considering, at a late stage in life, to pursue a career.[71]

To facilitate the many women who wrote to her home at Cunningham Place for such information, in July 1862 Davies printed a flysheet listing the subjects required for the preliminary examination. They included Latin, algebra and mathematics, thus highlighting the fact that, irrespective of their gender, the inadequate state of schooling of girls rendered them unlikely candidates. It also advised that the 'Diploma of Doctor of Medicine can only be obtained from a University'. While it noted that a diploma or licence from the Apothecaries' Hall could be obtained by women who had undergone training at a recognised school, it concluded: 'no school in England or Scotland is as yet open to women'.[72] Davies continued to print similar information leaflets, often at her own expense, throughout her campaign for higher education for women. This corpus of literature reveals that Davies recognised the importance of disseminating not only general facts about female education, but crucial details about the reasons *why* women were debarred from higher education. Thus, for example, while her flysheet on the Diploma of Doctor of Medicine (1862) ostensibly outlined the requirements for such a Diploma to readers, it also made them aware of the key reasons why women were not awarded such a Diploma. The reasons were several, and included the paucity of good schooling for girls, the complete lack of medical schooling for women and the fact that the universities were not prepared to accept women as examination candidates.

In the same year Davies also wrote a paper, 'Medicine as a Profession for Women,' which was read for her by Mr Russell Gurney[73] at the annual meeting of the National Association for the Promotion of Social Science (1862). At this meeting the question of opening university examinations to women was raised, and a special meeting of the Association was called at which Frances Power Cobbe read her paper on 'University Degrees for Women'.[74] The Association resolved unanimously that 'measures ought to be provided for testing and attesting the education of women in the middle and higher classes'.[75] It was also decided that, as the University of London did not wish to be repeatedly used as a *corpus vile*, Emily Davies should make an attempt to persuade one of the older Universities to make a gesture towards the education of women and girls.

Davies opted to request that the Local Examinations,[76] designed as an external test and standard administered by Cambridge and Oxford Universities to middle-class boys' schools, should be opened to girls. This move was consonant with her general desire to improve formal schooling for girls, and with her belief that examinations and certification were, for girls as much as for women, the absolute measure intellectual parity between the sexes. She had considered the tactic of using the entrance of girls to the Local Examinations as a route to eventual participation by women in University Examinations as early as July 1862, when she wrote to her close friend Anna Richardson:

> Are you inclined to give any help or advice in the matter of the Middle Class, or as they are now called, Local Examinations of the Universities? We are going to make a try for them, and it has occurred to me that a Memorial from ladies actually engaged in tuition would have considerable weight. If you think it a good plan, will you send me the names of any heads of Schools, or governesses, whom you think likely to be interested. I have been looking at the subjects and they seem to me as suitable for girls as for boys, and that the examinations would be worth having, tho' I do not care *very* much for them in themselves, because I think the encouragement to learning is most wanted *after* the age of eighteen. It seems however that if we could get these Examinations, it would be a great lift towards getting the University of London.[77]

In the letters of Emily Davies there are a few rare glimpses of her steely determination, and toward the close of this business-like missive to Richardson it is possible to see what drove Davies on in the face of much hostility:

> This agitation is hateful work, but it becomes clearer every day that incessant and unremitting talking and pushing is the only way of gaining our ends. I stop sometimes and ask whether the ends are worth such horridly disagreeable means, and if one had only a personal interest in the matter, I am sure it would be impossible to persevere. But we are fighting for people who cannot fight for themselves.[78]

In her pursuit of Local Examinations for girls, Davies met with opposition from Mr Griffiths of Oxford, who wrote back that 'the University Statute which gives us our authority gives it to us only in respect of boys . . . the

University would think the examination of young ladies a matter altogether beyond its sphere of duty.[79]

However at Cambridge Dr Liveing offered to present a memorial on her behalf to the members of the Cambridge Local Examination Syndicate of which he was Secretary. Davies began her lengthy battle by forming a University Examinations Committee, consisting of Barbara Bodichon, Lady Goldsmid (Treasurer),[80] Mr Russell Gurney, Mr Hastings, Miss Bostock, Miss Craig, and Mr Heywood, on 23 October 1862, at a meeting at 3 Waterloo Place.[81] Most of these people would play key roles in the founding of Girton College, and the opening of the University of Cambridge to women. They were also closely associated with the Social Science Association, which continued to keep female education on its agenda. Following this meeting, Davies drew up a document, 'Reasons for the Admission of Women to University Examinations,' which was signed by 132 public figures including George Grote, Vice-Chancellor of the University of London, Herbert Spencer, Mary Somerville, Harriet Martineau, the Dean of Canterbury, the Earl of Chichester, the Recorder of London QC, Lord Lyttleton, and the Marchioness of Londonderry. One thousand copies were printed and circulated among members of the Convocation of the University of London.

The Committee called together the Local Committees for both the Oxford and Cambridge Local Examinations, and managed to get a consensus that they would get up a memorial to the Universities. At Oxford, again, the response was negative: the Oxford Local Examinations were not to be opened to girls until 1870. At Cambridge, the Secretary to the London Centre, Mr R.H. Tompkinson proved a reliable and valuable ally who enlisted support from the Committee for the London Centre, and offered Emily Davies advice on the wording of circulars. By October 1863, the Cambridge Syndicate had agreed to allow girls to be examined on an experimental basis, and the Committee began to organise their own centre for girls. The examination date was set for December 14th. Writing to Anna Richardson, Davies was both excited and daunted by what she had achieved:

> 17 Cunningham Place
> Monday Evening.
> October 26th 1863

My dear Anna

Our breath was taken away on Saturday by receiving quite unexpectedly a favourable answer from the Cambridge Syndicate to our application. I fully expected they would politely get rid of us by saying it was 'beyond their powers'. It has thrown us into dreadful agitation. We

have only six weeks to work up our candidates. . . . Do come to the
rescue. We shall look unspeakably foolish if we have no candidates,
after all, and people won't understand the reason. . . . I will send you a
packet of circulars as soon as possible, and please send them about. If
any country girls like to come up, we will arrange to receive them and
take good care of them during Examination week. . . . I am afraid no
girls will come who are not certain to pass, whereas hundreds of boys
failed the first year.

Yours ever,
E.D.[82]

Davies drafted and printed a circular, informing teachers and governesses
of the forthcoming examinations. Without much difficulty, Davies's friends
brought together a group of candidates representing the more prominent
girls' schools. Twenty-five candidates came from the North London Collegiate School, and a number came from Queen's College, and Miss Octavia
Hill's School. Lady Goldsmid and Mr Heywood made donations to cover the
expenses of having the examiners mark the scripts. The results, together with
statistical tables, were published in a *Report of an Examination of Girls held in
Connexion with the Local Examinations of the University of Cambridge*, and 1000
copies of a *Report of a Discussion on the Proposed Admission of Girls to University
Local Examinations*[83] were also printed and circulated, as plans developed to
make the examinations a permanent feature of girls' education. The examinations were welcomed by headmistresses. Octavia Hill, writing to Davies in
February 1864, eagerly awaited the results of her students while acknowledging that the girls greatly benefitted from the opportunity to meet students
from other parts of England. Davies, whose long-term ambition was to foster
female collegiate spirit and the sharing of intellectual interests must have been
heartened by Hill's letter which said that she was extremely pleased with the
effect on her pupils, as 'they were much invigorated by the examination..and
the intercourse with other students gave them a feeling of working with a
large body of learners all over England, which was very good'.[84]

The results of this pioneering venture had long-term implications for
higher education generally. By Michaelmas Term, 1864, a memorial was sent
to the Vice-Chancellor and Senate of the University of Cambridge, request-
ing that the Local Examinations could be officially extended to include girls.
On 24 November, a Syndicate was appointed to consider the memorial and
in February 1865 they considered that the examinations could be extended to
girls through intermediary local committees 'composed of ladies, and care
being taken to prevent undue publicity or intrusion'.[85] The measure was
carried by 55 votes to 51, and Emily Davies commented that 'with but little

prevision of the far-reaching consequences of its action, the Senate of the University of Cambridge took its first step in recognition of duties and responsibilities in regard to the higher education of women'.[86]

The year 1864 also saw the start of the investigations of the Schools Inquiry Commission (Taunton). The neglect by the earlier Public Schools Commission of girls' education had caused Emily Davies to criticise its Report at the annual meeting of the N.A.P.S.S.:

> National and British Schools for girls are inspected, mistresses are trained, female pupil-teachers are apprenticed, and speaking generally, the education of the daughters of the labouring classes is as carefully watched over as that of their sons. Why is the case altered when we advance a few steps higher in the social scale?[87]

The S.I.C., which had been issued for enquiry into the education given in schools not included in former Commissions, included in its inquiry the education of middle class girls. The inclusion of girls schools in the scope of the inquiry was a result of petitioning by the London Association of Schoolmistresses and the submitting of a Memorial by Emily Davies and the University Education Committee. The memorialists offered to place at the disposal of the Commissioners any information which might be found helpful. In his reply, the Secretary to the Commission, Henry J. Roby, stated:

> The endowments appropriated to the education of the middle and upper classes . . . will form an important part of the Commissioners' inquiry. Neither the number nor the value of the endowments, which belong either in whole or in part to the education of girls, is at all comparable to that of those which are provided for boys. This . . . diminishes the share which the former can claim in the investigations of the present Commission.[88]

Roby continued by saying that the Commissioners would, however, 'instruct the Assistant Commissioners . . . to report upon the state and prospects of girls' education,' and they would also 'be ready to include [as witnesses] such persons as may be recommended to them as best qualified to express opinions n the subject'.[89]

In 1867 and 1868 the 'Reports and Evidence of the Commissioners' were issued in twenty volumes. While it was generally accepted that the scope of the Commission allowed it to devote only 'about one twentieth'[90] of the Reports to the education of girls, Dorothy Beale took it upon herself to collate and publish some of the evidence on the education of girls.[91] Nine women involved in education were invited to give evidence, namely: Miss

Porter, Miss Kyberd, Miss King, Miss Martin, Miss Smith, Miss Davies, Miss Buss, Miss Wolstenholme, and Miss Beale.

The Commission took a direct and honest look at the general doubt and prejudices of the time, launching into an overview of the contemporary so-cial climate in the first paragraph of the introductory chapter, and reminding readers of 'the enormous number of unmarried women in the middle class who have to earn their own bread' and the 'lateness of marriage' due to increasing numbers of men either entering the army, leaving for the colonies, or exercising caution about the 'expensiveness' of supporting a wife and fam-ily. From the outset, then, the Commission consolidated the opinion of a number of women writers who had used these very points to buttress their arguments in favour of education and employment.

It also acknowledged the 'long-established and inveterate prejudices . . . that girls are less capable of mental cultivation, and less in need of it, than boys; and . . . that as regards their relations to the other sex and the probabili-ties of marriage, more solid attainments are actually disadvantageous than the reverse'.[92] The Commission, however, suggested that these ideas had 'a very strong root in human nature,' and that 'it would be idle to suppose that they would ever cease to have a powerful operation'.[93] What the Reports did challenge was the practice of keeping middle-class daughters in genteel idle-ness, arguing that their training should render them useful to their future husbands in the conduct of business, and that in them should rest the respon-sibility to create 'a higher and more cultivated tone in society'.[94]

The Reports of the S.I.C. indicated clearly that 'the state of middle-class female education [was], on the whole, unfavourable'. The commissioners agreed unanimously that the deficiencies included: 'Want of thoroughness and foundation, want of system; slovenliness and showy superficiality; inat-tention to rudiments; undue time given to accomplishments, and those not taught intelligently or in any scientific manner'.[95] The standard of perform-ance of boys of the same age was used as the yardstick against which to meas-ure the performance of the girls. While the report found girls to be better in reading and writing than boys, it was widely agreed that girls performed very unfavourably, compared with boys, at mathematics. It was also noted that outmoded texts, such as Mrs Mangalls's reading book, were still in use, and rote-learning was much in evidence. The commissioners stated that 'the es-sential capacity is the same, or nearly the same, in the two sexes,'[96] but the blurring of sexual differences proved problematical, and the language of the document clearly indicates tensions arising from an attempt to re-define the female sphere while cognisant of the contemporary ideology of femininity:

> . . . the foundation, the main and leading elements of instruction, should
> be the same in the two cases, and further . . . ample facilities and en-

couragement, and far more than now exist, should be given to women who may be able and willing to prosecute these studies to a higher point; but . . . the complete assimilation of the education of the sexes . . . should not be attempted.[97]

Nonetheless, applauding the participation of girls in the Cambridge Locals, the Commissioners pointed out that 'the bold step of admitting girls to the same exams as boys is clearly justified'. The Commissioners also concluded favourably on the question of higher education for women, although it was outside the scope of the enquiries to address this in any depth. Queen's College and Bedford College were praised, but it was recognised that the deficiency lay in education 'for girls of seventeen upwards'.[98] The Commissioners also expressed 'cordial approval' of Emily Davies's proposal for a women's college, and of Anne J. Clough's proposed public lectures for ladies.

The S.I.C. had long-term implications for the higher education of women. It recognised the paucity of good schooling for middle and upper-middle class girls, it applauded the efforts of certain schoolmistresses, such as Miss Buss at North London Collegiate, who were proving that girls could perform well given good tuition, it viewed higher education for women in a positive light, and -most importantly − it gave to the higher education debate a certain *gravitas*: these were the opinions of learned and respected gentlemen. There were two immediate consequences of the inclusion of female education in the scope of the S.I.C. Firstly, attention was drawn to the question of appropriation by boys' schools of educational endowments which might, under the terms of the endowments, equally have been made available to girls' schools. Secondly, it became clear that formal higher education for girls and women was a pressing necessity. Emily Davies continued to play a central role in the debate over these two issues. It was she who raised the thorny question about the application of endowments to the education of girls, and it was she who set about founding a female college to be associated, at the earliest possible opportunity, with one of the old universities.

On 3 May 1865, Davies read a paper before the Education Department of the National Association for the Promotion of Social Sciences (N.A.P.S.S.). It was later published by Longman.[99] In it she argued that the paucity of endowed girls' schools had diminished the share which girls' schools could claim in the S.I.C. investigations. Davies, pointing out that the endowments appropriated to the education of the middle and upper classes belonged almost exclusively to boys, questioned 'how far such appropriation [was] in accordance with the intentions of the donors'.[100] Of the S.I.C. she then concluded:

If the education of girls is already so thorough and complete as to re-

quire no improvements, we need not trouble ourselves about founders'
intentions, and may well be content to leave things as they are. If, on
the contrary, it is found to be faulty and deficient in some very essential
points, and if the fault can be traced to the want of the pecuniary aid
which is so largely bestowed on boys' schools, it will then appear reasonable to apply any funds that may be available for educational purposes in the direction where assistance is most required.[101]

Davies had no doubt but that girls' schooling would be found wanting. Her
argument, worked out in her paper as an exercise in simple logic, concluded
with practical recommendations:

> Money might be spent upon the education of girls of the upper and
> middle classes in four ways – in building school-houses; in founding
> new schools . . . in the endowment of professorships for the teaching of
> particular subjects; in the foundation of scholarships tenable in the school
> itself, and exhibitions to some higher school or college.[102]

Davies was to turn her interests almost exclusively to the project of founding
an institution for the higher education of women worthy of the name of
'college'. Her paper acknowledged the founding of colleges such as Queen's
and Bedford, but she believed that another type of women's college was
needed: one which would approximate closely to the colleges for men at
Oxford and Cambridge. Such a college should be completely residential,
unlike Queen's and Bedford, and it should not house a school. It should
aspire towards university status, and its graduates should be awarded university degrees.

Two occurrences precipitated the decision of Emily Davies to found
such a college. Firstly, in April 1866 Davies was rejected for the position of
Assistant Secretary of Queen's College. This ended any hopes she held of
using Queen's to realise her aims. Secondly, by the end of 1866 she had given
up on the possibility of getting the University of London to allow women to
take degree examinations. Throughout 1866, the year in which she published
her book *The Higher Education of Women*, Davies and her Committee had
made a renewed effort to obtain admission to the London matriculation, but
with no success. The Senate voted instead that a special examination for
women, of a less difficult standard than the Matriculation, should be established. Davies and the Committee were adamant that such a measure was
undesirable. She wrote at once to Mr R. H. Hutton, the member of the
Senate who strongly supported this resolution:

> I am afraid the people who are interested in improving the education of

women are a thankless crew. Instead of accepting as a great boon the admission of women to the London University Examinations 'in the manner proposed', they have come to the conclusion that they do not consider a special examination any boon at all, and will have nothing to do with it. Please do not publish this, however, as we should not like to seem ungrateful. We are really obliged to Convocation for their kind intentions in offering us a serpent when we asked for a fish, tho' we cannot pretend to believe that serpents are better for us.[103]

Hutton's reply serves to highlight the ideological chasm that existed between the Senate, which was prepared to make a compromise in favour of women's education, and Davies who was interested only in equality of opportunity. He wrote:

I think you are thankless . . . what is proposed we did not propose for you Enlightened ladies, but for girls, and if girls accept the boon how can you middlewomen come in and cut them off from what we propose? We did not, as far as I know, grant you anything — we offered something to girls in general and I shall be surprised if your influence proves so mischievously great as to prevent it being accepted. As to the thing you wish for, I believe it to be (like some of the political wishes of some of you) altogether premature to say the least. When women in general are better educated it will be time enough to see whether the aims of education ought to be the same for them as for men.[104]

In her reply to Hutton can be seen the essence of Davies's position regarding female education:

All I maintain, is that neither the enlightened ladies nor the London University know what the intellectual differences between men and women may be, but what I argue from this is, that therefore existing examinations, having already a recognized standing, had better be thrown open without reservation and let us see what comes of it. The moment you begin to offer special things, you claim to know what the special aptitudes are . . . I am sorry to say my stock of beliefs is small, but on this point I have no doubt whatever.[105]

On 27 August 1867, a Supplemental Charter was drawn up by the University of London, which allowed that a Special Examination for Women could be held. On 18 March 1868, the scheme finally adopted for these examinations was drawn up. By this time, Emily Davies had turned her attention to starting a College Committee with the aim of founding a college for women.

That Davies published *The Higher Education of Women* as early as 1866
indicates that she had worked out, to a considerable degree, the rationale
behind her proposed college for women. *The Higher Education of Women* was
less a blueprint for such a college, and more a set of responses to conventional
arguments against female education. As Janet Howarth has noted, it was written at a time when it was unclear how her objectives could be achieved, but
the climate was at least prepared by debate.[106] *The Higher Education of Women*
challenged conventional notions of gender roles and attacked 'the tyranny of
custom and the anomalous treatment of women in a society professing civi-
lised values'.[107] Davies noted that in schemes of male education 'it is assumed
as a matter of course, that the great object is to make the best of a man in
every respect'.[108] She then claimed for women a similar educational objective: 'to produce women of the best and highest type, not limited by exclusive regard to any specific functions hereafter to be discharged by them'.[109]
Female worth, she argued, should not be predicated on the role a woman
traditionally expected to fulfil. Rather it should be self-determined, and she
linked female education to the process of self-determination. The contemporary theory 'that the human ideal is composed of two elements, the male
and the female'[110] was then questioned by Davies. The advocates of such a
view, she maintained, usually also believed that 'man's strength is in the head,
woman's in the heart'.[111] Associated with such a doctrine, Davies commented,
was a double moral code 'with its masculine and feminine virtues, and its
separate law of duty and honour for either sex'.[112] Again repudiating such a
theory, Davies then went on to argue that the church did not recognise any
such distinctions of sex, and that such distinctions damaged the moral fibre of
men and women:

> An ascetic contempt for wifely and motherly and daughterly ties is no
> part of the Christian ideal. But the view which teaches women to think
> of family claims as embracing their whole duty . . . sets before them a
> standard of obligation which . . . vitiates not their lives only, but those
> of the men on whom their influence might be of a far different sort.
> That such a theory is radically inconsistent with the divine order might
> easily be shown. That its action on society is profoundly demoralising is
> a lesson taught by mournful experience.[113]

On the other hand, arguing from the Christian stand-point that the law of
human duty is the same for both sexes, she concluded that the education
required was likely to be 'in its broader and more essential features, the same'.
This was the kind of education that Davies sought to make available to women
by founding a college of higher education associated with one of the great
universities.

In the 'Family Chronicle', Davies recorded that on 29 September 1866, Dr Plumptre, who had held hopes that Davies would get the Assistant Secretaryship at Queen's, wrote to her that Queen's was not likely to raise the age limit of admission nor to ask for advanced university examinations.[114] The need clearly existed for someone to found a college for young women, with university affiliation as its objective. Very shortly after, on 6 October, Davies attended a meeting of schoolmistresses at Manchester at which opinion was expressed that 'a place of higher education to which to transfer the more advanced pupils from school [was] wanted'.[115] Her journal records that as she drove from the meeting to the house at which she was staying, it was borne in upon her 'that the only way to meet the situation would be to found a new College, fulfilling the desired conditions'.[116]

Davies evidently went about seeking support for her general idea quite some time before she called a meeting of like-minded individuals. She told Anna Richardson of her ideas late in 1866, and drafted a 'programme' which she had copied and sent to twenty friends. It proposed that a college for young women should be established 'in a healthy locality, about equidistant between London and Cambridge,' and that while the religious services and instruction should be in accordance with the principles of the Church of England, attendance at services and instruction should not be obligatory for conscientious objectors. Reactions to the programme varied. Helen Taylor Mill wrote to Davies to say that she did not feel she could become associated with Davies's proposed college, believing that it was not right for people who were not members of the Church of England to subscribe money 'for the direct teaching of what they believed to be untrue'.[117] Early in 1867, she received a letter from H.J. Roby, who had corresponded with Dr Temple about the matter. Roby passed on Temple's words of caution, suggesting that 'the scheme deserves encouragement, but that it will fail, the Public not being yet in a right frame of mind to accept such schemes'.[118]

Close friends, such as Barbara Bodichon, were more encouraging. Early in 1867, in a lengthy letter to Bodichon, Davies laid out her dream that the scheme should be 'brought down from the clouds':

> I have drawn up the Programme of which I enclose a Proof . . . I believe the next step must be to get up a Committee . . . [the] best plan seems to be to have a rather large general Committee of distinguished people, to guarantee our *sanity,* and a small Executive, to do the work . . . if we can get Lord Lyttleton who has the reputation of being rather High Church, to be Chairman, and Lady Goldsmid to be Treasurer, I think the comprehensiveness of the scheme will be pretty well guaranteed.[119]

Davies was shrewd in deciding that the general committee should serve the function of creating a good image for the college, while the working committee should comprise a small group of like-minded individuals with energy and commitment to the idea of higher education for women. Members of the University Examination Committee, with whom she first discussed the idea, occasionally made suggestions with which Davies evidently had little patience, and it was therefore never her plan that the one committee should serve both projects. Recounting events at the meeting at which she advised the Examination Committee of her plans, she wrote to Bodichon:

> Miss Bostock's point was that whatever there is a demand for, Bedford College is ready to give, and we were rather embarrassed in replying, as it was awkward to insist that the people we expect to get have either never heard of Bedford College or despise it and won't think of going near it. . . . Mr Clay and Mr Tomkinson are almost too strong on our side and too determined to make the College a paradise. They insisted that the girls should have breakfast in their own rooms . . . as if the whole thing depended upon it.[120]

Davies set about drawing up a list of suitable people for a working committee early in 1867. The list of people, preserved with her papers, includes a note against each name indicating the particular characteristic for which that individual was desired. Beside Lady Goldsmid's name appears the word 'economy,' and indeed Lady Goldsmid would become a fine Treasurer. H.R. Tomkinson was desired for his 'conciliation,' Mrs Manning for her 'domestic morals,' and Davies noted herself as contributing 'principles' to the scheme. Lady Stanley of Alderly, who at first declined to become associated with the proposed college, was later to prove both a suitable ally (she was mother to a large family) and a useful aid. In addition to providing the college with much-needed financial support, she became very committed to its affairs upon the death of her husband, and was a source of support and advice to Davies.

From the outset, Davies was ambitious to associate the College with worthy public figures, lest it should be ridiculed. She asked Lady Stanley to seek the support of the Queen, in 1868. In a letter, Davies informed Barbara Bodichon of Lady Stanley's response:

> When I asked Lady Stanley if the Queen would do anything for us, she said she had no doubt she would as soon as we were on our legs, but not before. If we had a certain number of students actually collected together and at work, we could proclaim the astonishing fact, and show the thing is actually begun . . . we want by every substantial means to make ourselves look substantial.[121]

It would seem that the idea of starting on an ambitious scale, rather than a humble one, was strongly supported by George Eliot (M.E. Lewes), with whom Davies carried out a correspondence late in 1867. On 16 November 1867, Eliot invited Davies to tea to discuss 'the desirable project of founding a College for Women'.[122] Eliot wrote again, following their meeting, to say that she and Mr Lewes strongly objected to beginning the project on a 'small scale':

> To spend forces and funds in this way would be a hindrance rather that a furtherance of the great scheme which is pre-eminently worth trying for. Every one concerned should be roused to understand that a great campaign has to be victualled.[123]

Eliot advised Davies that she should aim to raise a fund of £50,000 to start the project, but the figure of £30,000 seems to have been agreed upon by the Committee from the start. In a letter to Bodichon, Davies outlined her plans to begin the project on a suitably 'substantial' scale:

> The next question will be to set about raising the money. We are told that we ought to ask for £30,000 at least, as besides the expense of building we ought to have something in hand, in case we do not at first get students enough to make the College pay. It is not a large sum, considering that there is to be but one College of this sort in Great Britain and Ireland and the Colonies, and considering how easy it is to raise immense sums for boys' schools. But considering how few people really wish women to be educated, it is a good deal. Everything will depend, I believe on how we start. If we begin with small subscriptions, a low scale will be fixed and everybody will give in proportion. I do not know yet what anybody is going to do, except myself. I mean to give £100. . . . As soon as I hear from you, I shall go to Lady Goldsmid, Mrs Russell Gurney, Mr James Heywood, the Westlakes and two or three other people who are likely to be interested, and we may then I hope make a beginning at looking for a site &c.[124]

Undaunted by the enormity of her task, Davies went ahead with her plans, and both Roby and Temple gave their support. The first meeting of this Committee was held at Regent Street, London, on 5th December 1867. The minutes of the meeting state that Mrs Manning, Revd Sedley Taylor and H.R. Tomkinson were present, while Lady Hobart, Lady Goldsmid, the Dean of Canterbury, Mrs Russell Gurney and Mr Heywood were unable to attend but wished to be a part of the new venture. At the meeting it was decided that all the above, together with G.W. Hastings, H.J. Roby, Miss

Metcalfe and Emily Davies, would 'form a Committee for the purpose of founding a College for the higher education of women'.[125] Davies was elected Hon. Secretary. The Resolutions clearly reflect the wishes of Emily Davies:

> . . . the College shall be if possible connected with the University of Cambridge, and . . . efforts shall be made to obtain, ultimately, the admission of the students, under suitable regulations, to the Examinations for Degrees of that University.[126]

At this meeting it was decided that a sum of £30,000 should raised for the purposes of the college, and the first subscriptions promised were noted. Barbara Bodichon pledged £1000, while Mrs Manning and Emily Davies each pledged £100.[127] H.R. Tomkinson later negotiated with the bank, and an account for the college was established.

The General Committee included three Bishops, two Deans and a number of prominent people, although not everyone whom Davies approached was interested in supporting the college. Davies wrote to Anna Richardson in December 1867, to say that they needed some High Church names on the Committee. 'Please get us some at once,' she concluded briskly. Anna Richardson suggested the well-known writer Charlotte Yonge.[128] Yonge wrote to Davies, refusing her support, stating her opinion that 'girls in large numbers always hurt one another in manner and tone if in nothing else. Superior women will teach themselves, and inferior women will never learn more than enough for home life'.[129]

Davies does not seem to have been overly concerned by the refusal of support from some quarters. She continued to send out circulars, to write letters, and to organize meetings. In February 1868, a meeting was held at which Lady Stanley and Professor Seeley of Cambridge University were added to the Executive Committee. Money continued to come in, with a subscription of £50 from George Eliot, £100 each from Lady Goldsmid, Mr Heywood, Mrs Manning and Mr Tompkinson, and a promise of £20 yearly from Elizabeth Garrett. By the middle of July 1868, £2000 had been raised. Further efforts were required in order to generate support. An advertisement was placed in the newspapers setting forth the scheme, and Davies wrote a paper, 'Some Account of a Proposed College for Women,'[130] for the Congress of the Social Science Association meeting at Birmingham in the autumn. In her paper, she argued that higher education was urgently needed for the sisters of Cambridge graduates, the sisters ' . . . scattered about in country houses and parsonages, and in the families of professional men and retired merchants and manufacturers'.[131]

The atmosphere at the Birmingham Congress seemed to suggest that the time was right for a measure of formal education for women to be encouraged. Davies wrote to Anna Richardson that she and Elizabeth Garrett 'did a great deal of conversion at Birmingham,' and to Barbara Bodichon she wrote that the college 'was a very new idea, but it was well received'.[132] Such public events greatly suited Davies's temperament, and she was buoyed up by the general response at Birmingham, after which she reflected that 'people are much more interested in the College when they have *seen* somebody who is concerned in it. And prejudice melts away beautifully'.[133]

Throughout 1868, Davies carried out her plans for the founding of a women's college against a backdrop of activity by the North of England Council for the Higher Education of Women. This was an organization founded in the autumn of 1867 by Anne Jemima Clough, with the aim of providing lectures for women in large towns. It also aimed to establish special examinations for women over eighteen, principally as a test for teachers though open to all women. This proposal was to be presented in a Memorial to the Senate of the University of Cambridge. Davies was frustrated by this development, as many potential supporters of her college began to think that the lectures and special examinations would suffice as formal higher education for women. Davies believed that college education was best, and wrote with concern to Anna Richardson that 'when you give the choice of the difficult best, or the easy second best, the latter is most likely to be taken'.[134] Concerned that the standard of lecturing at local colleges could not 'reach a high pitch of excellence,' she hoped that her college would not lose support. Additionally, the establishing of special examinations for women would greatly jeopardise the possibility of securing equal or identical examinations for men and women. Davies believed that the female examinations were likely to be popular with all who wished to tread a cautious middle-ground concerning rights for women. She wrote to Richardson of her concerns that 'the idea of the new scheme is not that it is easy and a stop-gap, but that it is to be womanly'.[135]

The University Examinations Committee supported Davies's point of view, and at a meeting on 22 March 1868 it resolved not to support the proposed Memorial to the University of Cambridge for examinations for women, on the grounds that such a scheme of examinations would 'keep down the level of female education'.[136] The Committee did not, however, take any public action on the matter, believing that squabbles among women about the education question would damage their cause. The scheme for special examinations was carried without opposition by the Cambridge Senate on 23 October 1868. While Davies was disappointed at this outcome, the examinations for women served to provide a supply of qualified teachers to improve standards at girls' schools and, thereby, to increase the supply of girls for Girton and Newnham in the coming years.

Plans for the founding of a women's college continued at this time, and were doubtless affected by the spirit of compromise that surrounded the instigation of special lectures for women. The earliest draft plans suggest that some of Davies's colleagues were prepared to settle for less than Davies had originally proposed. In the draft constitution for the college, drawn up by a sub-committee consisting of Mr Roby, Mr Tompkinson and Mr Sedley Taylor, no mention of granting Certificates or awarding of Degrees was made. Additionally, they proposed that the College should include representatives of the Universities of Oxford, London and Cambridge, rather than being a constituent College of any one University. This infuriated Davies who wrote a long letter to Tomkinson reminding him of the original aims:

> . . . the proposal to represent three Universities departs altogether from the fundamental idea of the College, which is, to be at the earliest possible moment, a constituent part of the University of Cambridge, and adopts the totally different (not to say antagonistic) idea, of a new, independent, female University . . . the real ground on which all separate schemes for women are objectionable [is] the extreme undesirableness of drawing lines of demarcation and setting up artificial distinctions.[137]

The Committee considered the objections raised by Davies, and drew up a fresh report which declared the intention of the council of the proposed college to 'obtain for the students of the College admission to the Examinations for degrees of the University of Cambridge and, generally, to place the College in connection with that University'.[138]

The curriculum of the college was drawn up by a sub-committee during August 1868, and it was decided that students would be prepared for the Poll, or Ordinary, Degree. As it was believed that the Poll Degree was inferior in that it omitted English, French and history, it was decided that the college students would also take an additional examination to be known as the college certificate. Professor Seeley of Cambridge University was the force behind this decision. He believed that the over-emphasis on the classics was a general fault of university education and that increased attention should be given to logic, English, political philosophy and physical science. Davies was critical of this innovation at the college, seeing it as an experiment which might further divide male and female educational aims. She allowed it to go ahead, however, on the grounds that it would be plain to see that women students were taking the Poll Degree and then supplementing it with a college certificate in some subjects. She clarified this position, remarking that 'the Ordinary Degree is obviously and notoriously adapted to ordinary men (or as some say, the refuse), and our students will not be ordinary women'.[139] From the outset, then, Davies was determined to associate the college with the examinations and practices of the university, believing that in this way the college would guarantee the highest educational standards for women and later, in 1881, she secured the right for Girton students to take the Tripos (honours) examinations.

The practical work of opening the college was undertaken by the Auxiliary Committee, a group of Cambridge men. Davies held the firm opinion that the college should not be located in Cambridge, but should be close by. This would ensure that the students would be free from distraction while also at a sufficiently safe remove from male students to allow some freedom. Additionally, she knew that parents were less likely to object to the college, if it was located at a distance from the men's colleges. In April 1868, Davies made an exploratory journey to Hitchin, outside Cambridge. It was decided to make a temporary beginning in a rented house there, and to buy a site on which to build a college. Miss Manning agreed to take up the temporary post of Mistress, and a college prospectus was drawn up and printed. Davies secured the teaching of some Cambridge lecturers of high standing, including Professor Seeley and Professor Liveing, and Dr Althaus of London University.

The College for Women, Benslow House, Hitchin, opened with five students in October 1869. The five young women were Miss Gibson, Miss Townshend, Miss Woodhead, Miss Lumsden and Miss Lloyd, and in the second term they were joined by Miss Cook. Of these women, Miss Gibson and Miss Lumsden (later Dame Louisa Lumsden) have left records of the early days at the college.[140] Of the students which entered during the next three years, Constance Maynard and Jane Frances Dove have also left accounts of college life.[141] Constance Maynard, who came to the college in 1872, recalled her excitement at first hearing about the college from her cousin, Professor Lewis Campbell. Cambell had, in turn, heard of it from Isabella Cook, whose sister was also to be among the early students. 'That's what you've been waiting for!' Maynard instantly thought. Her father, was less enthusiastic, and only allowed her to go to Hitchin if she first promised not to try for a degree but to come home after one year 'as if nothing had happened, and not take to teaching or anything eccentric'.[142] Maynard's parents quickly reviewed their feelings about Hitchin, and she stayed for three years to take the Moral Science Tripos. Thereafter she took up teaching, and became the first Principal of Westfield College. Starting out at Hitchin, Maynard had a keen sense that, together with the other early students, she was making history. Over forty years later, she recalled her first year:

> Not one waking half-hour through that summer did I forget what lay before me, the 14th October, 1872, was the day of my life, and is remembered every year without fail . . . the extraordinary happiness of

that first year at Hitchin, is a thing that cannot come twice in a lifetime. It was as though the keep of all knowledge were there ready to
hand.[143]

Emily Gibson, who came to Hitchin to read mathematics, had learned
about the College for Women through an article by Llewelyn Davies in
Macmillan's Magazine.[144] Gibson had been educated by Miss Pipe, at Laleham
School, Clapham Park. Miss Pipe, remembered by Gibson as a remarkable
teacher, had read the *Higher Education of Women* by Emily Davies to her students. Gibson wrote to Davies to enquire about the new college, and was
encouraged to apply for a place. Isabella Townshend and Lydia Woodhead
were awarded the first entrance scholarships, while Louisa Lumsden, who
came to read classics, declined to be considered for a scholarship on the basis
that she could afford to pay fees and did not wish to deprive another woman
of a place. From the start, Lumsden impressed Davies, who described her to
Barbara Bodichon as 'manifestly a lady, as well as an eager student'.[145]

The students each had a bedroom in which a sitting-room was also arranged. One room on the ground floor served as a common room and lecture
room, and the dining room was in the basement. Determined that the students would observe traditional college dining practice, Davies arranged the
dining hall so as the students sat in a row facing high table. Lumsden recalled
that the five students eventually rebelled against such formality at Hitchin,
though her memories of those early days suggest that from the outset Davies
intended to imitate the traditions of the great colleges for men. 'So academi-
cally formal . . . was the order imposed from the first at Hitchin', she recalled,
'we might have been fifty undergraduates instead of five harmless young
women'.[146] Emily Gibson similarly recalled in 1925 that 'it needed an effort
of imagination to recognize Dons and high table and undergraduates all complete, though as it were in embryo: but it was an effort that Miss Davies was
fully prepared to make and to insist upon'.[147]

Although Barbara Bodichon sent sketches to be hung in the library, and
Davies endeavoured to make Benslow House as comfortable as possible, the
first students had few amusements other than study and conversation. The
house, which was situated on a chalk cliff above Hitchin, with views of Hert-
fordshire, took an hour to reach by train from Cambridge. Occasional excur-
sions were taken, but otherwise the students amused themselves with country
walks and trips to the swimming bath in Hitchin. It was not part of Emily
Davies's scheme that the students should participate in Cambridge University
life: she saw contact with male students as neither desirable nor necessary.
Davies was sensitive to the fact that the pioneer students would be scrutinised
sharply for signs of unladylike behaviour, and she avoided all possibilities of
scandal. Simple amusements such as playing football on the lawn or dressing

in male costume for drama productions were forbidden. As it was, the students were often viewed as oddities. Jane Frances Dove recalled that when she first went to college it was 'an unheard-of event' among her neighbours and friends, and she 'was at once set apart by them as an eccentric and somewhat awesome person.'[148]

Despite the obstacles that early women students had to overcome in order to attend the college, they seem to have enjoyed the intellectual challenge and the freedom of college life. There was a strict daily routine which obliged the ladies to attend for prayers at 8 a.m. daily, to be followed by breakfast, and then lectures and study punctuated by luncheon at 12 a.m. and dinner at 6 p.m.. The college gates were closed at 6 p.m., after which time the students could read, write or entertain each other in their rooms. There was one lecture every day, the length of which was determined by the hours of the railway trains rather than by the capacities of the lecturer and students. Between October and December 1870, the first five students of the College took the 'Little Go' or 'previous' examinations. All five passed in Classics. Additionally, Miss Gibson and Miss Woodhead passed the Additional Mathematical Subjects. In Michaelmas term, 1871, the remaining three students took the Additionals.

The students were fond of Emily Davies, though she did not teach them and had as little as possible to do with the daily running of the College. As Constance Maynard recalled: 'She did not know us in any true manner, nor seek to guide us in even the least degree, but . . . the whole burden fell on her . . . she kept herself in the background, and acted chiefly as a strong unseen support to those whom she admired'.[149] Davies did not live at Benslow House, but the students enjoyed her visits and kept her informed of their activities in letters. Anna Lloyd concluded one such letter with the warm words, 'if I say we are getting on well, that does not mean but that we should get on still better if you were here'.[150] In a similar vein, Louisa Lumsden wrote to her: 'Everything is going on here pleasantly – but I think we shall all be the better of having you among us to cheer us on'.[151] Lydia Woodhead wrote to Davies on 4th March, 1870, to thank her for her advice on 'the use of mathematics,'[152] while Emily Gibson wrote to her two days later with suggestions of what books they should have in the library.[153]

It was never the intention of Emily Davies that the college would remain at Hitchin in the somewhat inadequate Benslow House. As early as 1867, she had written to Barbara Bodichon that she hoped to build a very grand college, and 'to get Waterhouse, the architect of the Manchester Assizes Courts'.[154] She believed that this would confer much-needed status on the venture, adding: 'I am anxious that the building should be as beautiful as we can make it. As we can not have traditions and associations we shall want to get dignity in every other way that is open to us'.[155] Davies was rigid in her determination to employ Alfred Waterhouse.[156] It is not known when they first met, but it seems likely, however, that he came to Benslow House to discuss building extensions in 1869 or 1870.[157] At this time the Committee were considering possible sites for a new college, and Waterhouse may have been asked for his advice about plans to erect a temporary iron building at Benslow house. This building, known as the 'tin tabernacle,' housed the growing number of students until the move to Girton. The site chosen by the newly formed Building Committee was situated two miles from Cambridge, and comprised sixteen acres of open fields near Girton village. Waterhouse was chosen to design the buildings, and every detail of the college was worked out with Davies and the Committee. The plans were finalised late in 1872, and building began. By September 1873, the first phase, part of Old Wing, was completed and Davies moved in to see about furnishings. The Committee had set a target of £30,000 as the building budget, and while Waterhouse calculated that the actual cost would be close to £26,500, it was difficult to raise even a small portion of that sum. The Committee had raised £7,200 since the project had first been set up. Some £2000 had been spent at Hitchin, and the site at Girton cost £2000. Nonetheless, it was agreed that the building should begin on a scale that would allow for expansion, and that would enable the college to take in increasing numbers. The layout of the college contrasted with that of the older foundations of Cambridge and Oxford. Girton College was built in long wings with corridors down one side, rather than in the traditional staircase system. As Prudence Waterhouse has since commented, many early visitors to the college questioned the use of a corridor system.[158] It was chosen partly because the medieval system of vertical division with pairs of sets and gyp rooms at each landing of a staircase was more expensive to build. But, more importantly, such staircases, opening into a quad or square, allowed easy access to the students' rooms. Davies recognised that the corridor system provided a more secure layout, which would appeal in particular to the parents of young women who had not lived away from home before. The corridor system broke the buildings into small, safe communities. It also allowed for good cross ventilation, as rooms were built only on one side of each corridor. The system also allowed for all parts of the college to be connected from within, and made for flexibility in terms of adding on new wings over the succeeding decades.

Davies planned that every student would have two rooms to herself: a bedroom and a sitting room. Eventually, economy dictated that in some cases the young women were supplied with one large room, with a curtained off bedspace. Each room had a fireplace, creating much work for the maids. The students were encouraged to make their rooms homely. Photographs of the early rooms suggests that they were much-loved sanctuaries for young women enjoying new-found freedom.

In 1873, with the College ready to open, Davies published a leaflet advertising the College and inviting support. In the leaflet she took pains to highlight the links between Girton College and Cambridge University. 'The teaching, being given by men engaged in University and College tuition at Cambridge is of the very highest class,' she advised.[159] She also stressed the importance of examinations at Girton, reminding the public that 'it is desired as far as possible to connect the College with the University of Cambridge, and the degree Certificates given by the College will be really, though not formally, equivalent to University degrees, and will be practically useful in a similar manner'.[160]

Not only the educational aims, but also the building of Girton College, which continued at a steady pace, reflected Davies's wish that Girton should indeed resemble the great colleges for men. It eventually included chapel, hall and library. In 1886, sixteen acres of land to the east of the college were bought, and a scheme of landscaping was put in place. An avenue of chestnut trees behind the College was the present of Lady Stanley, and a grander approach, in the form of Tower Wing, was built as the College entrance. The tudor detail of the tower, echoing the older college gateways, provided the element of stature and tradition that Davies had feared the College lacked. The completed design, not finished until 1900, comprised three courts: Emily Davies Court, Cloisters Court, and Woodlands Court, with Cloisters Court at the centre of the College. The work of Alfred Waterhouse was continued in 1898 by his son Paul Waterhouse, and building projects begun in the 1930s were designed by Alfred's grandson, Michael Waterhouse, together with Sir Giles Gilbert Scott.

Once installed in Girton College, the students resumed the daily routine begun at Hitchin. The routine changed little over the next ten years, as published accounts of life at Girton testify.[161] Students were expected to rise at seven o'clock in the morning, at which time water cans were brought to each room for washing. Prayers continued to be read at eight o'clock. All meals were served in the fine new dining hall, which had a proper high table at which the Mistress and resident lecturers sat. A portrait of Davies, and one of Lady Stanley of Alderly were completed, thus the traditional Oxbridge practice of displaying portraits of college founders and principals in Hall was begun. Each student was required to observe 'marking roll': the practice of signing a register three times daily. Lectures by resident lecturers were given in the College in the mornings, and in the afternoons visiting lecturers from Cambridge came to the College. The practice of providing informal luncheon between twelve and three was begun, while dinner continued to be served with typical college formality at six o'clock. Societies, notably the Debating Club, the Bookworm's Club, the Lawn Tennis Club, the Cricket Club (see fig. 8) and the Choral Society were started. One college society of noted status was the Girton Fire Brigade (see fig.9), which comprised a group of fit and trained students who could fight any unexpected fire within the college, since it would have taken quite some time for a Cambridge fire brigade to reach the scene. Happily the society, which lasted for many years, was never called upon to fight a fire. New students were expected to settle in quickly, and become part of the college life, Davies had little patience for girls who suffered from homesickness, or who expected a cosy family life at the college. She wrote to Barbara Bodichon that the College was 'not a place for 'young girls', any more than the other Colleges are for young boys. It is a place for young women. As to their feeling lonely, I am afraid that cannot be helped'.[162]

This was the point at which Girton College departed from the vision of education for women which had a tradition dating back at least two centuries. Far from seeking to create a female community of learned and pious women, as Astell had done in the seventeenth century, one such as was seen in Sarah Scott's *Millenium Hall* of the eighteenth century, Davies wished to closely replicate the men's colleges and open to women the educational rights of men. Far from merely running a second 'home' for young ladies, Davies began the battle to open up the degrees and privileges of Cambridge University to women.

It proved to be a lengthy battle, hard fought and hard won, and it has been documented elsewhere by historians including M.C. Bradbrook, Rita McWilliams Tullberg and June Purvis.[163] Davies did not live to see women become full members of the University of Cambridge, but in founding Girton College and in initiating the process by which it became a university college for women, she realised Mary Astell's dream that women should be allowed to 'court Truth' and pursue knowledge.

The second half of the nineteenth century, then, witnessed the opening up of higher education to women in England. In addition to the scientific and cultural societies, mechanics' institutes and the working men's colleges, colleges for women provided tuition and certification. The founding of Queen's College in 1848, under the auspices of the Governesses' Benevolent Institution, was the first move taken in the direction of formal college education for women. It was followed quickly by the opening of Bedford College in 1849. In 1856, the first attempt by a woman to gain admission to the University of London for the sake of obtaining a medical degree was made. In 1878, this privilege was granted to women, along with admission for women to all degrees of the university. The first college for women connected to Cambridge, Girton College, was founded in 1869, while Newnham was founded in 1871. At Oxford, Somerville and Lady Margaret Hall were founded in 1879. Cambridge opened the honour degree examinations of the University to the women of Girton and Newnham in 1881, while Oxford opened

Fig. 8 Girton College Cricket Team, 1898

Fig. 9 Girton College Fire Brigade, 1887

some of its examinations to Oxford women in 1884. These colleges appeared in many discussions published in contemporary print culture and their founders wrote and published on higher education for women. In these founding of these institutions, we see the realisation of a proposal, some two hundred years old, that there should be college education for women. What they each later became is of importance and of interest to the history of education, but is not part of this study. In successive decades, Queen's, Bedford and Girton were shaped by new Mistresses and Principals, and by the demands of students and of a changing society. But in their early years, they were the fruition of some two hundred years of debate dating back to Anna van Schurman's sixteenth century disstertation on 'whether a maid may be a scholar'. In-sofar as the founders of Queen's and Bedford aimed at providing female education at a 'college,' they also represent a realisation of Mary Astell's seventeenth century *Proposal*. But it is Emily Davies whose ideas most closely represent a development from Astell's. Mary Astell's 'female monastery' offered women seclusion, intellectual stimulation, and the pursuit of 'Truth'. Queen's College and Bedford College, both originally non-residential, did not place the same emphasis on individual study and contemplation, nor on the pursuit of universal truths, as Emily Davies did when she planned her 'university' college for women. As she wrote in 1874:

> College life supplies what may perhaps be regarded as the two great needs for moral, intellectual, and physical development – the need of solitude the need of sympathy and companionship.[164]

The opening of the first colleges for women was justified, for many, by the growing need to train women of the middle and upper middle classes to earn their own living. Thus, the original educational aims of Queen's and Bedford were consonant with a growing tolerance for training ladies to teach. The broader aims of Girton College were more controversial, since they threatened a traditionally male bastion:

> The College aims at giving to women what the universities give to men. It is a college in the Oxford and Cambridge sense of the word.[165]

Davies, through her work with the University Examinations Committee and later with the College Committee, saw examinations and certification as central to the female education question. This vision, in particular, distinguished her writing from earlier works. The notion of university degrees for women raised a fundamental question about the equality of the sexes, but the demand for places at the first colleges for women pointed clearly to the fact that they were much needed. The following of a university curriculum seemed, to

Davies, the most obvious way of testing women's suitability for university education. Having found that such a curriculum was within the capabilities of women, it seemed fair and reasonable to request that such women should be awarded degrees upon successful completion of the same examinations as male students, and that the doctrine of separate spheres should have no place in the pursuit of knowledge and truth. As Davies summarised:

> . . . the real ground on which all separate schemes for women are objectionable [is] the extreme undesireableness of drawing up lines of demarcation and setting up artificial distinctions.

Queen's College, Bedford College and Girton College represented distinct stages in the gradual opening up of higher education to women. Through Queen's, it was made clear that certification for governesses was necessary and that girls and women could benefit from a system of good formal education. Bedford represented a development of this idea in that it was founded to offer a liberal education to girls and women without emphasising either vocational or academic qualifications. In Girton was developed the idea of a residential university college education for women, an education which had, as its aim, the pursuit of Truth.

Appendix

CATEGORIES OF PRINT CULTURE RELATED TO WOMEN
AND LEARNING 1600-1900

Advice: Publication in which advice or guidance is offered in one or more of the following: curriculum for girls; curriculum for women; reading for girls or women; principles of education suited to the female sex.

Attack: Publication in which one or more of the following are criticised: female learning; learned women; female reason; female pedantry; institutions for female education.

Conduct: Publication in which advice or instruction is given on behaviour appropriate to the female sex.

Defence: Publication in which one or more of the following are defended: female learning; learned women; female reason; female pedantry; institutions for female education.

Drama: Publication for theatre performance related to the theme of female education or learning.

Entertainment: Publication written for amusement, and with no direct educational aim.

Ephemerides: Diary and/or almanac for women, in which general information was sometimes included.

Epistolary: Publication in form of letters related to theme of female education.

Medical: Publication discussing women and education from a medical perspective; publication teaching women about health and medicine.

Miscellany: Publication containing miscellaneous information for the entertainment and general education of females, and usually comprising stories, riddles, verses and letters.

Other: Publication of which no details are known, or which does not fit into any of these categories.

Praise: Publication in which women are praised for their learning (usually containing examples of women from antiquity).

Proposal: Publication outlining a proposal for the education of women, or for a college for women.

Religious: Publication basing a discussion of female education/female behaviour on the lessons of scripture; publication by clergyman treating of the theme of female virtue in the light of Church teachings.

Satire: Publication in which learned women/women and education are ridiculed, either directly or indirectly.

Text book: School text book; manual for self-instruction; text book for use by private tutor or governess.

Verse: Publication related to the theme of women and learning, written in verse.

1600-1700

Author/Entry	Title	Date	Category
Agrippa, Henricus Cornelius	The Glory of Women	1652	Praise
Allestree, Richard	The Ladies calling	1673, 1693, 1700	Conduct
Astell, Mary	A Serious Proposal for Ladies	1694	Proposal
B.M.	The Ladies Cabinet	1654	Entertainment
B.R.	Female Excellency	1688	Praise
Boyer, Abel	The Compleat French Master for Ladies	1694	Text book
Boyle, Francis	Discourses and Essays	1696	Text book
Cavendish, Margaret	The Philosophical and Physical Opinions	1655, 1663	Text book
Chamberlayne, Edward	An Academy or College . . . Ladies	1671	Proposal/Religious
Chudleigh, Marys	The Female Advocate	1700	Defence
Closet	A Closet for Ladies and Gentlewomen	1608	Entertainment
Cockayne, Aston	The Obstinate Lady	1657	Satire/Drama
Crouch, Nathaniel	Female Excellency	1688	Praise
Dialogue	A Dialogue between two Young Ladies	1696	Entertainment
Dialogue	Continuation of a Dialogue . . . Young Ladies	1696	Entertainment
Digby, Kenelm	A Conference with a Lady	1638	Religious
Directory	A Directory for the Female Sex	1684	Other
Drake, Judith	Essay in Defence of the Female Sex	1696, 1697	Defence
Du Bosc, Jacques	A Secretary of Ladies	1638	Other
Ephemerides	The Woman's Almanack	1659	Almanac
Eugenia	The Female Advocate	1700	Defence

1600-1700

Author/Entry	Title	Date	Category
Evelyn, Mary	*Mundus Muliebris*	1690	Entertainment
Excellence	*Female Excellence*	1697	Defence
Fenelon, Abbot de	*The education of young gentlemen*	1699	Proposal
Fyge, Sarah	*The Female Advocate*	1686	Defence
Lady	*To a vertuous and judicious Lady*	1660	Religious
Ladies	*The Ladies Behaviour*	1693	Entertainment
Norris, James	*The accomplish'd Lady*	1684	Defence
Masham, Damaris	*A Discourse concerning the Love of God*	1696	Religious
Philaret	*The Female War*	1697	Attack
Philogynes	*The Freedom of the Fair Sex Asserted*	1700	Defence
Platt, Hugh	*Delights from the Ladies*	1602, 1605 1608, 1630	Entertainment
Rich, Barnaby	*My Ladies Looking Glass*	1616	Other
Richardson, Elizabeth	*A Ladies Legacie to her Daughers*	1645	Religious
Savile, George	*The Lady's New-Years Gift: or, Advice*	1699	Conduct
Shirley, John	*The Accomplished Ladies Rich Closet*	1696	Conduct
Sowerby, Leonard	*The Ladies Dispensatory*	1652	Advice/Medical
Tate, Nahum	*A Present for the Ladies*	1693	Defence
Theodidactus, Eugenius	*The Ladies Champion*	1660	Other
Toll, Thomas	*The Female Duel, or the Ladies Looking Glass*	1661	Entertainment
Triumphs	*Triumphs of Female Wit*	1683	Verse
Various	*The Ladies Mercury*	1693	Miscellany
Woolley, Hanah	*The Gentlewoman's Companion*	1673	Advice
Wright, Thomas	*The Female Virtuosoes*	1693	Satire/Drama

1700–1800

Author/Entry	Title	Date	Category
Academy	*The Polite Academy*	1765	Conduct
Address	*Address to a Young Lady*	1796	Advice
Ancourt, (d'), Abbé	*The Lady's Preceptor*	1743	Conduct
Aubigne, (d'), Françoise	*The Ladies Monitor*	1758	Advice/Text book
Behn, Aphra	*A Companion for the Ladies-Closets*	1712	Other
Bennett, John	*Strictures on Female Education*	1787	Advice/Conduct
Biographium Faemineum	*The Female Worthies*	1766	Praise
Blackett, Mary Dawes	*The Monitress*	1791	Epistolary/Advice
Bland, James	*An Essay in Praise of Women*	1733, 1736 1767	Praise
Brown, John	*One Female Character and Education*	1765	Advice/Religious
Burton, J.	*Lectures on Female Eduation and Manners*	1793, 1794	Advice/Conduct
Butler, William	*Arithmetical Questions . . . for Female Pupiles*	1786	Text book
C.M.	*An Account for Fair-Intellectual Club*	1720	Other
Cartwright, Mrs	*Letters on Female Education*	1777	Epistolary/Advice
Chapone, Hester	*Letters on the Improvement of the Mind*	1780	Epistolary/Advice
Cherub	*The Cherub or, Guardian of Female Innocence*	1792	Conduct
Chudleigh, Mary	*The Ladies Defence*	1701	Defence
Cowley, Charlotte	*The Ladies History of England*	1780	Text book
Cresswick	*The Lady's Preceptor*	1792	Text book
Damarville	*The Young Lady's Geography*	1765	Text book
Defence	*A Defence for the Ladies*	1720	Defence/Satire
Dodd, William	*An Epistle to a Lady*	1753	Religious

1700-1800

Author/Entry	Title	Date	Category
Donovan, Timothy	*The Whimsical Lady*	1770, 1780	Text book
Du Bois, Dorothea	*The Lady's Polite Secretary*	1765	Text book
Duncombe, John	*The Feminead: or, Female Genius*	1757	Verse/Praise
Green, Sarah	*Mental Improvement for a Young Lady*	1793	Text book
Grieg, John	*The Young Lady's New Guide to Arithmetic*	1800	Text book
Harris, John	*Astronomical Dialogues . . . Lady*	1719	Text book
Haywood, Eliza	*Epistles for the Ladies*	1749	Epsitolary/Advice
Essay	*An Essay for the education of young Ladies*	1798	Advice
Fielding, Sarah	*The Governess, the Little Female Academy*	1781	Novel
Fordyce, James	*The Character and conduct of the female sex*	1776	Conduct
G.R.	*The accomplish'd female instructor*	1704	Advice/Text book
Gisborne, Thomas	*An Enquiry into the duties of the Female Sex*	1797, 1798 1801, 1806	Conduct
Haywood, Eliza	*Ladies for Ladies*	1756	Epsitolary
Honoria	*The Female Mentor*	1793, 1802	Advice/Ephemerides
Horde, Thomas	*The Female Pendant*	1782	Satire/Drama
Horne, George	*A Picture of the Female Character*	1794	Advice/Conduct
Horne, George	*Reflections on . . . Female Character*	1796	Advice/Conduct
Jenkyns, Soame	*The Modern Fine Lady*	1751	Satire/Verse
Kenrick, William	*The Whole Duty of Woman*	1797	Conduct
Ladies	*The Ladies dispensatory*	1739, 1740, 1770	Advice/Medical

1700–1800

Author/Entry	Title	Date	Category
Lady	*Female Restoration*	1780	Defence
Lady	*Female Rights Vindicated*	1758	Defence
Lady	*The Progress of a Female Mind*	1794	Verse/Epistolary
Lady	*The Female Guardian*	1784	Conduct
Lady	*The Lady's Preceptor*	1790	Conduct
Lady	*The Whole Duty of a Woman*	1701, 1712, 1739	Advice/Conduct
Lady	*The Young Lady's Parental Monitor*	1790	Conduct
Lady	*To a Lady on Education*	1791	Advice
Lady	*Amusement Hall*	1794	Advice
L.F., Esq.	*The Virgin's Nosegay, or . . . Duties*	1744	Conduct
Marriott, Thomas	*Female Conduct*	1759, 1760	Conduct/Verse
Moir, John	*Female Tuition*	1784	Advice
Monster	*The Female Monster*	1705	Verse/Satire
Murray, Ann	*Mentoria: or, the Young Ladies Instructor*	1779	Text book
Physician	*The Female Physician*	1770	Advice/Medical
Pilkington, Mary	*A Mirror for the Female Sex*	1798, 1799 1800	Conduct
Portia	*The polite lady: or, a course of female education*	1763, 1769 1775, 1788	Epistolary
Radcliffe, Mary Ann	*The Female Advocate*	1799	Defence
Rice, John	*A Lecture . . . female education*	1773	Advice
Rice, John	*A Plan for Female Education*	1779	Advice
Robertson, Joseph	*An Essay on the education of young ladies*	1798	Advice
Savile, George	*The Lady's New-Years Gift: or, Advice*	1701, 1707 1784	Conduct
Scott, Mary	*The Female Advocate*	1774, 1775	Verse/Defence
Scott, Mrs	*Complete Etiquette for Ladies*	1754	Conduct

1700-1800

Author/Entry	Title	Date	Category
Scally, John	*The Lady's Encyclopedia*	1788	Text book
Taverner, William	*The Female Advocates*	1713	Drama
Various	*Annual Present for the Ladies*	1787	Ephemerides
Various	*The Gentlemen's and Ladies Diary*	1799-1808	Ephemerides
Various	*Harris's British Ladies Complete Pocket Book*	1791	Ephemerides
Various	*The Ladies' Complete Pocket Book*	1769	Ephemerides
Various	*The Ladies Daily Companion*	1785	Ephemerides
Various	*The Ladies Diary: or, the women's Almanack*	1706, 1839	Ephemerides
Various	*A Companion to the Ladies Diary*	1781	Ephemerides
Various	*The Diarian Miscellany*	1775	Ephemerides
Various	*The Diarian Repository*	1774	Ephemerides
Various	*A Supplement to the Ladies Diary*	1788-1806	Ephemerides
Various	*The Ladies Mirror, or Mental Companion*	1785-1814	Ephemerides
Various	*The Ladies Miscellany, or . . . Useful Knowledge*	1788	Ephemerides
Various	*The Ladies Museum, or Complete Pocket Book*	1773-1814	Ephemerides
Various	*The Ladies' Own Memorandum Book*	1771-1779	Ephemerides
Various	*The Ladies Physiognomical Mirror*	1798	Ephemerides
Various	*The Ladies Pocket Journal*	1786	Ephemerides
Various	*The Female . . . Intelligence*	1716	Miscellany
Eliza Haywood/ Various	*The Female Spectator*	1744	Miscellany
Various	*The Lady's Magazine*	1770-1818	Miscellany

1700–1800

Author/Entry	Title	Date	Category
Various	*The Lady's Magazine, or Polite Companion*	1759–1763	Miscellany
Various	*The Lady's Monthly Museum*	1798–1806	Miscellany
Various	*The Ladies Monthly Museum, Improved*	1817–1828	Miscellany
Various	*The Lady's Museum*	1760, 1761	Miscellany
Various	*The Lady's New and Elegant Pocket Magazine*	1795	Miscellany
Various	*The Monthly Miscellany*	1774	Miscellany
Various	*The New Lady's Magazine*	1786–1797	Miscellany
Various	*The New Royal and Universal Magazine*	1759	Miscellany
Various	*The Repository, and Ladies Weekly Museum*	1805, 1806	Miscellany
Various	*Town Talk, in a Letter to a Lady*	1715, 1716	Miscellany
Various	*The Young Gentleman's and Lady's Magazine*	1799, 1800	Miscellany
Various	*The Lady and Gentleman's Pocket Magazine*	1796	Miscellany
Various	*The Lady's . . . Scientific Magazine*	1782–1784	Miscellany
Various	*The Ladies Magazine and Repository*	1792, 1793	Miscellany
Various	*The Lady's Magazine*	1792, 1793	Miscellany
Wakefield, Priscilla	*Reflections . . . Female Sex*	1798, 1817	Advice
Wilkes, Wetenhall	*A Letter of Genteel and Moral Advice to a Lady*	1753, 1760	Conduct
Wollstonecraft, Mary	*The Female Reader*	1789	Text book
Wollstonecraft, Mary	*Thoughts on the Education of Daughters*	1787	Advice
Woty, William	*The Female Advocate*	1770	Verse
Wright, George	*The Lady's Miscellany*	1793, 1797	Text book
W.W.	*A Letter . . . in Praise of Female Learning*	1739	Praise

1800–1900

Author/Entry	Title	Date	Category
Appleton, Elizabeth	*Private Education . . . for Young Ladies*	1815, 1816	Advice
Anderson, William	*Female Education*	1851	Essay
Anon.	*The Female Instructor*	1817, 1830 1845	Advice/Conduct
Arthur, Timothy	*Advice to the Ladies on . . . Conduct*	1856	Conduct
Aytres, Henry	*Conversions on Aritihmetic . . . Ladies*	1843	Text book
Bakewell, Mrs.	*Parting Precepts to a Female Sunday Scholar*	1847	Advice/Religious
Beaman, Edmund	*The True Principles of Education . . . Female*	1848	Advice
Beecher, Catherine	*Suggestions Respecting . . . Education*	1829	Advice/Other
Bennet, Giorgiana	*Remarks on Female Education*	1842	Advice
Brenner, Lucie	*Gymnastics for Ladies*	1870	Advice/Text book
Brewster, Margaret	*Household Economy . . . for female training*	1858, 1878	Text book
Broadhurst, Frances	*A Word in Favour of Female Schools*	1813	Defence
Broadhurst, Thomas	*Advice to Young Ladies . . . Conduct*	1808, 1810	Advice/Conduct
Brown, James	*The Work of a Ladies College*	1857	Essay
Brunetiere, C.	*An Essay on Female Education*	1840	Other
Bureaud-Riofry, Antoine	*Physical Education . . . for Young Ladies*	1838	Advice/Text book
Burton, J.	*Lectures on Female Education and Manners*	1802	Advice/Conduct
Butler, William	*Exercises on the Globes . . . for young ladies*	1803, 1808, 1816, 1818 1837	Text book
Butler, William	*Geographical Exercises . . . for young ladies*	1811, 1818, 1848 (27th edn.)	Text book

1800–1900

Author/Entry	Title	Date	Category
Butler, William	*An Introduction to Arithmetic . . . ladies*	1838	Text book
Cary, Virginia	*Letters on Female Character*	1830	Epistolary/ Conduct
Chirol, J. Louis	*An Enquiry . . . System of Female Education*	1809	Other
Cockle, Mary	*Important Studies, for the Female Sex*	1809	Cockle
Cohen, Joseph	*Copies for the Instruction of Ladies*	1839	Text book
Cox, Francis Augustus	*Female Scripture Biography*	1817	Religious
Coxe, E.H.	*The Female Mentor*	1847	Other
Craik, George Lillie	*The Pursuit of Knowledge . . . Females*	1838	Other
Davidson, Lillias	*Cycles and Cycling . . . for ladies*	1890	Other
Erskine, F.J.	*Bicylcing for Ladies*	1896	Other
Erskine, F.J.	*Tricycling for Ladies*	1885	Other
Farquhar, Barbara H.	*Female Education*	1851	Defence
Garnett, James Mercer	*Seven Lectures on Female Education*	1824	Other
Gisborne, Thomas	*Enquiry into the Duties of the Female Sex*	1816 (11th edn.)	Advice
Gregory, John	*A Father's Legacy to his Daugher*	1822, 1828 1868	Conduct
Green, James	*Woman, or the . . . duties of the female*	1857	Praise/Conduct
Hatfield, S.	*Letters on the Importance of the Female Sex*	1803, 1813	Epistolary/Defence
Hopa, Louisa	*The Female Teacher*	1853	Advice
Ireland, Dept. of State	*Reading Book for the Use of Female Schools*	1850	Text book
Johnson, Robert	*Lecture . . . a System of Female Education*	1851	Advice
[Lady, By a]	*A Word in favour of Female Schools*	1826	Defence

1800-1900

Author/Entry	Title	Date	Category
Mab, Queen [pseud]	*The Modern Minerva*	1810	Satire/Verse
Mackey, James	*Essay on Female Education*	1819	Other
[Mother, By a]	*Female Excellence; or, Hints to Daughters*	1840	Advice/Conduct
[Mother. By a]	*Importance of Female Education*	1827	Advice/Conduct
Newman, Catherine	*Practical Hints on Female Education*	1824	Advice
Nicolay, Charles	*Queen's College, London*	1849	Other
Palmer, Samuel	*Apostolical Directions . . . Female Education*	1809	Religious
Pascoe, Charles	*Schools for Girls & Colleges for Womenr*	1879	Other
Pendered, Anne Eliza	*Remarks on female education*	1823	Advice
Phelps, Almira	*The female student*	1844	Other
Scott, Alexander	*Suggestions on Female Education*	1849	Other
Various	*The Christian Ladies Pocket Book*	1842-44	Ephemerides
Various	*The Emerald, or Ladies' Pocket Book*	1855	Ephemerides
Various	*The Evangical Museum*	1814	Ephemerides
Various	*Findlater's Ladies Housekeeping Book*	1889	Ephemerides
Various	*Fulcher's Ladies Memorandum Book*	1834-76	Ephemerides
Various	*The Garnet, or Ladies Useful Pocket Book*	1858	Ephemerides
Various	*Gedge's Town and Country Ladies*	1802	Ephemerides
Various	*The Gentlemen's and Ladies Diary*	1799-1880	Ephemerides
Various	*The Governess: a Repertory*	1855	Ephemerides
Various	*Graham's Ladies Pocket Souvenir*	1844	Ephemerides
Various	*The Keepsake or Ladies Diary*	1858	Ephemerides

1800–1900

Author/Entry	Title	Date	Category
Various	*The Keepsake or Ladies Pocket Book*	1854	Ephemerides
Various	*The Ladies' and Gentleman's Diary*	1819–1822	Ephemerides
Various	*The Ladies' Annual Diary and Almanack*	1842–1844	Ephemerides
Various	*The Ladies' Annual Journal*	1814	Ephemerides
Various	*The Ladies New and Elegant Pocket Book*	1814	Ephemerides
Various	*The Ladies Own Memorandum Book*	1842–1846	Ephemerides
Various	*The Ladies Pearl Pocket-book Almanack*	1842–1844	Ephemerides
Various	*The Ladies' Pocket Book Almanack*	1862	Ephemerides
Various	*The Ladies' Polite Remembrancer*	1838	Ephemerides
Various	*The Ladies' Polite Remembrancer*	1842–1844	Ephemerides
Various	*The Ladies Superb Pocket Book Almanack*	1842–11844	Ephemerides
Various	*Penny's Ladies' . . . Diary and Almanack*	1877	Ephemerides
Various	*Poole's Juvenile Ladies' Pocket . . . Book*	1842–1844	Ephemerides
Various	*Poole's London Annual Repository*	1843–1846	Ephemerides
Various	*The Rainbow, or Ladies' Pocket Book*	1855	Ephemerides
Various	*The Ruby, or Ladies Boudoir Pocket Book*	1842	Ephemerides
Various	*The Sapphire, or the Juvenile Ladies . . . Book*	1842	Ephemerides
Various	*The Suffolk Ladies' Memorandum Book*	1813	Ephemerides
Various	*The Wreath; or, Ladies Pocket Book*	1854	Ephemerides

Notes

ABBREVIATIONS

L = Letter;   AL – Autograph letter;   ALS = Autograph letter signed;
AMs = Autograph manuscript;   AMsS = Autograph manuscript signed;
n.p. = no place;   n.d. = no date

INTRODUCTION

1   See for example Gillian Avery, *The Best Type of Girl: A History of Girls' Independent Schools* (London, 1991); Margaret Bryant, *The Unexpected Revolution: A Study in the Education of Women and Girls in the Nineteenth Century* (London, 1979); Joan Burstyn, *Victorian Education and the Ideal of Womanhood* (London: Croom Helm, 1980); Sarah Delamont and Lorna Duffin *The Nineteenth Century Woman, her Cultural and Physical World* (London, 1978); Ann Digby, "New Schools for the Middle Class Girl," in *Educating the Victorian Middle Class*, ed. P. Searby (Leicester: History of Education Society, Proceedings of the 1981 Annual Conference of the History of Education Society of Great Britain); Carol Dyhouse, *Girls Growing up in Late Victorian and Edwardian England* (London, 1981); Sheila Fletcher, *Feminists and Bureaucrats: A Study in the Development of Girls' Education in the Nineteenth Century* (Cambridge, 1980); Felicity Hunt, *Lessons for Life: The Schooling of Girls and Women 1850-1950* (Oxford, 1987); June Purvis, *A History of Women's Education in England* (Milton Keynes, 1991); Judith Rowbotham, "Education for Model Maidens," chap. in *Good Girls Make Good Wives* (Oxford, 1989); Gillian Sutherland, "The movement for the higher education of women: its social and intellectual context in England, c.1840-80," in *Politics and Social Change in Modern Britain*, ed.

Peter Waller (Brighton, 1987).

2   This term was used by Margaret Bryant in her study *The Unexpected Revolution: A Study in the Education of Women and Girls in the Nineteenth Century*).

3   Anna Maria van Schurman, *Dissertatio, de Ingenii Muliebris ad Doctrinam, et Meliores Litteras Apptitudine* (1641) DT, trans. Clement Barksdale, *The Learned Maid, or Whether a Maid may be a Scholar* (1659).

4   Lawrence Stone, *The Family, Sex and Marriage in England, 1500-1800* (London, 1979), p.25.

5   Nina Auerbach, *Communities of Women* (Mass., and Conn., 1978), p.5.

6   Elizabeth Nestor, *Female Friendships and Communities* (Oxford, 1985), p.7.

7   For a discussion of the nineteenth century movement for the establishment of Anglican nunneries see Elizabeth Nestor, *Female Friendships and Communities*. Nestor notes that in 1868, public attention was drawn to the court case of *Saurin v. Starr, and Others* when it was brought before the Queen's Bench. The longest case ever heard by the Queen's Bench, it was sensationalised in the popular press. It involved the action of a nun against her Mother Superior for unfair dismissal, and revelations included charges of broken vows and assignations with an elderly gentleman. It was quickly viewed as a "woman's squabble" and, as Nestor points out, detractors lost no opportunity to ridicule communities of women.

1: WHETHER A MAID MAY BE A SCHOLAR

1 Shirley Nelson Kersey, ed., *Classics in the Education of Girls and Women* (New Jersey and London, 1981), p.19.

2 Foster Watson, *Vives and the Renaissance Education of Women* (London, 1912), pp.3-4, cited in Betty Travitsky, *The Paradise of Women: Writings by English Women of the Renaissance* (Connecticut, 1981), p.240.

3 Travitsky, *The Paradise of Women*, p.3. See also Julia O'Faolain and Laura Martines, eds., *Not in God's Image* (New York, 1973).

4 Travitsky, *The Paradise of Women*, p.7.

5 Juan Luis Vives, *Instruction of a Christian Woman* (1523) trans. Richard Hyrde, 1540; *De Ratione Studii Puerilis and Satellitium sive Symbola* (1523), trans. Foster Watson, 1912; *Office and duetie of an husband* (1529) trans. Thomas Paynell, 1553; Richard Hyrde, 'Dedicatory Letter' to *A devoute treatise upon the Pater Noster*, translated by Margaret More Roper from the Latin of Erasmus, 1524; Sir Thomas More, 'Letter to William Gonell' (1518?); and Sir Thomas Elyot, *The Defence of Good Women* (1545).

6 Juan Luis Vives, 'The Instruction of a Christian Woman', in *Classics in the Education of Girls and Women,* ed. Kersey, p.38.

7 John Amos Comenius, *The Great Didactic* (1657), ed. M.W. Keating (1910), quoted by David Cressy, *Education in Tudor and Stuart England* (Cambridge, 1980), p.111.

8 Ibid.

9 Vives, *Instruction*, in *Classics in the Education of Girls and Women*, ed. Kersey, p.41.

10 Joan Kelly, 'Did Women Have a Renaissance?'(1977), chap. in *Women, History and Theory* (Chicago, 1984).

11 Kersey, *Classics in the Education of Girls and Women*, p.19.

12 See Merry E. Weisner, 'Women's Defense of their Public Role', in *Women in the Middle Ages and the Renaissance,* ed. Mary Beth Rose (Syracuse, 1986).

13 Kelly, *Women, History and Theory*, p.2.

14 Simon Shepherd, *The Women's Sharp Revenge: Five Women's Pamphlets from the Renaissance* (London, 1985), pp. 17-18.

15 Janis Butler Holm, 'The Myth of a Feminist Humanism', in *Ambiguous Realities: Women in the Middle Ages and Renaissance,* ed. Carole Levin and Jeanie Watson (Detroit, 1987), p.198.

16 Shepherd, *Women's Pamphlets*, p.17.

17 Travitsky, *The Paradise of Women*, p.5.

18 Ian Maclean, *The Renaissance Notion of Woman: A Study in the Fortunes of Scholasticism and Medical Science in European Intellectual Life* (Cambridge, 1980), p.1.

19 Ibid., p.5. For a discussion of the influence of *Il libro del Cortegiano* see Margaret L. King, *Women and the Renaissance* (Chicago and London, 1991), p.163.

20 Maclean, *The Renaissance Notion of Woman*, p.13.

21 Unidentified source cited by Maclean, *The Renaissance Notion of Woman*, p.42.

22 Maclean, *The Renaissance Notion of Woman*, p.41.

23 Aristotle, *De Generationa Animalium*, IX.I, quoted in Maclean, *The Renaissance Notion of Woman*, p.42.

24 Maclean, *The Renaissance Notion of Woman*, p.64.

25 Jane Tibbetts Schulenburg, 'The Heroics of Virginity', in *Women in the Middle Ages and the Renaissance*, ed. Mary Beth Rose, p.31.

26 Henderson & McManus, *Half Humankind*, p.82.

27 Vives, *The Instruction of a Christian Woman* in *Classics in the Education of Girls and Women*, ed. Kersey, p.40.

28 Ibid.

29 Vives, *The Office and Dutie of an Husband*, quoted in *Silent but for the Word: Tudor Women as Patrons, Translators and Writers of Religious Works*, ed. Margaret P. Hannay (Ohio, 1985), p.25.

30 Travitsky, *The Paradise of Women*, p.7.

31 Ibid.

32 Thomas Becon, *New Catechisme* (1564) quoted in Travitsky, *The Paradise of Women*, p.7.

33 Travitsky, *The Paradise of Women*, p.7.

34 See Maclean, *The Renaissance Notion of Woman*, p.63.

35 John Knox, *The First Blast of the Trumpet Against the Monstrous Regiment of Women* (1558) in *The Works of John Knox*, iv, ed. David Laing (1855), p.374.

36 Stephen Gosson, *Quipps for Upstart New-fangled Gentle-women*, AM 1595, MS Malone 17, Bodleian Library, Oxford.

37 This included the following: I.G., *An Apology for Womankind* (1605); Ludowick Lloyd, *The Choice of Jewels* (1607); William Heale, *An Apology for Women* (1609); Barnaby Rich, *The Excellency of Good Women* (1613); Joseph Swetnam, *The Arraignment of Lewd, Idle, Froward and Unconstant Women* (1615); Daniel Tuvil, *Asylum Veneris, or a Sanctuary for Ladies* (1616); Rachel Speght, *A Muzzle for Melastomus* (1617); Esther Sowernam [pseud.], *Esther hath hanged Haman* (1617); and Constantia Munda [pseud.], *The Worming of a Madde Dogge* (1617).

38 Kelly, *Women, History and Theory*, p.91.

39 *Hic Mulier; or , The Man-Woman; Haec Vir; or, The Woman-Man; Mulled Sack; or the Apology of Hic Mulier to the late Declamation against her*. For a study of these, see Henderson and McManus, *Half Humankind*.

40 Margaret P. Hannay, *Silent but for the Word: Tudor Woment as Patrons, Translators, and Writers of Religous Works* (Ohio, 1985), p 1.

41 For an account of the earliest publications by English women see Patricia Crawford, 'Women's Published Writings, 1600-1700' and Sara Heller Mendelson, 'Stuart Women's Diaries', in *Women in English Society, 1500-1800*, ed. Mary Prior (London, 1985).

42 Patricia Crawford in 'Women's Published Writings, 1600-1700' notes that 'from 1640 to 1700, women's publications amounted to 1.2. per cent of the total publications, which more than doubled their pre-Civil-War contribution of around 0.5 per cent'. See *Women in English Society, 1500-1800*, ed. Mary Prior, p.266.

43 Ibid.

44 Relevant research in this area includes David Cressy, *Literature and Social Order: Reading and Writing in Tudor and Stuart England* (Cambridge, 1980); Mary Mahl and Helen Koon, *The Female Spectator: Women Writers Before 1800* (Indiana, 1977); and Alison Adburgham, *Women in Print: Writing Women and Women's Magazines from the Restoration to the Accession of Victoria* (London, 1972), though none of these offers an examination of publications on the education of women.

45 See *An Account of the Charity Schools Lately Erected in England, Wales and Ireland* (1706). See also J. Lawson and Harold Silver, *A Social History of Education in England* (London, 1973) and Joan Simon, *Education and Society in Tudor England* (Cambridge, 1966)

46 *An Account of the Charity Schools*, p.8.

47 David Cressy in *Literature & Social Order: Reading and Writing in Tudor and Stuart England* (1980) and in *Education in Tudor and Stuart England* (1975) notes that masters at the grammar schools occasionally supplemented their income with additional 'petties' which girls attended. This possibly accounts for the woodcut illustration, showing both boys and girls being tutored, in the widely used English grammar text *The English School Master* by Edmund Coote (1596), although it is noteworthy that while the boys are depicted writing, the girls are reading: girls who attended the petty schools learned to read but rarely to write.

48 For accounts of schooling for upper-class girls see Dorothy Gardiner, *English Girlhood at School* (London, 1929), Josephine Kamm, *Hope Deferred* (London, 1965), Roger Thompson, *Women in Stuart England* (London, 1974) and M.C. Borer, *Willingly to School* (London, 1975).

49 John Evelyn, *Diary*, 20 April 1667, cited by Roger Thompson, *Women in Stuart England*, p.189.

50 See Kamm, *Hope Deferred*, and Gardiner, *English Girlhood at School*.

51 David Cressy in *Literature and Social*

Order: Reading and Writing in Tudor and Stuart England and Patricia Crawford in 'Women's Published Writings, 1600-1700" have examined these two areas, respectively. There exists no analysis of the significance of the emergence of women's education as a theme in seventeenth century writing.

52 Cressy, *Literature and Society*, p.147.

53 S.A. Richards, *Feminist Writers of the Seventeenth Century* (London, 1914), p.8.

54 See Richards, *Feminist Writers of the Seventeenth Century*.

55 Gardiner, *English Girlhood at School*, p.271.

56 Anna Maria van Schurman, *Dissertatio, de Ingenii Muliebris ad Doctrinam, et Meliures Litteras Apptitudine* (1641), p.9.

57 Patricia Phillips, *The Scientific Lady: A Social History of Woman's Scientific Interests, 1520-1918* (London, 1991), p.33.

58 Mahl & Koon, *The Female Spectator*, p.117. Mahl and Koon also record that two letters among van Schurman's papers are signed Bathsua Makin, and that both are written in Greek.

59 Bathsua Makin, *An Essay to Revive the Ancient Education of Gentlewomen* (1673), reprinted in Mahl & Koon, *The Female Spectator*, p.126.

60 Ibid.

61 Ibid., p.130.

62 Hannah Woolley, *The Gentlewoman's Companion* (1675), p.1.

63 Florence M. Smith, *Mary Astell* (1915; this edn., New York, 1966), Introduction.

64 See Ralph Thoresby, *Diaries*, quoted by Smith, *Mary Astell* , p.10.

65 Mary Astell, *A Serious Proposal to the Ladies for their True and Greatest Interest* (London, 1697), p.6.

66 Ibid., p.11.

67 Ibid., p.13.

68 Ibid., p.20.

69 Ibid., p. 40.

70 Elizabeth Elstob to George Ballard, ALS 13 July 1738, MS Ballard 43, 10829, f.29, Bodleian Library, Oxford. Elstob wrote: 'I don't remember that I ever heard Mrs [*sic*] Astell mention the Good Lady's name you desire to know, but I very well remember she told me it was Bishop Burnet that prevented that good Design by dissuading that Lady from encouraging it'.

71 Ruth Perry, *The Celebrated Mary Astell* (London & Chicago, 1986).

72 Karl D. Bulbring, *Mary Astell: An Advocate of Woman's Rights Two Hundred Years Ago* (1891).

73 Mrs McIlquham, 'Mary Astell: A Seventeenth Century Advocate for Women', *The Westminster Review* 149 (1898), p.445.

74 Smith, *Mary Astell*.

75 Joan K. Kinnaird, 'Mary Astell and the Conservative Contribution to English Feminism', *Journal of British Studies* 19 (1979), p.75.

76 Perry, *The Celebrated Mary Astell*, p.12.

77 Ibid., p.329.

78 Bulbring, 'Mary Astell', p.4.

79 Kersey, Introduction to Mary Astell in *Classics in the Education of Women and Girls*, p.96. In addition to this error, Kersey attributes another piece, 'An Essay in Defence of the Female Sex' to Astell. The author of this piece was decided, as early as 1915, to be Judith Drake.

2: STRICTURES AND VINDICATIONS

1 Alice Brown, *The Eighteenth Century Feminist Mind* (Detroit, 1987), p.20. For a discussion of the socio-political background of this period see Miriam Brody, Introduction to Mary Wollstonecraft, *A Vindication of the Rights of Woman* (Middlesex, 1992).

2 See Roy Porter, *English Society in the Eighteenth Century* (London, 1982).

3 Janet Todd, *A Dictionary of British and American Women Writers, 1660-1800* (London, 1987), p.1.

4 Phillips, *The Scientific Lady*, p.ix.

5 *The Athenian Mercury*, no.18, (1691).

6 Hannah Woolley, *The Gentlewoman's Companion* (1675), quoted by M.C. Borer, *Willingly to School* (London, 1975), p.108.

7 Ibid.

8 *The Athenian Mercury*, no. 18, (1691).

9 Phillips, *The Scientific Lady*, p.28.

10 Ibid., p.33.

11 Makin, *Essay to Revive the Ancient Education of Gentlewomen*, quoted by Patricia Phillips, *The Scientific Lady*, p.39.

12 Makin, Postscript to *Essay to Revive the Ancient Education of Gentlewomen*, printed in full in *First Feminists*, ed. Moira Fergusson, pp. 141-42.

13 Ibid., p.142.

14 John Harris, *Astronomical Dialogues Between a Gentleman and a Lady: Wherein The Doctrine of the Sphere, Uses of the Globes, And the Elements of Astronomy and Geography are Explain'd, in a Pleasant, Easy and Familiar Way* (1719), p.6.

15 Ibid.

16 Elizabeth Carter, *All the Works of Epictetus which are now Extant* (2nd edn., London: 1753).

17 Mary Somerville, MS Somerville Notebook, 1859, Somerville Papers, Bodleian Library, Oxford. In her Notebook, Somerville reflected that her conversation had given the idea to the contemporary scientist Adams to compute the orbit of Neptune, concluding '. . . if I had possessed originality or genius I might have done it, a proof that originality or discovery is not given to women?'

18 *The Female Spectator* (April, 1744), quoted in Frances Gees Black, *The Epistolary Novel in the late Eighteenth Century: a Descriptive and Bibliographical Study* (Eugene, 1940), p.85.

19 "On the Female Mind' in *The Female Preceptor* (London, 1813), p.1.

20 See Black, *The Epistolary Novel in the late Eighteenth Century*, p.215.

21 Lady Pennington, *An Unfortunate Mother's Advice to her Absent Daughters*, in *The Young Lady's Parental Monitor* (London, 1790), p.70.

22 The Marchioness de Lambert, *Advice of a Mother to a Daughter*, in *The Young Lady's Parental Monitor* (1790), p.137.

23 Mary Wray, *The Ladies Library* (London, 1714), p.23.

24 Ibid., p.22.

25 Ibid., p.439, and also in Astell, *A Serious Proposal*, p.24.

26 Ibid., p.28.

27 Clara Reeve, *Plans of Education; with Remarks on the Systems of Other Writers* (1792) in *Women in the Eighteenth Century*, ed. Vivien Jones (London, 1990), pp. 116-17.

28 Ibid., p.117.

29 Ibid.

30 Maria Edgeworth, *A Practical Education*, vol. 2 (1801), p.123.

31 John Bennet, *Strictures on Female Education* (1787), p.138.

32 Ibid., p.142.

33 *The Female Guardian*, by a Lady (London, 1784), title page.

34 *The Female Monitor*, by a Lady (London, 1800), p.85.

35 Thomas Gisborne, *An Enquiry into the Duties of the Female Sex* (London, 1797), p.11.

36 Ibid., pp 12-13.

37 Ibid., p.34.

38 George Saville, Marquis of Halifax, *Advice to a Daughter* (1688), in *Women in the Eighteenth Century*, ed. Vivien Jones, p.18.

39 Jones, *Women in the Eighteenth Century*, p.15.

40 Ibid.

41 Dr. John Gregory, *A Father's Legacy to his Daughters*, in *The Young Lady's Parental Monitor* (1790), p.29.

42 Hannah More, *Thoughts on the Cultivation of the Heart and Temper in the Education of Daughters*, in *Works*, vol. VI, p.326.

43 Lady Pennington, *An Unfortunate Mother's Advice to Her Absent Daughters*, in a *Letter to Miss Pennington*, in *The Young Lady's Parental Monitor* (1790), p.72.

44 Miriam Brody, Introduction to *A Vindication of the Rights of Woman*, p.21.

45 Ibid., p.22.

46 Ibid.

47 Mary Wollstonecraft, *Thoughts on the Education of Daughters* (1787), *Mary, A Fiction* (1788), *Original Stories from Real Life* (1788), *The Female Reader* (1789), *A Vindication of the Rights of Men*, in a *Letter to the Right Honourable Edmund*

Burke (1790), *A Vindication of the Rights of Woman* (1792), *A Historical and Moral View of the Origin and Progress of the French Revolution* (1794), *Letters Written During a Short Residence in Sweden, Norway, and Denmark* (1796), *Posthumous Works of the Author of a Vindication of the Rights of Woman*, (1798), and *The Wrongs of Woman, or Maria*, published with *Posthumous Works* (1798) and later reprinted as *Maria, or the Wrongs of Woman* (London, 1975).

48 Horace Walpole to Hannah More, 24 January 1795, in *The Letters of Horace Walpole*, ed.Peter Cunningham (1859), quoted in *A Study of Mary Wollstonecraft and The Rights of Woman*, Emma Rauschenbasch Clough (London, 1898), p.43.

49 Clough, *A Study of Mary Wollstonecraft*, p.26.

50 It would be very trite indeed, to explain away the failure of some of her personal relationships with the few short references to her childhood that this chapter can include; neither is it within the scope of this study to account for the writings examined, in relation to the psychological make-up of each writer. Biographical details can merely be used to inform the reader of intellectual interests and occupational involvements that might have shaped the writers philosophy of education, therefore reference to Wollstonecraft's childhood is perfunctory.

51 Richard Price, *A Review of the Principle Questions and Difficulties in Morals* (London, 1758), p.23.

52 Mary Wollstonecraft, *Vindication of the Rights of Women*, in *A Wollstonecraft Anthology*, ed. Janet Todd (Cambridge, 1989), p.98.

53 Mary Wollstonecraft, *A Vindication of the Rights of Woman* (London, 1792), pp. 81-2.

54 Price, *A Review of the Principle Questions and Difficulties in Morals*, p.24.

55 Mary Poovey, *The Proper Lady and the Woman Writer: Ideology as Style in the Works of Mary Wollstonecraft, Mary Shelley, and Jane Austen* (London &

Chicago, 1984), p.48.

56 Mary Wollstonecraft to Everina Wollstonecraft, 9 October [1786], in *Collected Letters of Mary Wollstonecraft*, ed. Ralph M. Wardle (Ithaca & London, 1979), p.117.

57 Mary Wollstonecraft to Everina Wollstonecraft, 30 October [1786], in Wardle, *Collected Letters*, p.120.

58 Mary Wollstonecraft to Eliza Wollstonecraft Bishop, 5 November [1786], in *Collected Letters*, pp. 123,124.

59 Mary Wollstonecraft, *Analytical Review* III (Jan-April, 1798) in *A Wollstonecraft Anthology*, ed. Janet Todd, p.219.

60 Ibid.

61 Ibid.

62 Mary Wollstonecraft, *Mary, A Fiction*, in *A Wollstonecraft Anthology*, ed. Janet Todd, p.184.

63 Ibid., p.183.

64 C.S. Salzmann, *Moralisches Elementarbuch*. Wollstonecraft's translation appeared in two volumes in 1790 (reprinted: 1792, 1793, 1811, 1821).

65 See Chapter Three.

66 Mary Wollstonecraft, Review of Catherine Macaulay's *Letters on Education*, *Analytical Review* (November, 1790), in *A Wollstonecraft Anthology*, ed. Janet Todd, p.116.

67 Brody, *A Vindication of the Rights of Woman*, Introduction, p.11.

68 Todd, *A Wollstonecraft Anthology*, Introduction, p.10.

69 Mary Wollstonecraft, *An Historical and Moral View of the Origins and Progress of the French Revolution* (London, 1795), p.73.

70 Wollstonecraft, *Origins and Progress of the French Revolution*, p.5.

71 Miriam Brody notes that Imlay had travelled to Paris 'to interest the French government in a land speculation scheme in the territory of Kentucky.' See Brody, Introduction to *A Vindication of the Rights of Woman*, p.14.

72 William Godwin, *Memoirs of the Author of A Vindication of the Rights of Woman*, p.190, quoted in Clough, *A Study of Mary Wollstonecraft and the Rights of Woman*, p.61.

73 *The Gentleman's Magazine* 38, no.3 (1798), pp. 186-87.
74 *Anti-Jacobin Review* 9 (1797) quoted *A Wollstonecraft Anthology*, ed. Janet Todd, p.17.
75 John Locke, *An Essay Concerning Human Understanding* I.4.2 (1690; this edn., London, 1977), p.24.
76 Ibid., I,4,23, p.28.
77 Ibid.
78 Mary Wollstonecraft, *Thoughts on the Education of Daughters*, in *A Wollstonecraft Anthology*, ed. Janet Todd, p.28.
79 Ibid., p.29.
80 Ibid., p.32. Todd notes that 'Beauty washes were intended to improve the complexion; they were made from a variety of ingredients ranging from bean water to minced pigeon. Olympian dew was probably a cleansing agent, while liquid bloom was a vegetable extract designed to give an instant lasting rosy hue to the cheeks. . . . Lead and bismuth were used to give whiteness and polish to the face; they were absorbed by the skin and eventually poisoned the system.'
81 Astell, *A Serious Proposal*, p.6.
82 Wollstonecraft, *Thoughts on the Education of Daughters*, in *A Wollstonecraft Anthology*, ed. Janet Todd, p.36.
83 Astell, *A Serious Proposal*, p.24.
84 Wollstonecraft, *Thoughts on the Education of Daughters*, in *A Wollstonecraft Anthology*, ed. Janet Todd, p.36.
85 Astell, *A Serious Proposal*, p.19.
86 Wollstonecraft, *A Vindication of the Rights of Woman*, in *A Wollstonecraft Anthology*, ed. Janet Todd, p.88.
87 Ibid., p.34.
88 Astell, *A Serious Proposal*, p.20.
89 While in Ireland, Wollstonecraft wrote to her sister that she was reading *Émile*. Letter No. 55 (24 March 1787), *Collected Letters*, p.145.
90 Sarah Fielding, *The Governess, or Little Female Academy* (1749; this edn.: London, 1987), p.viii.
91 Mary Wollstonecraft, *Original Stories from Real Life*, in *A Wollstonecraft Anthology*, ed. Janet Todd, p.41.
92 Mary Wollstonecraft, *A Vindication of the*

Rights of Men, in *A Wollstonecraft Anthology*, ed. Janet Todd, p.75.
93 Ibid., p.76.
94 Ibid., p.71.
95 Ibid., p.53.
96 Locke, *Essay Concerning Human Understanding*, IV, 19, 4.
97 Wollstonecraft, *A Vindication of the Rights of Woman*, in *A Wollstonecraft Anthology*, ed. Janet Todd, p.85.
98 Ibid., p 86.
99 Dr James Fordyce, *Sermons to Young Women* (1765).
100 Gregory, *A Father's Legacy to His Daughters* (1774).
101 Wollstonecraft, *A Vindication of the Rights of Woman*, p.192.
102 Ibid., p.198.
103 Ibid., p.144.
104 Ibid., p.262.
105 Brody, *A Vindication of the Rights of Woman*, Introduction, pp. 1-2.
106 William Roberts, *Memoirs of the Life and Correspondence of Hannah More* (London: 1834), p.13.
107 Newspaper cutting, untitled, n.d., Hannah More Papers, BL 42511, f.37.
108 See Roberts, *Memoirs of the Life and Correspondence of Hannah More*, p.48
109 Sarah More to her sisters (1774), in Roberts, *Memoirs*, p.48.
110 Sarah More to one of her sisters (1775), in Roberts, *Memoirs*, p.54.
111 Ibid., p.52.
112 Hannah More to one of her sisters (1776), in Roberts, *Memoirs*, p.63.
113 Hannah More Papers, BL 42511, f.38.
114 R. Brimley Johnson, ed., *The Letters of Hannah More* (London, 1925), p.9.
115 Hannah More, *Essays on Various Subjects Principally Designed for Young Ladies* in *The Works of Hannah More* (1833), vol. 3, p.261.
116 See J.C. Colquhoun, *Wilberforce: His Friends and Times* (London, 1867), p.122.
117 Hannah More, Preface to *The Fatal Falsehood* (1779) in *Works*, vol. 5, p.172.
118 Hannah More quoted in Roberts, *Memoirs*, vol.3, pp. 96-7.
119 Hannah More, *Diary*, 21 January 1798,

in Roberts, *Memoirs*, vol. 3, p.55.
120 Hannah More, *Diary*, 28 January 1794, in Roberts, *Memoirs*, vol. 3, p.56.
121 Hannah More, *Diary*, 2 February 1798, in Roberts, *Memoirs*, vol. 3, p.57.
122 Hannah More quoted in *Hannah More*, Jeremy and Margaret Collingwood (Oxford), p.77.
123 Hannah More, *Essays on Various Subjects, Principally Designed for Young Ladies* (1777) in *Works*, vi, p.264.
124 Ibid.
125 Ibid., p.268.
126 Hannah More, *Thoughts on the Manners of the Great* (1788) in *Works*, vol. 2, pp. 279-80.
127 Hannah More to the Bishop of Bath and Wells (1801) in Roberts, *Memoirs*, vol.3, p.133.
128 Hannah More to Sir William Pepys (1821), quoted in Collingwood, *Hannah More*, p.77.
129 Hannah More, quoted in Collingwood, *Hannah More*, pp. 111-12.
130 Hannah More, *Strictures on the Modern System of Education, with a view of the Principles and Conduct Prevalent among Women of Rank and Fortune* (1799).
131 Hannah More, *Strictures* in *Works*, iii, pp.11-12.
132 Ibid., pp. 49-50.
133 Ibid., p.51.
134 Ibid., p.69.
135 Ibid., p.204.
136 Hannah More, *Strictures* in *Women in the Eighteenth Century*, ed. Vivien Jones, p.137.
137 More, *Strictures* in *Works*, vol. 3, p.14.
138 Ibid., p.207.
139 Ibid., p.130.
140 Wollstonecraft, *Vindication of the Rights of Woman*, in *A Wollstonecraft Anthology*, ed. Janet Todd, p.3.
141 Hannah More to Horace Walpole, quoted in Clough, *A Study of Mary Wollstonecraft*, p.44.
142 Horace Walpole to Hannah More, quoted in Roberts, *Memoirs*, pp. 354-5.
143 More, *Strictures, in Works*, vol. 3, p.47.
144 Ibid., p.12.
145 Jean Jacques Rousseau, *Émile*, p.328.

3 : THE EDUCATION OF WOMEN IN ENGLISH LITERATURE

1 See Deirdre Raftery, 'Educational Ideologies and Reading for Girls in England, 1815-1915' (U.K., *History of Education Society Bulletin*, April 1997).
2 Christine de Pizan, *Le Livre de la Cité des Dames* (1405), trans. Bryan Anslay, *The Boke of the Cyte of Laydes* (1591). Next trans.: Earl Jeffrey Richards, ed., *The Book of the City of Ladies* (New York, 1982). The edition referred to hereafter is Richards, ed., (1982).
3 Marina Warner, *The Book of the City of Ladies*, Foreword.
4 Earl Jeffrey Richards, *The Book of the City of Ladies*, Introduction.
5 Christine de Pizan, *The Book of the City of Ladies*, p.62.
6 Ibid., p.63.
7 Ibid.
8 The French translation by Laurent de Premierfait was completed around 1401. An English translation was published by Guido Guarino, *Concerning Famous Women* (New Brunswick: 1963).
9 Earl Jeffrey Richards, *The Book of the City of Ladies* (1982), Introduction.
10 Elaine V. Beilin, *Redeeming Eve: Women Writers of the English Renaissance* (New Jersey, 1987), Introduction.
11 Christine de Pizan, *The Book of the City of Ladies* (1982), p.12.
12 Ibid., p.14.
13 Ibid., p.99.
14 *The Schole house of Women* (1541), in Henderson and McManus, *Half Humankind*, pp.137,155.
15 As the *Schole house* contains references to *Mulierum Paean* by Edward Gosynhill, scholars have argued that he wrote both works. The *Short-title Catalogue* attributes the *Schole house* to Gosynhill.
16 See Chapter One, pp. 32-3.
17 *The Schole house of Women* (1541), in Henderson and McManus, *Half Humankind*, p. 138.
18 Ibid., pp. 139-40.
19 Ibid., p.142.
20 Finding fault.
21 Have at their command.

22 *The Schole house of Women* (1541), in Henderson and McManus, *Half Humankind*, p.144.
23 Ibid., p.151.
24 *Joseph Swetnam, An Arriagnment of Lewd, idle, froward* [sic], *and unconstant women* (1615) in Henderson and McManus, *Half Humankind*, pp. 190-216.
25 See *Kissing the Rod: An Anthology of Seventeenth Century Women's Verse*, Germaine Greer et al., eds. (London, 1988), p.68.
26 Rachel Speght, From *The Dreame* (1641) in *Kissing the Rod: An Anthology of Seventeenth Century Women's Verse*, Germaine Greer et al., eds., p.69.
27 Ibid., p.71.
28 Ibid.
29 Katherine M. Rogers, *The Troublesome Helpmate: A History of Misogyny in Literature* (Seattle and London, 1966), p.131.
30 Quoted in Rogers, *The Troublesome Helpmate*, p.129.
31 Ibid., p.130.
32 Sir Thomas Overbury, 'A Wife' (1614) quoted in Rogers, *The Troublesome Helpmate*, p.131.
33 André Lagarde et Michard Laurent, *XVII Siècle: Les grands auteurs Francais du programme* (Paris, 1962), p.174.
34 See Dorothy Gardiner, *English Girlhood at School* (London, 1929).
35 Thomas Wright, *Female Virtuoso* (Act III, sc.i.) quoted in Dorothy Gardiner, *English Girlhood at School*, p.273
36 Rae Blanchard, 'Richard Steele and the Status of Women', in *Studies in Philology*, vol. 26, no. 3, (North Carolina, July 1929), p.327.
37 See Florence Smith, *Mary Astell* (1914).
38 See Ruth Perry, *Women, Letters and the Novel* (New York, 1980), Introduction.
39 Ibid.
40 Ibid.
41 Ibid.
42 Ibid.
43 For a chronological list titled 'English Letter Fiction, 1660-1740' see Robert Adams Day, *Told in Letters: Epistolary Fiction Before Richardson* (Ann Arbor, 1966), pp. 237-58.

44 Ruth Perry, *Women, Letters and the Novel*, p.8.
45 Clive T. Probyn, *English Fiction of the Eighteenth Century* (London, 1987), p.6.
46 Ibid.
47 Janet Todd, *A Dictionary of British and American Women Writers, 1600-1800* (London, 1987), Janet Todd and Dale Spender, *Anthology of British Women Writers from the Middle Ages to the Present Day* (London, 1989), Dale Spender, *Mothers of the Novel* (London, 1987), and Patricia Crawford, 'Women's Published Writings, 1600-1700' in *Women in English Society, 1500-1800*, ed. Mary Prior.
48 For example, Anne Conway's *Opscula Philosophica* (1690) was ascribed to van Helmont, who had merely transcribed it into Latin. See Patricia Crawford, 'Women's Published Writings, 1600-1700' in *Women in English Society, 1500-1800*, ed. Mary Prior, p.209.
49 Crawford, 'Women's Published Writings' *Women in English Society*, ed. Mary Prior, p.214.
50 David Cressy, *Literature and Social Order: Reading and Writing in Tudor and Stuart England* (Cambridge, 1980).
51 Patricia Crawford, 'Women's Published Writings, 1600-1700', in *Women in English Society* , ed. Mary Prior, p. 213.
52 Bathsua Makin, *Essay to Revive the Ancient Education of Gentlewomen* (1673), Preface.
53 Janet Todd, ed., *A Dictionary of British and American Writers, 1600-1800*, Janet Todd and Dale Spender, eds., *Anthology of British Women Writers from the Middle Ages to the Present Day*, Robert W. Uphaus and Gretchen M. Foster, eds., *The Other Eighteenth Century: English Women of Letters, 1660-1800* (East Lansing, 1991), Katherine M. Rogers and William McCarthy, eds., *The Meridian Anthology of Early Women Writers* (New York and Ontario, 1987).
54 Janet Todd, *A Dictionary of British and American Women Writers, 1660-1800*, p.3.
55 Ibid., p.4.
56 Ibid., p.247.
57 Virginia Woolf, *A Room of One's Own*

(1929; this edn., 1977), p.60.

58 Margaret Cavendish, Duchess of Newcastle, *Preface to Observations on Experimental Philosophy* (1666), quoted by Dale Spender, *Mothers of the Novel*, p.38.

59 Moira Ferguson, *First Feminists*, p.17.

60 For example, Richard Samuel, *The Nine Living Muses of Great Britain*, oil on canvas, *c.*1779, National Portrait Gallery, London. This canvas depicts Hannah More, Catherine Macaulay, Elizabeth Montagu, Charlotte Lennox, Angelica Kauffman, Elizabeth Carter, Anna Laetitia Barbauld, and Elizabeth Griffith.

61 A recent 'Bluestocking' study, in which the origins of the term are traced, is Sylvia Harcstark Myres, *The Bluestocking Circle* (Oxford, 1990).

62 Hester Chapone, *Letters on the Improvement of the Mind* (1775), in *The Works of Mrs Chapone* (London, 1807), vol. 3, p.86.

63 Ibid., p.169.

64 Ibid., pp. 171, 172.

65 Ibid., p.199.

66 Ibid., pp. 76-7.

67 *Analytical Review* (November, 1790).

68 Mary Wollstonecraft, quoted in Dale Spender, *Women of Ideas*, p.95.

69 Doris Stenton, *The English Woman in History* (New York, 1977), p.306.

70 W.E.H. Lecky, *The History of England in the Eighteenth Century*, vol. 3, p.256, quoted in Dale Spender, *Women of Ideas*, p.95.

71 In 1778, at the age of forty-seven, she married a man twenty-six years her junior.

72 Catherine Macaulay, *Letters on Education, with Observations on Religious and Metaphysical Subject* (1790), pp. 49-50.

73 Ibid., p.221.

74 Ibid., p.47.

75 Ibid., p.49.

76 Laetitia Matilda Hawkins, *Letters on the Female Mind, its Powers and Pursuits* (1793) in *Women in the Eighteenth Century*, ed. Vivien Jones, p.118.

77 Ibid., pp. 118-19.

78 Ibid., p.119.

79 Ibid., p.120.

80 Ibid., p.117.

81 Mary Robinson, *A Letter to the Women of England, on the Injustice of Mental Subordination* (1799) in *Women in the Eighteenth Century*, ed. Vivien Jones, p.240.

82 Ibid.

83 Ibid.

84 Ibid.

85 Ibid., pp. 241-2.

86 See Jane Spencer in Sarah Scott, *Millenium Hall* (1762; this edn.: London, 1985), Introduction.

87 Sarah Scott, *Millenium Hall*, p.64.

88 See Chapter One.

89 See Jane Spencer, *Millenium Hall*, Introduction.

90 *Monthly Review* (1890), quoted in Cheryl Turner, *Living by the Pen: Women Writers in the Eighteenth Century* (London and New York, 1992), p.31.

91 Judy Simons, *Fanny Burney* (London, 1987), p.18.

92 Ibid.

93 See Cheryl Turner, *Living by the Pen*, p.133. See also Paul Kaufman, 'The Community Library: A Chapter in English Social History', *Transactions of the American Philosophical Society* (N.S. 57, Pt.7, 1967).

94 See Cheryl Turner, *Living by the Pen*.

95 For a bibliography of women's fiction between 1696-1796 see Cheryl Turner, *Living by the Pen*, pp. 154-211.

96 Ibid., p.34.

97 Judy Simons, *Fanny Burney*, p.34.

98 Ibid.

99 Ibid., p.50.

100 Ibid., p.51.

101 Ibid., p.82.

102 Ibid., p.86.

103 Quoted in Simons, p.55.

104 See Simons, *Fanny Burney*, p.22.

105 David Douglas Devlin, *Jane Austen and Education* (London, 1975), p.1.

106 Jane Austen, *Northanger Abbey*, quoted in Devlin, *Jane Austen and Education*, p.2.

107 Jane Austen *Pride and Prejudice* (1813; this edn.: Middlesex, 1986), pp. 236-37.

108 David Devlin, *Jane Austen and Education*, p.6.

109 Elizabeth Joyce, 'Jane Austen' in *Dictionary of British Women Writers*, ed. Janet Todd, p.22.

110 Ibid., p.23.

111 Richard Simpson, *North British Review* (April, 1870), quoted in S. Evans, *Educational Trends Between 1775 and 1880 as Revealed in the Novels of Jane Austen and George Eliot* (unpublished M.Ed. thesis, University of Swansea, 1980), p.20.

112 Jane Austen, *Emma* (1816; this edn.: Oxford, 1981), p.18.

113 Ibid., p.55.

114 Ibid., p.17.

115 Jane Austen *Pride and Prejudice*, p.84.

116 Jane Austen, *Sense and Sensibility* (1811; this edn.: London, 1986), p.179.

117 Jane Austen, *Pride and Prejudice*, p.113.

118 Ibid.

119 Ibid., p.105.

120 Ibid., p.67.

121 Ibid.

122 Ibid., p.114.

123 Jane Austen, *Mansfield Park* (1814; this edn.: Middlesex, 1984), p.448.

124 Ibid.

125 See Chapter Five, *Infra*.

126 John Killham, 'Feminism at Cambridge', in Killham, *Tennyson and 'The Princess':Reflections of an Age* (University of London, 1958), pp. 67–85.

127 Carol A. Martin, 'George Eliot' in *Dictionary of British Women Writers*, ed. Janet Todd, p.217.

128 George Eliot, *Middlemarch* (1872; this edn.: London, 1920), p.161.

129 Ibid.

130 See S. Evans, *Educational Trends Between 1775 and 1880*.

131 George Eliot, *Middlemarch*, p. 205.

132 George Eliot, *The Mill on the Floss* (1860; this edn.: London, 1987), p.303.

133 George Eliot, *Daniel Deronda* (1876; this edn.: London, 1971), p.156.

134 Carol A. Martin, 'George Eliot', in *Dictionary of British Women Writers*, ed. Janet Todd, p.217.

135 Hallam, Second Baron Tennyson, *Alfred, Lord Tennyson, a Memoir*, i (London, 1897), p.248.

136 Add. MSS 6345, 6346 and 2588 (E)

585. CAM, and Sir Charles Tennyson, *Cornhill Magazine*, vol. cliii (1936) p. 673, cited in *The Poems of Tennyson* vol. 2, ed. Christopher Ricks (Essex, 1987), p.219.

137 W.Ward, *Aubrey de Vere* (1904) p.71, cited in *The Poems of Tennyson*, vol. 2, ed. Ricks, p.219.

138 Elizabeth Barret Browning to Robert Browning, in E. Kintner (ed.), *Letters* vol. 1, ed. F. Kintner (1969), p.427, cited in *The Poems of Tennyson*, ii, ed. Ricks, p.219.

139 Ibid.

140 Sir Alfred Lord Tennyson, *The Princess*, in *The Poems of Tennyson*, ii, ed. Ricks, p.226.

141 Ibid.

142 Ibid., pp. 260–61.

143 Ibid., p.261.

144 Ibid., p.245.

145 Ibid., p.241.

146 Ibid., p.250.

147 Ibid., p.253.

148 'Tennyson's Princess', *The Quarterly Review* vol. 82 (March, 1848).

149 See 'Colleges for Girls', *Englishwoman's Journal,* vol. 2, no.12 (1859), p.361, and 'An American University for Women', *Englishwoman's Journal* 12, no. 67 (1863), p.47.

150 Deborah Gorham, 'The Ideology of Femininity and Reading for Girls', in *Lessons for Life: the Schooling of Girls and Women, 1850-1950,* ed., Felicity Hunt, p.55.

151 Angela Brazil, *St. Catherine's College*, in *Omnibus of Schoolgirl Fiction*, ii (London, 1959), p.15.

152 David Rubenstein, *Before the Suffragettes: Women's Emancipation in the 1890s* (Brighton, 1986).

153 Elaine Showalter, *A Literature of their own: British Women Novelists from Brŏnte to Lessing* (London, 1982).

154 David Rubenstein, *Before the Suffragettes*, p.17.

155 *Punch* (26 May, 1894), p.252, quoted in Rubenstein, *Before the Suffragettes*, p.22.

4: ANATOMIZING FEMALE REASON

1 See Chapter One.
2 See Chapter Two.
3 Four doctors were most prominent in the debate about women's suitability for education: Clouston, Maudsley, Playfair and Thorburn. Sir Thomas Clouston, Physician-Superintendent of the Royal Edinburgh Asylum, and the first Lecturer on Mental Disease in the University of Edinburgh, published the influential *Female Education from a Medical Point of View* in 1882, and his *Clinical Lectures on Mental Disease* in 1883 (it had reached its sixth edition by 1904). Henry Maudsley, who had been medical Superintendent of Manchester Lunatic Hospital, Professor of Medical Jurisprudence at University College, London, published 'Sex in Mind and Education' (*Fortnightly Review*, 1874). W.S. Playfair, Professor of Obstetric Medicine at King's College, London, published *A Treatise on the Science and Practice of Midwifery* (1876) and, together with T.C. Allbutt, produced the key text *A System of Gynaecology* in 1896. John Thorburn, Professor of Obstetrics at Manchester, published *A Practical Treatise on the Diseases of Women* (1885), and had contributed to the female education question with 'Female Education in its Physical Aspect' in *Six Introductory Lectures* (1884). Other influential doctors include Thomas Laycock, Professor of Medicine and Lecturer on Medical Psycology and Mental Disease at Edinburgh, whose *A Treatise on the Nervous Disorders of Women* had appeared in 1840; David Tuke MD, author of *A Manual of Psychological Medicine* (1874); Edward Tilt MD, President of the Obstetrical Society of London, and author of *A Handbook of Uterine Theraputics, and of Diseases of Women* (4th edn., 1878), *On the preservation of the health of Women* (1850) and Alfred Lewis Galabin MD, Obstetric Physician and Lecturer in Midwifery and the Diseases of Women to Guy's Hospital, who wrote *Elements of Health and Principles of Female Hygiene* (1852); and the influential text *Diseases of Women* (5th edn., 1893). Other key works include, Dr Michael Ryan, *A Manual of Midwifery*, (4th edn., 1841), Dr Charles Waller, 'Lectures on the Function and Diseases of the Womb' (*Lancet*, 14 December 1839), Samuel Mason, *The Philosophy of Female Health* (1845), Walter Johnson, *The Morbid Emotions of Women* (1850), Robert Carter, *On the Influences of education and Training in preventing diseases of the Nervous System* (1855), F.C. Skey, *Hysteria* (1867), J.M. Allan, 'On the Differences in the Minds of Men and Women' (1869), Dr Robert Barnes 'Lumleian Lectures on the Convulsive Diseases of Women' (*The Lancet*, 12 April 1873), and J.C. Webster, *Puberty and the Change of Life* (1892).

4 See Pat Jalland and John Hooper, *Women from Birth to Death: The Female Life Cylce in Britain, 1830-1914* (New Jersey, 1986) p.53.
5 Jalland and Hooper, *Women from Birth to Death*, p.58.
6 Alfred Lewis Galabin MD, *Diseases of Women*, 5th edn., (London: 1893), p.473.
7 Jalland & Hooper, *Women from Birth to Death*, p.3.
8 Ibid. p.5.
9 The most controversial publication which brought this argument to the general public was Dr Henry Maudsley, 'Sex in Mind and in Education', *Fortnightly Review* 15 (1874).
10 J.M. Allan, 'On the Differences in the Minds of Men and Women', *Journal of the Anthropological Society* 7 (1869), pp. cxcvi-cxcviii, in Jalland and Hooper, *Women from Birth to Death*, p.22.
11 J.C. Webster, *Puberty and the Change of Life* (1892), pp. 28-31, in Jalland and Hooper, *Women from Birth to Death*, p.82.
12 Joan N. Burstyn, *Victorian Education and the Ideal of Womanhood* (London: 1980), p.87
13 Ian Maclean, *The Renaissance Notion of Woman*, p.41.

14 See Chapter One.

15 Thomas Laycock, *A Treatise on the Nervous Diseases of Women* (1840), pp. 140-2, in Jalland and Hooper, *Women from Birth to Death*, p.77.

16 Ibid.

17 Ibid.

18 Dr Michael Ryan, *A Manual of Midwifery*, 4th edn. (1841), p.61., in Jalland and Hooper, *Women from Birth to Death*, p.20.

19 Richard Carlile, *Every Woman's Book, or What is Love?* (1838), pp. 35-6, in Jalland and Hooper, p.32.

20 See Walter Johnson, *The Morbid Emotions of Women* (1850), E.J. Tilt, *Elements of Health and Principles of Female Hygiene* (1852), Robert Barnes, 'Lumleian Lectures on the Convulsive Diseases of Women', *The Lancet,* (12 April, 1873), all in Jalland and Hooper, *Women from Birth to Death*.

21 J.C. Webster, *Puberty and the Change of Life* (1892), pp. 28-31, in Jalland and Hooper, *Women from Birth to Death*, p.82.

22 E.J. Tilt, *Elements of Health and Principles of Female Hygiene* (1852), 175-76, in Jalland and Hooper, *Women from Birth to Death*, p.79.

23 Anne Digby, 'Women's Biological Strait-jacket', in Susan Mendes and Jane Rendall, *Sexuality and Subordination* (London, 1989), pp. 208, 209.

24 See note 3 above.

25 Henry Maudsley, 'Sex in Mind and in Education'.

26 Elizabeth Garret Anderson MD, 'Sex in Mind and Education: A Reply', *Fortnightly Review* 15 (May, 1874).

27 T.S. Clouston MD, *Female Education from a Medical Point of View* (Edinburgh, 1882), p.33..

28 Ibid., p.31.

29 Ibid., p.29.

30 Ibid., p.32.

31 Ibid., p.38.

32 Ibid.

33 Ibid., p.41.

34 Ibid., p.45.

35 Digby, 'Women's Biological Strait-jacket', in *Sexuality and Subordination,*

eds. Mendes and Rendall, p.211.

36 J. Thorburn, *A Practical Treatise on the Diseases of Women* (London, 1885), p.102.

37 *The Times,* 15 April 1880, 17 February 1881.

38 Sophie Bryant, *Overwork: From the Teacher's Point of View, with special reference to the Work in Schools for Girls,* (London, 1885), pp. 14, 15.

39 Digby, 'Women's Biological Strait-jacket', in eds. Mendes and Rendall, *Sexuality and Subordination*; Carol Dyhouse, 'Social Darwinistic ideas and the Development of women's education in England, 1880-1921', in *History of Education,* 5, no. 1 (1976), pp. 41-58.

40 Digby, 'Women's Biological Strait-jacket', in *Sexuality and Subordination,* eds. Mendes and Rendall, p.213.

41 Dyhouse, 'Social Darwinistic ideas and the Development of women's education in England, 1880-1921', p.41.

42 Ibid.

43 Havelock-Ellis, *The Task of Social Hygiene* (London, 1912), *Man and Woman* (London, 1894); E.S. Chasser, *Perfect Health for Women and Children* (London, 1912); W.C.D. Whetham and C.D. Whetham, *Heredity and Society* (London, 1912); Dr C.W. Saleeby, *Parenthood and Race Culture* (London, 1906), *Woman and Womanhood* (London, 1912), and *Evolution the Master-Key* (London, 1906).

44 Herbert Spencer, *The Principles of Biology,* II (London, 1867), pp. 485-6, quoted in Dyhouse, 'Social Darwinistic ideas and the Development of women's education in England, 1880-1921', p.43.

45 Herbert Spencer, *Education; Intellectual, Moral and Physical* (London, 1861), p.187, quoted in Dyhouse, 'Social Darwinistic ideas and the Development of women's education in England, 1880-1921', p.43.

46 Dr Whithers-Moore, Presidential Address to the Annual Meeting of the British Medical Association, reported in the *British Medical Journal,* 14 (1886), quoted in Dyhouse, 'Social Darwinistic ideas and the Development of women's edu-

cation in England, 1880-1921', p.45.

47 Digby, 'Women's Biological Strait-jacket', in *Sexuality and Subordination*, eds. Mendes and Rendall, p.214.

48 Ibid.

49 Dr E.H. Ruddock wrote: 'In no department of the healing art . . . is quackery and mismanagement more evident as in that which appertains to the ailments peculiar to women.' *The Common Diseases of Women* (6th edn., London, 1888), p.iv.

50 Isaac Barker Brown was known as one of the best Victorian surgeons, and was elected President of the Medical Society of London in 1865. He believed in the curative power of clitoridectomy, in the treatment of epilepsy and other ailments in women. His work came under severe scrutiny from members of his profession, who believed that he performed too many clitoridectomies without proven successful results, that he did so before invited visitors, and that he performed this operation without first obtaining the consent of his patients. In 1866 a debate about Barker Brown began in the *Lancet* and other medical journals, which revealed confused and differing views about female physiology and sexuality. Barker Brown was expelled from the Obstetrical Society in April 1867 as a result of having failed to obtain consent to operate from his patients, but the Society did not question the merit of the operation itself.

51 For a discussion of this see Margaret Bryant, *The Unexpected Revolution: A Study in the History of Education of Women and Girls in the Nineteenth Century* (London, 1979).

52 Patricia Hollis, *Women in Public, 1850-1950: Documents of the Victorian Women's Movement* (London, 1979), p.45.

53 Ibid., p.47.

54 M. Jeanne Peterson, 'The Victorian Governess : Status Incongruence in Family and Society', in *Suffer and Be Still: Women in the Victorian Age,* ed. M. Vicinus, (London, 1980), p.5.

55 Emily Davies, *English Woman's Journal*

(March, 1858).

56 Revd J. Stephens, 'The Importance of Female Character', in *The Female Preceptor,* vol. 1, no. 1 (London, 1813-15), p.11.

57 See Chapter One.

58 Mrs John Sandford, *Woman, in her Social and Domestic Character,* 3rd edn. (London, 1833), p.2.

59 Sara Ellis, The Daughters of England (1842), in *Women in Public,* ed. Hollis, p.15.

60 For a brief biographical sketch of Sara Stickney Ellis see Janet Todd, *Dictionary of British Women Writers* (London, 1989), pp. 221-3.

61 Ibid.

62 Barbara Bodichon, A *Brief Summary of the Laws* (1851), in *Women in Public,* ed. Hollis, p.171.

63 Ibid.

64 Thomas Gisborne, *An Enquiry into the Duties of the Female Sex* (London, 1797), pp. 12-13.

65 Ibid., p.22.

66 Ibid., p.23.

67 Ibid., p.32.

68 Ibid., p.58.

69 Ibid., p.333.

70 Revd John Bennet, *Strictures on Female Education* (London, 1787), pp. 140-2.

71 *The Cherub or Guardian of Female Innocence* (London, 1792), p.16.

72 Revd John Bennet, *Strictures on Female Education,* p.142.

73 *Quarterly Review* (1869), p.464.

74 Henry Maudsley, 'Sex in Mind and in Education'.

75 Thomas Gisborne, *An Enquiry into the Duties of the Female Sex,* p.22.

76 Ibid., pp.12, 13.

77 Mary Poovey, *The Proper Lady and the Woman Writer* (London & Chicago, 1984), p.9.

78 Asa Briggs, *The Age of Improvement, 1783-1867* (London, 1979), p.73.

79 Deborah Gorham, 'The Ideology of Femininity and Reading for Girls, 1850-1914)' in *Lessons for Life,* ed. Hunt, p.46.

80 See Raftery, 'Educational Ideologies and Reading for Girls, 1815-1915', *History of Education Bulletin* (1997).

81 See Mary Cadogan and Patricia Craig, *You're a Brick, Angela!,: A New Look at Girls' Fiction, 1839-1975* (London, 1976), p.45.

82 *The Female Preceptor*, 1, no. 7 (1813-15), p. 219.

83 J. Burgeon, *Sermon* (1884) in *Women in Public*, ed. Hollis, p.8.

84 Mr. Bouverie, speaking on the Women's Disabilities Bill, House of Commons *Hansard*, 3 May 1871.

85 *The Ladies Penny Gazette*, 1, no. 1 (London, 1832), pp.5,6.

86 Judith Rowbotham, *Good Girls Make Good Wives: Guidance for Girls in Victorian Fiction* (Oxford, 1989), p.6.

87 Ibid.

88 See Edward J. Bristow, *Vice and Vigilance: Purity Movements in Britain Since 1700* (Dublin, 1977).

89 Phillipa Levine, *Feminist Lives in Victorian England* (Oxford, 1990), p.87.

90 The Contagious Diseases Acts were introduced quietly into garrison towns in England in 1864. They allowed that an alleged prostitute could be held for medical examination and, if infected with a venereal disease, treated in hospital. If she refused she was liable to imprisonment. Led by Mrs. Josephine Butler, a body of opposition challenged the Acts.

91 F.K Prochaska, 'Philanthropy', in *The Cambridge Social History of Britain, 1750-1950*, vol 3, ed. F.M.L. Thompson (Cambridge, 1990), p. 358.

92 Ibid., p.359.

93 Hollis, *Women in Public*, p.223.

94 See for example Michael Anderson, 'Marriage Patterns in Victorian Britain: An Analysis Based on Registration District Data for England and Wales, 1861' in *Journal of Family History* 1 (1976) pp.55-79; J.A. Banks, *Prosperity and Parenthood: A Study in Family Planning among the Victorian Middle Classes* (London, 1954); Angus McLaren, 'Abortion in England, 1890-1914' in *Victorian Studies* 20 (1977), pp. 379-400, and Ann Oakley, 'Wise Women and Medicine Men: Changes in the Management of Childbirth' in *The Rights and Wrongs of Women*, eds. Juliet Mitchell and Ann Oakley (Harmondsworth, 1976).

95 Eliza Linn Linton, 'Womanliness' from *The Girl of the Period* (1883), in *Women in Public*, ed. Hollis, p.20.

96 Ibid.

97 See for example 'Queen Bees or Working Bees', *Saturday Review* (12 November 1859) which argued that 'Married life is woman's profession . . . , by not getting a husband . . . she has failed in business.'

98 W.R. Gregg, 'Why are women redundant?', *National Review* (April, 1862), in Patricia Hollis, *Women in Public*, p.12.

99 Elizabeth Garret Anderson MD, 'Sex in Mind and Education: A Reply', *Fortnightly Review*, vol. 15 (May, 1874).

100 Henry Maudsley, 'Sex in Mind and in Education', *Fortnightly Review* 15 (1874).

101 Grant Allen, 'Plain Words on the Woman Question', *Fortnightly Review* (October, 1889), in *Women in Public*, ed. Hollis, p.28.

102 Ibid.

103 Ibid., p.29.

104 See Dale Spender's biographical sketch of Eliza Linn Linton in Todd, *Dictionary of British Women Writers*, pp. 422-5.

105 Eliza Linn Linton, 'Womanliness' from *The Girl of the Period* (1868), in *Women in Public*, ed. Hollis, p.20.

106 Eliza Linn Linton, *Ourselves. A Series of Essays on Women* (London & New York, 1869), p.42.

107 Ibid.

108 Ibid.

109 Thomas Gisborne, *An Enquiry into the Duties of the Female Sex*, p.20.

110 Ibid.

111 *Punch* (n.d.) quoted in Delamont and Duffin, *The Nineteenth Century Women: Her Cultural and Physical World* (London, 1978), p.121.

112 Allen, 'Plain Words on the Woman Question', *Fortnightly Review* (1889) in *Women in Public*, ed. Hollis, pp. 29-30.

113 Ibid., p.30.

114 Linton, *Ourselves. A Series of Essays on Women*, p.41.
115 Linton, 'Womanliness', in *Women in Public,* ed. Hollis, p.234.
116 Revd Benjamin Parson, *The Mental and Moral Dignity of Woman* (London: 1842), p.4.
117 *Quarterly Review* (1869), p.465.
118 Beatrice Webb, Diary (8 March 1889), in *Women in Public,* ed. Hollis, p.21.
119 Ibid.
120 *Quarterly Review* (1869), p.465.
121 Bryant, *The Unexpected Revolution*, p. 59.
122 Richard D. Altick, *The Common Reader: A Social History of the Mass Reading Public, 1800-1900* (Chicago, 1957).
123 Ibid., p.83.
124 Ibid., p.99.
125 Ibid., p.85.
126 Alvar Ellegard, 'The Readership of the Periodical Press in Mid-Victorian Britain', *Göteborgs Universiets Årsskrift* 33 (1957), pp. 1-40.
127 Ibid.,p.1.
128 Ibid., p.6.
129 Ibid., p.8.
130 Ibid., p.30.
131 *Christian Observer* 38 (1832).
132 *Christian Observer* 65 (1966), p. 94.
133 For a list of articles on women in these publications see E.M. Palmegiano, *Women and British Periodicals, 1832-1867: A Bibliography* (London, 1989).
134 Ellegard, 'The Readership of the Periodical Press in Mid-Victorian Britain', p.28.
135 Sir Walter Scott, *Life*, vol.3, p.142 (letter to George Ellis, November 2, 1808), quoted in *The Wellesley Index to Victorian Periodicals*, pp. 696-7.
136 *The Wellesley Index*, pp. 697, 698.
137 Ellegard, 'The Readership of the Periodical Press in Mid-Victorian Britain', p.28.
138 Elizabeth Eastlake, 'The Englishwoman at School', *Quarterly Review* 146 (1878).
139 'Queen's College', *Quarterly Review* 86 (1850).
140 See Todd, *Dictionary of British Women Writers*, pp.201-202.
141 James Davies, 'Female Education', *Quarterly Review* 119 (1866), pp. 510-11.
142 Ibid., p.510.
143 Ibid.
144 Ibid.
145 Ibid., p.513.
146 Ibid., p.509
147 Montagu Burrows, 'Female Education', *Quarterly Review* 126 (1869).
148 Ibid., p.456.
149 Ibid., p.472
150 Ibid.
151 Ibid.
152 Ibid., pp. 472-3.
153 Ibid., p.474.
154 T.H. Lister, 'The Rights and Conditions of Women', *Edinburgh Review* 73 (1841).
155 *Wellesley Index*, p.421.
156 Ellegard, 'The Readership of the Periodical Press in Mid-Victorian Britain', p.27.
157 T.H.Lister, 'The Rights and Conditions of Women', *Edinburgh Review* 73 (1841), p.193.
158 Harriet Martineau, 'Female Industry', *Edinburgh Review* 109 (1859).
159 T.H. Lister, 'The Rights and Conditions of Women', *Edinburgh Review* 73 (1841), p.189.
160 Ibid., p.189.
161 Ibid., pp. 190-1.
162 Ibid.
163 Martineau, 'Female Industry.'
164 'Lectures to Ladies on Practical Subjects' (unsigned), *Edinburgh Review*, 103 (1856).
165 Ibid., p.149.
166 See *The Wellesley Index,* p.210.
167 Ellegard, 'The Readership of the Periodical Press in Mid-Victorian Britain', p.27.
168 Thomas Markby, 'The Education of Women', *Contemporary Review* 1 (1866).
169 Ibid., p.396.
170 Ibid.
171 Ibid., pp. 397, 399.
172 Ibid., p.400.
173 Ibid., p.401.

174 Ibid., p.403.

175 Ibid., p.404.

176 Thomas Markby, 'On the Education of Women', *Contemporary Review* 7 (1868).

177 Ibid., 242.

178 Ibid., pp. 242-3.

179 Ibid., p.245.

180 Ibid., p.261.

181 Emily Davies, 'Some account of a proposed new College for Women', *Contemporary Review* 10 (1869), and this edition reprinted in Emily Davies, *Questions Relating to Women* (London: 1910).

182 Royal Commission to Inquire into Education in Schools in England and Wales, 1864-1866. The Reports of the S I C. (Taunton) were gradually issued in 1867-68. The Reports of the findings on girls' education appear in Volume V: Minutes of Evidence, Pt. II [3966 - IV].

183 Emily Davies, 'Some account of a proposed new College for Women', p.88.

184 Ibid., p.90.

185 Ibid., p.98.

186 Ibid., p.101.

187 Ellegard, 'The Readership of the Periodical Press in Mid-Victorian Britain', p.33.

188 Omega, 'Men and Women: A brief hypothesis concerning the difference in their genius', *Blackwood's* 16 (1824); Jasper Sussex (pseud.) 'Letter to Mrs M. on the equality of the Sexes', *Blackwood's* 20 (1826); John Wilson 'Characteristics of Women', (Parts I - IV) *Blackwood's* vols. 33-34 (1833).

189 Margaret Oliphant, 'The Laws Concerning Women', *Blackwood's* 79 (1856); Margaret Oliphant, 'The Condition of Women', *Blackwood's* 83 (1858).

190 Emily Davies, 'The Influence of University Degrees on the education of women', *Victoria Magazine* (1863) and this edition reprinted in Davies, *Questions Relating to Women*.

191 Ibid., pp. 48-9.

192 Ibid., p.51.

193 Ibid., p.59.

194 Maudsley, 'Sex in Mind and in Education'.

195 Ibid., p.466.

196 Ibid., p.467.

197 Ibid., p.468.

198 Ibid., p.473.

199 Ibid.

200 Elizabeth Garret Anderson, 'Sex in Mind and Education: A Reply'.

201 Ibid., p.582.

202 Ibid.

203 Ibid., pp. 584, 594.

204 For a history of the Girls' Public Day School Company (later Trust) see Gillian Avery, *The Best Type of Girl: A History of Girls' Independent Schools* (London, 1992).

205 Emily Davies, in 'Higher Education in connexion with the Universities', *Journal of the Women's Education Union* 2, no. 14 (1874), p.27.

206 Ibid.

207 Ibid.

208 Ibid.

209 Ibid. pp. 27, 28.

210 Ibid., p.28.

211 Ibid.

212 'University Degrees for Women', *Journal of the Women's Education Union* 2 (1874), p.82.

213 'Oxford and the Higher Education of Women', *Journal of the Women's Education Union* 7 (1879), pp. 53-5.

214 'Thirty Years Progress in Women's Education', *Journal of the Women's Education Union* 7 (1879), pp. 119-20.

215 See for example Hollis, *Women in Public*; Rita McWilliams Tullberg, *Women at Cambridge* (London, 1975); Barbara Stephen, *Emily Davies and Girton College* (London, 1927); Jennifer Uglow, 'Josephine Butler: From Sympathy to Theory', in *Feminist Theorists*, ed. Dale Spender; S.R. Herstein, *A Mid-Victorian Feminist, Barbara Leigh Smith Bodichon* (New Haven and London, 1985), and Ray Strachey, *Millicent Garrett Fawcett*. For a biographical study of Cobbe see Deirdre Raftery, 'Frances Power Cobbe' in *Women, Power and Consciousness in Nineteenth Century Ireland*, eds. Mary Cullen and

Maria Luddy (Dublin, 1995).

216 Emily Davies founded the College for Women at Hitchin in 1869 and it transferred to Girton, Cambridge, in 1873. The first three 'Girton Pioneers' took Tripos in 1873 by private arrangements with the examiners. In 1881 women were admitted to Cambridge University undergraduate examinations on the same terms as men. They did not become full members of the University until 1945.

217 Janet Horrowitz and Myra Stark, *The Englishwoman's Review: An Index* (New York, 1980), Introduction.

218 Ibid.

219 Ibid.

220 Ibid.

221 Elizabeth Blackwell, 'Letters to Young Ladies Desirous of Studying Medicine', *English Woman's Journal* (February,1860). This edition reprinted in *Barbara Leigh Smith and the Langham Place Group,* ed. Candida Ann Lacey (New York and London, 1987), p.456.

222 Elizabeth Blackwell, 'Medicine as a Profession for Women', *English Women's Journal* (May, 1860). This edition in *Barbara Leigh Smith and the Langham Place Group,* ed. Lacey, p.472.

223 'Female Education in the Middle Classes', *English Woman's Journal* (June, 1858), pp. 217-27.

224 Ibid., p.219.

225 Ibid., p.220.

226 Ibid.

227 Ibid., p.223.

228 'Why boys are cleverer than girls', *English Woman's Journal* (October, 1858), pp. 116-18.

229 'Are men naturally cleverer than women?', *English Woman's Journal* (January, 1859), pp. 333-6.

230 Ibid., p.334.

231 Ibid., p.335.

232 'Colleges for Girls', *English Woman's Journal* (February 1859), pp. 361-374.

233 Ibid., pp. 364-5.

234 Ibid, p.365.

235 Ibid.

236 Ibid., p.372.

237 Ibid.

238 Bessie Rayner Parkes, 'The Market for Educated Female Labour', *English Woman's Journal* (November, 1859) in *Barbara Leigh Smith and the Langham Place Group,* ed. Lacey, p.143.

239 Ibid.

240 Bessie Rayner Parkes, 'What Can Edu-cated Women Do?' (Part I), *English Woman's Journal* (December, 1859), in *Barbara Leigh Smith and the Langham Place Group,* ed. Lacey, p.157.

241 Ibid.

242 Isa Craig, 'Insanity its Cause and Cure', *English Woman's Journal* (September 1859) in *Barbara Leigh Smith and the Langham Place Group,* ed. Lacey, pp. 317-18.

243 See *The English Women's Journal* (October 1862), p.123; *The English Woman's Journal* (December, 1862), p.286; and *The English Woman's Journal* (January 1863), p.325. See also Stephen, *Emily Davies and Girton College,* pp. 73-4.

244 'The University of London and the Graduation of Women', *English Woman's Review* (June 1863), p.270.

245 Ibid., p.271.

246 Ibid., p.274.

247 For details of the Local Examinations Board see Stephens, *Emily Davies and Girton College,* p.83.

248 'The University of Cambridge and the Education of Women', *The English Woman's Journal* (December, 1863), pp. 277-80.

249 Ibid., p.278.

250 See Horrowitz and Stark, *The Englishwoman's Review: An Index,* Introduction.

5: 'BRINGING THE DREAM DOWN FROM THE CLOUDS'

1 See June Purvis, *A History of Women's Education in England* (Milton Keynes, 1991), p.96.

2 Ibid., p.97.

3 The Sheffield Literary and Philosophi-

cal Society admitted women from its inception in 1823 if they were of the family relations of full members (see Purvis, *A History of Women's Education in England*, p.97).

4 Purvis, *A History of Women's Education in England*, p.100.

5 Ibid.

6 Ibid., p.102.

7 The National Society for promoting the education of the poor in the principles of the Established Church.

8 See Elaine Kaye, *A History of Queen's College London, 1848-1972* (London, 1972), p.16.

9 Frances Mary Buss to Dorothea Beale (1889), quoted in Elizabeth Raikes, *Dorothea Beale of Cheltenham* (London, 1898), p.25.

10 R.C. Trench, Preface to *Lectures on Mediaeval Church History* (1877), quoted in Kaye, *Queen's College London*, p. 55.

11 Frederick Denison Maurice, 'Female Education', *Metropolitan Quarterly Magazine* 2 (November 1825), pp. 265-82, quoted in Kaye, *Queen's College London*, pp. 23-4.

12 Revd Frederick Denison Maurice, 'Queen's College, London: its objects and methods.' Lecture delivered in the Hanover Square Rooms on Wednesday, 29 March, 1848 (London, 1848), p.1.

13 Ibid., p.5.

14 Ibid., p.8

15 Ibid.

16 Ibid., p.17.

17 Ibid., p.10.

18 Kaye, *Queen's College London*, p.52.

19 Ibid.

20 Quoted in Raikes, *Dorothea Beale of Cheltenham*, p.27.

21 *Quarterly Review* 86 (March, 1850), pp. 364-82.

22 F.D. Maurice, MS letter in the possession of Queen's College, and quoted by Kaye, *A History of Queen's College London*, p.72.

23 See Anne V. O'Connor and Susan M. Parkes, *Gladly Learn and Gladly Teach: A History of Alexandra College and School, Dublin* (Dublin, 1983), p.8.

24 Dorothea Beale, 'Recollections of the Early Years of Queen's College', p.38.

25 Frances Buss to Dorothea Beale, L n.d, n.p., quoted in Kaye, *Queen's College London*, p.81, no source.

26 See Kaye, *Queen's College London*, p.82.

27 Report of the Committee of Education Meeting, 17 November 1863, Queen's College, London, quoted in Kaye, *Queen's College London*, p.83.

28 Emily Davies to Dr Plumptre, L September 1866, quoted in AMsS Family Chronicle, f. 489, Davies Papers, Girton College, Cambridge.

29 Ibid.

30 Emily Davies, AMsS Family Chronicle, quoted in Kaye, *Queen's College London*, p.85.

31 Kaye, *Queen's College London*, p.58.

32 Report of a Governesses' Benevolent Institution Committee Meeting, 1849, cited in Kaye, *Queen's College London*, p.58.

33 John de Soyres won the Hulsean Prize while at Cambridge, and upon graduation came to Queen's College to lecture on the History of the French reformed Church 1659-1685. He was considered by his students to be an inspiring teacher. He was particularly encouraging to Gertrude Bell, one of the most brilliant students Queen's ever had, who went on to read history at Lady Margaret Hall, Oxford, where she gained an excellent first.

34 Emily Davies to Barbara Bodichon, 1874, n.p., quoted in Kaye, *Queen's College London*, p.107.

35 Queen's College Annual Report, 1882, cited in Kaye, *Queen's College London*, p.115.

36 Elizabeth Jesser Reid to Eliza Bostock and Jane Martineau, 1860, n.p., quoted in Margaret J. Tuke, *A History of Bedford College for Women, 1860-1937* (London, 1939), p.3.

37 Tuke, *A History of Bedford College for Women*, p.62.

38 Elizabeth Jesser Reid to Eliza Bostock and Jane Martineau, 1860, n.p., quoted in Tuke, *A History of Bedford College for Women*, p.21.

39 'Statement Respecting the Ladies' College, Bedford Square' (1852), quoted in Tuke, *A History of Bedford College for Women*, p.21.

40 Francis William Newman was the Honorary Secretary to the first Council and Board at Bedford College, as well as the Professor of Ancient History and of mental and Moral Science together with Political Economy. He ended his association with Bedford in 1851, following a controversy about the manner used to appoint teaching staff when trying to maintain the non-sectarian character of the College. See Linna Bentley, *Educating Women: A Pictorial History of Bedford College, University of London, 1849-1985* (London, 1991), p.5.

41 Tuke, *A History of Bedford College for Women*, p.99.

42 Ibid., p.111.

43 Emily Davies, AMsS Family Chronicle, Davies Papers, Girton College.

44 Emily Davies, AMsS Family Chronicle, Davies Papers, Girton College, quoted in Stephen, *Emily Davies and Girton College*, p.24.

45 Emily Davies, AMsS Family Chronicle, Davies Papers, Girton College Archives, quoted in Stephen, *Emily Davies and Girton College*, p.25.

46 Emily Davies, AMsS Family Chronicle, p.159, Davies Papers, Girton College.

47 Annie and Barbara Leigh Smith were the daughters of Benjamin Leigh Smith and Anne Longdon. They were firstly known in society as the illegitimate cousins of Florence Nightingale, but Barbara came to prominence in her own right through her association with the Langham Place circle. A co-founder and some-time editor of the *English Woman's Journal*, she also toured Europe, was a successful painter, and initiated the married women's property rights campaign. In 1857 she married a Frenchman, Eugene Bodichon, and thereafter divided her time between their home in Algiers, and London where she her was at the centre of the activities of the Langham Place circle. Her country house at Scalands was a popular retreat for her friends and for early Girton students.

48 For details of the Langham Place circle, see Chapter Four.

49 Bessie Rayner Parkes (1829-1925) was the daughter of Joseph Parkes of Birmingham, an active politician with Whig and Radical sympathies. She co-founded the *English Woman's Journal* with Barbara Bodichon, and was an active member of the Langham Place circle. She married M. Belloc in 1868. Her son was Hillaire Belloc, the poet. Parkes published a number of books, including *Essays on Women's Work* (1865).

50 Jessie Merton White (1832-1906) applied in 1856 to all the London hospitals (14 in number) for leave to enter as a medical student. She was refused by every hospital, and was also refused leave to take the examinations of the University of London. She later became a news correspondent in Genoa.

51 Davies Papers, Girton College Archives.

52 For a detailed discussion of this see Stephen, *Emily Davies and Girton College*.

53 See McWilliams Tullberg, *Women at Cambridge*.

54 Elizabeth Garrett to Emily Davies, 12 April 1861, in AMsS Family Chronicle, quoted in Stephen, *Emily Davies and Girton College*, p.6.

55 Elizabeth Garrett to Emily Davies, 17 August 1860, in AMsS Family Chronicle, quoted in Stephen, *Emily Davies and Girton College*, p.58.

56 Elizabeth Garrett to Emily Davies, n.p., n.d., quoted in Stephen, *Emily Davies and Girton College*, p.59.

57 Elizabeth Garrett to Emily Davies, 5 September 1860, in AMsS Family Chronicle, quoted in Stephen, *Emily Davies and Girton College* p.59.

58 Emily Davies, 'Female Physicians', *English Woman's Journal*, 1861; 'Medicine as a Profession for Women', (N.A.P.S.S., 1862) published in Emily Davies, *Questions Relating to Women* (1910).

59 Jessie Merton White to Barbara Leigh Smith, L 3 March 1857, in Lacey, *Barbara Leigh Smith and the Langham Place Group*, pp. 68-9.

60 Emily Davies, AMsS Family Chronicle, p.251, Davies Papers, Girton College.

61 Bodichon Papers, Girton College.

62 Emily Davies to Barbara Bodichon, ALS 1862, Bodichon Papers, B301, Girton College.

63 Ibid.

64 Ibid.

65 Mary Somerville to Emily Davies, L 1862, in AMsS Family Chronicle, p. 254a, Davies Papers, Girton College.

66 See *English Woman's Journal*, October 1862, p. 123; December 1862, p. 286; January 1863, p. 325. See also Stephen, *Emily Davies and Girton College*, pp. 73-4.

67 Appeal to the University of London not to Exclude Women (1862), Davies Papers, ED3/24, Girton College.

68 Ibid.

69 Ibid.

70 See Davies Papers, Box III, Girton College.

71 For examples, see Sophia Clapton to Emily Davies, ALS 30 August 1862, Davies Papers, ED3/5, Girton College.

72 Flysheet on the Diploma of Doctor of Medicine (July, 1862), Davies Papers, ED3/3a, Girton College.

73 Russell Gurney (1804-1978) Q.C., Recorder of London 1857-1878, Conservative M.P. for Southampton 1865-1878, took charge of the Married Women's Property Bill in the House of Commons in 1870. He was a committed supporter of higher education for women.

74 Published by Emily Faithful as 'Female Education and how it would be affected by University Examinations' (1862).

75 Transactions of the National Association for the Promotion of Social Science (1862), p.339, Girton College Archives. See also Emily Davies, 'Family Chronicle, 1905' AMsS pp.259-261, Girton College.

76 For details of the Local Examinations Board see Stephen, *Emily Davies and*

Girton College, p.83.

77 Emily Davies to Anna Richardson, ALS July 1862, Davies Papers, ED VII/LOC 7, Girton College.

78 Ibid.

79 John Griffiths to Emily Davies, L 19 July 1862, in AMsS Family Chronicle, p.266, Davies Papers, Girton College.

80 Lady Louisa Goldsmid (1835-1909), was the wife of Sir Francis Goldsmid, the first Jew to become a member of the House of Commons. The Goldsmids had wide philanthropic interests, and they supported the movements for the education and enfranchisement of women. Lady Goldsmid was among the first Members of Girton College, to which she gave a number of generous benefactions.

81 Minutes of the first meeting of the University Examinations Committee, 23 October 1862, in AMsS Family Chronicle, p.270, Davies Papers Girton College.

82 Emily Davies to Anna Richardson, ALS 26 October 1863, Davies Papers, ED VII/LOC 48, Girton College.

83 Cambridge Local Examinations, *Report of an Examination of Girls, held in Connexion with the Local Examinations of the University of Cambridge in 1863* (London, 1863).

84 Octavia Hill to Emily Davies, L 18 February 1864, in AMsS Family Chronicle, p. 339, Davies Papers, Girton College.

85 Emily Davies, 'Women in the Universities of England and Scotland' (1896), re-printed in Davies, *Questions Relating to Women* (1910), p.166.

86 Ibid.

87 Emily Davies, 'On Secondary Education as Relating to Girls' (N.A.P.S.S., 1864), re-printed in Davies, *Questions Relating to Women*, p.63.

88 Henry J. Roby to E.A. Bostock, L 28 February 1865, Davies Papers, Girton College.

89 Ibid.

90 Dorothy Beale, Introduction, *Reports Issued by the Schools Inquiry Commission on the Education of Girls* (1869),

Blackburn Collection, Girton College.
91 Ibid.
92 Ibid., p.1.
93 Ibid., p.2.
94 Ibid.
95 Ibid.,p.3.
96 Ibid., p.6.
97 Ibid.
98 Ibid., p.18.
99 Emily Davies, *The Application of Funds to the Education of Girls* (London, 1865).
100 Ibid., p.4.
101 Ibid., p.8.
102 Ibid., p.9.
103 Emily Davies to R.H. Hutton, AL 2 June 1866, in AMsS Family Chronicle, pp. 461-4, Davies Papers, Girton College.
104 R.H. Hutton to Emily Davies, L June 1866, in AMsS Family Chronicle, pp. 461-4, Davies Papers, Girton College.
105 Emily Davies to R.H.Hutton, AL June 1866, in AMsS Family Chronicle, 1905, AMsS p. 472, Davies Papers, Girton College.
106 See Janet Howarth, ed., Introduction to Emily Davies, *The Higher Education of Women* (London, 1988).
107 Ibid., p.xxxv.
108 Ibid., p.7.
109 Ibid., p.8.
110 Ibid., p.10.
111 Ibid., p.12.
112 Ibid.
113 Ibid., pp. 30-1.
114 Emily Davies, AMsS Family Chronicle, p.500, Davies Papers, Girton College.
115 Ibid.
116 Ibid.
117 Helen Taylor Mill to Emily Davies, ALS 26 October 1866, Davies Papers, EDXVII, Girton College.
118 H.J. Roby to Emily Davies, L 27 February 1867, in AMsS Family Chronicle, p.516, Davies Papers, Girton College.
119 Emily Davies to Barbara Bodichon, ALS 29 January 1867, Bodichon Papers, B5, Girton College.
120 Emily Davies to Barbara Bodichon,

ALS 6 April, 1867, Bodichon Papers, B8, Girton College.
121 Emily Davies to Barbara Bodichon, ALS 3 June, 1867, Bodichon Papers, Girton College.
122 George Eliot to Emily Davies, ALS 16 November 1867, Davies Papers, BOX III, ED5/1, Girton College.
123 George Eliot to Emily Davies, ALS 16 November 1867, Davies Papers, BOX III, ED5/2, Girton College.
124 Emily Davies to Barbara Bodichon, ALS 29 January 1867, Bodichon Papers, B5, Girton College.
125 Minutes of the first meeting of the College Committee, AMs 5 December 1867, Bodichon Papers, B323, Girton College.
126 Ibid.
127 Ibid.
128 See Stephen, *Emily Davies and Girton College*, p.167.
129 Charlotte Yonge to Emily Davies, L 22 July 1868, in AMsS Family Chronicle, pp. 622-3, Davies Papers, Girton College.
130 Reprinted in Emily Davies, *Thoughts on Some Questions Relating to Women*.
131 Emily Davies, 'Some Account of a Proposed New College for Women', quoted in Stephen, *Emily Davies and Girton College*, p.175.
132 See Stephen, *Emily Davies and Girton College*, p.178.
133 Emily Davies to Barbara Bodichon, AL September 1868, Bodichon Papers, Box I, B 15, Girton College.
134 Emily Davies to Anna Richardson, AL 21 February 1868, in AMsS Family Chronicle p. 579, Girton College.
135 Emily Davies to Anna Richardson, AL 23 March 1868, in AMsS Family Chronicle, p 594, Girton College.
136 See Stephen, *Emily Davies and Girton College*, p.192.
137 Emily Davies to Mr. Tompkinson, ALS 6 January 1869, ED Box XVII-GC1/7, Girton College.
138 See Stephen, *Emily Davies and Girton College*, p.196.
139 Emily Davies to Miss Manning, L 2 June 1869, n.p., quoted in Barbara

Stephen, *Emily Davies and Girton College,* p.199.

140 For Miss Gibson's recollections of the College for Women, Hitchin, see Stephen, *Emily Davies and Girton College,* pp. 214-221. See also L.I. Lumsden, 'The Ancient History of Girton College', *The Girton Review* (Michaelmas Term, 1907).

141 See C.L. Maynard, *Between College Terms* (London, 1910), and for Jane Frances Dove's recollections see Barbara Stephen, *Emily Davies and Girton College,* pp. 223, 224.

142 Constance Maynard to Lady Barbara Stephen, ALS 3 March 1925, MS Lady Barbara Stephen, Girton College.

143 Ibid.

144 Llewelyn Davies, 'A New College for Women', *Macmillan's Magazine* (June, 1868).

145 Emily Davies to Barbara Bodichon, ALS 4 June 1869, Bodichon Papers, B25, Girton College.

146 See L.I. Lumsden, 'The Ancient History of Girton College', *The Girton Review* (Michaelmas Term, 1907).

147 Communicated by Emily Gibson to Barbara Stephen, 1925, and quoted in Stephen, *Emily Davies and Girton College,* p.221.

148 Jane Frances Dove, n.d., n.p., quoted in Barbara Stephen, *Emily Davies and Girton College,* p.226.

149 Constance Maynard to Lady Barbara Stephen, ALS 3 March 1925, MS Lady Barbara Stephen, Girton College.

150 Anna Lloyd to Emily Davies, ALS 26 February 1869, Davies Papers, ED XVII, 1/3b, Girton College.

151 Louisa Lumsden to Emily Davies, ALS 28 February 1869, Davies Papers, ED XVII, 5/14, Girton College.

152 Lydia Woodhouse to Emily Davies, ALS 4 March 1870, Davies Papers, ED XVII, 5/15, Girton College.

153 Emily Gibson to Emily Davies, ALS 6 March 1870, Davies Papers, ED XVII, 5/16, Girton College.

154 Emily Davies to Barbara Bodichon, ALS 29 January 1867, Bodichon Papers, B5, Girton College.

155 Ibid.

156 Alfred Waterhouse was born in Liverpool in 1830 of Quaker parents. He trained in Manchester, and won the competition to build the Manchester Assize Courts in 1859. This brought him considerable fame, and he set up a prosperous business in London in 1865. Among his most important commissions were extensions to Balliol College, Oxford, and to Gonville and Caius, Trinity Hall, Jesus College and Pembroke College, Cambridge.

157 See Prudence Waterhouse, *A Victorian Monument: The Buildings of Girton College* (Cambridge, 1990).

158 See Waterhouse, *The Buildings of Girton College,* p. 8.

159 'Girton College'. Leaflet, 1873. Davies Papers, Ed XVIII, 10/18, Girton College.

160 Ibid.

161 See for example, *Life at Girton College by a Girton Student* (London: 1882) and 'Some Experiences of a Girton Graduate', *The Lady* (19 February, 1885), and reprinted in *The Lady* (21 February, 1985). For a description of Girton in the early twentieth century see A. Cunningham, 'A Day of my Life at Girton', *The Empire Annual for Girls* (London, 1910).

162 Emily Davies to Barbara Bodichon, ALS 12 June 1874, Davies Papers, ED XVII, 11/1b, Girton College.

163 See M.C. Bradbrook, *That Infidel Place: A Short History of Girton College, 1869-1969* (London, 1969); Barbara Stephen, *Girton College, 1869-1932* (Cambridge, 1932); McWilliams Tullberg, *Women at Cambridge,* Daphne Bennett, *Emily Davies and the Liberation of Women* (London, 1990), and Purvis, *A History of Women's Education in England.*

164 Emily Davies, 'Higher Education in Connexion with the Universities', *Journal of the Women's Education Union* 2, no.14 (15 February, 1874), p.28.

165 Ibid., p.27.

Bibliography

MANUSCRIPT MATERIAL

Bodleian Library, Oxford
  Somerville Papers
  Ballard Papers
  MS Malone 17

British Library, London
  Hannah More Papers

Girton College, Cambridge
  Bodichon Papers
  Davies Papers
  Parkes Papers
  MS Lady Barbara Stephen
  Girton College Official Records

Huntington Library, San Marino, Calif.
  Cobbe Papers

Schlesinger Library, Harvard
  Agassiz Papers

PARLIAMENTARY PAPERS

Royal Commission to Inquire into Education in Schools in England and Wales (Taunton),
  H.C, 1864–68, vols. I–XXI [3966] XXVIII.

NON-FICTION PRINT SOURCES PUBLISHED BEFORE 1900

Pamphlets, tracts and essays

Bulbring, Karl Daniel, *Mary Astell*, London: 1897.
Case, Thomas, *A brief history of the proposal to admit women to degrees at Cambridge, in 1887-8*, Oxford: 1896,
Davies, Emily, *Women in the Universities of England and Scotland*, Cambridge: 1896.
Fénélon, François de Salignac, *Treatise on the Education of Daughters* (1687). In *Women in the Eighteenth Century*, ed. Vivien Jones, London: Routledge, 1990.

Gosson, Stephen, *Pleasant Quippes for Upstart, Newfangled Gentlewomen*, London: 1595.
Gosynhill, Edward, *The Scholehouse of Women* (1541). In *Half Humankind: Contexts and Texts of the Controversy about Women in England, 1540-1640*, eds. Katherine Usher Henderson and Barbara F, McManus, Urbana and Chicago: University of Illinois, 1985.
—*Mulierum Paean* (1542). In *Half Humankind: Contexts and Texts of the Controversy about Women in England, 1540-1640*, eds. Katherine Usher Henderson and Barbara F. McManus.
Hic Mulier (1620), and *Haec Vir* (1620). In *Half Humankind: Contexts and Texts of the Controversy about Women in England, 1540-1640*, eds. Katherine Usher Henderson and Barbara F, McManus.

Text books, advice books and conduct literature

Algarotti, Francesco, *The Philosophy of Sir Isaac Newton Explained. In Six Dialogues on Light and Colours, Between a Lady and the Author*, Glasgow: 1735.
Allestree, Richard, *The Ladies' Calling*, Oxford: 1673.
Angleica's Ladies' Library, London: 1794.
Ascham, Roger, *The Schoolemaster*, London:1589.
Bennet, John, *Strictures on Female Education*, London: 1787,
The Cherub or Guardian of Female Innocence, London: 1792.
Coote, Edmund, *The English School Master*, London: 1596.
Cresswick, Mr, *The Female Reader*, London: J. Johnson, London: 1789,
The Female Instructor, or Young Woman's Companion: being a Guide to all the Accomplishments which adorn the Female Character, Liverpool: 1815.
Fordyce, James, *Sermons to Young Women*, London: 1765.
Gisborne, Thomas, *An Enquiry into the Duties of the Female Sex*, London: 1797.
Gregory, John, *A Father's Legacy to his Daughters*, London: 1790.
Harris, John, *Astronomical Dialogues Between a Gentleman and a Lady*, London: 1719.
Marcet, Jane, *Conversations on Chemistry*, 2 vols., London: 1805.
The Ladies' Cabinet, Enlarged and Opened. London: 1655.
The Ladies' Dictionary, London: 1694.
The Ladies' Dispensatory: or, Every Woman her own Physician, London: 1739.
The Ladies's Library, 3 vols. London: 1714.
The Ladies' Physical Directory, London: 1742.
The Ladies' Pocket Book of Etiquette, London: 1838.
The Ladies' Preceptor, London :1768.
More, Hannah, *Thoughts on the Cultivation of the Heart and Temper in the Education of Daughters*. In *The Works of Hannah More*, vol, 6, London: 1833,
—*Essays on Various Subjects, Principally Designed for Young Ladies* (1777). In *The Works of Hannah More*, vol, 6, London: 1833.
Pennington, Lady, *An Unfortunate Mother's Advice to her Absent Daughters*, London: 1790.
Reeve, Clara, *Plans of Education; with Remarks on the Systems of other Writers* (1792). In *Women in the Eighteenth Century*, ed. Vivien Jones, London: Routledge, 1990,
Saville, George (Marquis of Halifax), *The Ladies New Years Gift, or Advice to a Daughter*, Dublin: 1699.
[Lady, By a], *The Female Guardian*, London: 1784.

[Lady, By a], *The Female Monitor*, London: 1800.

Wollstonecraft, Mary, *Thoughts on the Education of Daughters*, London: 1787.

The Young Lady's Parental Monitor, London: 1790.

Publications on the education of women

Astell, Mary, *A Serious Proposal to the Ladies for the Advancement of their True and Greatest Interest* London:1697,

Davies, Emily, *The Higher Education of Women* (1866), London: Hambledon, 1988.

—*Thoughts on Some Questions (Mainly Educational) Relating to Women*, Cambridge: 1910.

Drake, Judith, *An Essay in Defence of the Female Sex* , London:1696,

Makin, Bathsua, *An Essay to Revive the Ancient Education of Gentlewomen (1673)*. In *The Female Spectator: English Woman Writers Before 1800*, eds. Mary Mahl and Helen Koon, Indiana: Indiana University Press, 1977.

More, Hannah, *Strictures on the Modern System of Education, with a view to the Principals and Conduct Prevalent among Women of Rank and Fortune* (1799). In *The Works of Hannah More*, vol, 3, London: 1833.

Schurman, Anna Maria van, *Disertatio de Ingenii Muliebris ad Doctrinam et Meliores Litteras Aptitudine*, 1641.

Wollstonecraft, Mary, *A Vindication of the Rights of Woman (1792)*, London: Penguin, 1992.

Woolley, Hannah, *The Gentlewoman's Companion; or, a Guide to the Female Sex*, London: 1675.

Reports and memorials

Flysheet on the Diploma of Doctor of Medicine, Emily Davies, private circulation, July 1862,

Report of an Examination of Girls, held in Connexion with the Local Examinations of the University of Cambridge in 1863, London: Emily Faithfull, 1863.

Reports Issued by the Schools Inquiry Commission on the Education of Girls (1869), ed. Doroethea Beale, London: 1869.

Articles from nineteenth century periodicals

'Are Men Naturally Cleverer than Women?' *English Woman's Journal* 2, no. 11 (January 1859).

Burroughs, Montagu, 'Female Education'. *Quarterly Review* 126, (April 1869).

'Colleges for Girls'. *English Woman's Journal* 2, no.12 (February, 1859).

Craig, Isa, 'Insanity, its Cause and Cure'. *English Woman's Journal* (September 1859). In *Barbara Leigh Smith and the Langham Place Group*, ed. Candida Ann Lacey, London: Routledge and Kegan Paul, 1987.

Davies, Emily, 'Some account of a proposed new College for Women', *Contemporary Review* 9 (December 1868).

— 'Higher Education in Connexion with the Universities', *Journal of the Women's Education Union* 2, no.14 (February 1874).

Davies, James Llewelyn, 'Female Education', *Quarterly Review* 119, no. 238 (April 1866).

— 'A New College for Women', *Macmillan's Magazine*, 18 (June 1868).

Fawcett, Millicent Garrett, 'The Education of Women of the Middle and Upper Classes', *Macmillan's Magazine* 17 (April 1868).

'Female Education in the Middle Classes', *English Woman's Journal* 1, no. 4 (June 1858).

Lister, T.H., 'The Rights and Conditions of Women', *Edinburgh Review* 73 (1841)

Markby, Thomas, 'The Education of Women', *Contemporary Review* 1 (March 1866).

Martineau, Harriet, 'Female Industry', *Edinburgh Review* 109, no. 222 (April 1859).

Parkes, Bessie Rayner, 'What Can Educated Women Do?' *English Woman's Journal* (November 1859). In *Barbara Leigh Smith and the Langham Place Group*, ed. Candida Ann Lacey.

— 'The Market for Educated Female Labour', *English Woman's Journal* (November 1859). In *Barbara Leigh Smith and the Langham Place Group*, ed. Candida Ann Lacey.

Shirreff, Emily, 'College Education for Women', *Contemporary Review* 15 (August 1870).

'The University of Cambridge and the Education of Women', *English Woman's Journal* 12, no. 70 (December 1863).

'Thirty Years Progress in Women's Education', *Journal of the Women's Education Union* 6, no. 80 (August 1879).

'Women Physicians', *Macmillan's Magazine* 18 (September 1868).

Medical books and articles

Allbutt, Thomas Clifford and W.S, Playfair, *A System of Gynaecology*, London: 1896.

Anderson, Elizabeth Garrett, M.D., 'Sex in Mind and Education: A Reply', *Fortnightly Review* 15 (May 1874).

Barnes, Robert, M.D., 'Lumleian Lectures on the Convulsive Diseases of Women', *The Lancet* (12 April 1873). In *Women from Birth to Death: The Female Life Cycle in Britain, 1830-1914*, eds. Pat Jalland and John Hooper, New Jersey: Humanities Press International, Inc., 1986.

Bucknill, John Charles, M.D., and Daniel Hack Tuke, M.D., *A Manual of Psychological Medicine*, London: 1874.

Clouston, Thomas Smith, M.D., *Female Education from a Medical Point of View*, Edinburgh: 1882.

Galabin, Alfred Lewis, M.D., *Diseases of Women*, London: 1893.

Johnson, Walter, *The Morbid Emotions of Women* (1850). In *Women from Birth to Death: The Female Life Cycle in Britain, 1830-1914*, eds. Pat Jalland and John Hooper.

Laycock, Thomas, M.D., *A Treatise on the Nervous Diseases of Women* (1840). In *Women from Birth to Death: The Female Life Cycle in Britain, 1830-1914*, eds. Pat Jalland and John Hooper.

Maudsley, Henry, M.D., 'Sex in Mind and in Education', *Fortnightly Review*, 15 (April, 1874),

Ryan, Michael, M.D., *A Manual of Midwifery* (1841). In *Women From Birth to Death: The Female Life Cycle in Britain, 1830-1914*, eds. Pat Jalland and John Hooper.

Thorburn, J, M.D., *A Practical Treatise on the Diseases of Women*, London: 1885.

Tilt, E.J, *Elements of Health and Principles of Female Hygiene* (1852). In *Women From Birth to Death: The Female Life Cycle in Britain, 1830-1914*, eds. Pat Jalland and John Hooper.

— *A Handbook of Uterine Theraputics, and of Diseases of Women*, London: 1878.

Webster, J.C, *Puberty and the Change of Life: A Book for Women* (1892). In *Women From Birth to Death: The Female Life Cycle in Britain, 1830-1914,* eds. Pat Jalland and John Hooper.

CONTEMPORARY NEWPAPERS, JOURNALS, MISCELLANIES AND ALMANACS

Analytical Review (November, 1790).
Lady's Monthly Museum (July 1798–June 1799).
Athenian Mercury 18 (23 May 1691); 6 (13 June 1691).
English Woman's Journal (March 1858–August 1864)
Female Preceptor 1, 2 (1813, 1814).
Female Spectator 4 vols. (1775).
Gentleman's Magazine 38 (13 March 1798).
Ladies' Companion, vols. 1, 2 (1849, 1850).
Ladies' Complete Pocket-Book (1760).
Ladies' Complete Pocket Book (1830)
Ladies' Diary (1707-08; 1712-17; 1719-1840).
Lady's Library (1714).
Ladies' Monthly Museum 15 (1805).
Ladies' Penny Gazette (27 October 1832).
Ladies' Pocket Magazine (1824-35).
Quarterly Review 82 (1848); 86 (1850); 146 (1878).
The Times, 15 April 1880; 17 February 1881.

CONTEMPORARY ENGLISH LITERATURE

Epistolary works

Cartwright, Mrs, *Letters on Female Education,* London: 1777,
Chapone, Hester, *Letters on the Improvement of the Mind* (1775). In *The Works of Mrs Chapone,* vol. 3, London: 1807.
Graham, Catherine Macaulay, *Letters on Education,* London: 1790,
Macaulay, Catherine, *Letters on Education, with Observations on Religious and Metaphysical Subjects,* London: 1790,
Robinson, Mary, *A Letter to the Women of England, on the injustice of Mental Subordination* (1799). In *Women in the Eighteenth Century,* ed. Vivien Jones,

Novels

Austen, Jane, *Northanger Abbey,* London: Everyman's Library, 1992.
—*Sense and Sensibility* (1811), London: Penguin Books, 1986.
—*Mansfield Park* (1814), Middlesex: Penguin Books, 1984.
—*Emma* (1816), Oxford: Oxford University Press, 1981.
—*Pride and Prejudice* (1823), Middlesex: Penguin Books, 1986.
Eliot, George, *The Mill on the Floss* (1860), London: Hamlyn, 1987.
—*Middlemarch* (1872), London: W. Blackwood and Sons, 1920.

—*Daniel Deronda* (1876), London: Zodiac Press, 1971.

Fielding, Sarah, *The Governess or Little Female Academy* (1749), London: Pandora Press, 1987.

Scott, Sarah, *Millenium Hall* (1762), London: Virago, 1985.

OTHER CONTEMPORARY PUBLICATIONS

Chapone, Hester, *The Works of Hester Chapone,* London: 1807.

Clough, Emma Rauschenbusch, *A Study of Mary Wollstonecraft and The Rights of Woman,* London: 1898.

Linton, Eliza Lynn, *Ourselves, A Series of Essays on Women,* London and New York: 1869.

More, Hannah, *Works,* vols. I–VI, London: 1883.

Parkes, Bessie Rayner, *Essays on Women's Work,* London: 1865.

Pizan, Christine de, *Le Livre de la Cité des Dames* (1405), trans, Earl Jeffrey Richards, *The Book of the City of Ladies,* New York: Persa Books, 1982.

Rousseau, Jean Jaques, *Émile* (1762), Cambridge: Dent & Sons, 1966.

Sandford, Mrs, J, *Woman, in her Social and Domestic Character,* London: 1833.

Tennyson, Sir Alfred, Lord, 'The Princess'. In Christopher Ricks, ed. *The Poems of Tennyson,* vol. 2, Essex: Longman, 1987.

Wakefield, Priscilla, *Reflections on the Present Condition of the Female Sex* (1798). In *Women in the Eighteenth Century,* ed. Vivien Jones,

Woolley, Hannah, *The Gentlewoman's Companion,* London: 1675,

SECONDARY SOURCES

College histories, biographies and published papers

Collingwood, Jeremy and Margaret, *Hannah More,* Oxford: Lion Publishing, 1990,

Hallam, 2nd Baron Tennyson, *Alfred, Lord Tennyson, a Memoir,* vol. 1, London: 1897.

Johnson, R, Brimley, ed. *The Letters of Hannah More,* London: 1825.

Kaye, Elaine, *A History of Queen's College, London, 1848-1972,* London: Chatto and Windus, 1972.

O'Connor Anne V, and Susan M, Parkes, *Gladly Learn and Gladly Teach: A History of Alexandra College and School, Dublin,* Dublin: Blackwater Press, 1983.

Perry, Ruth, *The Celebrated Mary Astell,* Chicago: University of Chicago Press, 1986.

Raikes, Elizabeth, *Dorothea Beale of Cheltenham,* London: 1898.

Roberts, William, ed. *Memoirs of the Life and Correspondence of Hannah More,* London: 1834.

Smith, Florence, *Mary Astell,* New York: AMS Press, 1966.

Stephen, Barbara, *Emily Davies and Girton College,* London: Constable, 1927.

—*Girton College, 1869-1932,* Cambridge: Cambridge University Press, 1932.

Tuke, Margaret, *A History of Bedford College for Women, 1849-1937,* London: Oxford University Press, 1939.

Wardle, Ralph M, *Collected Letters of Mary Wollstonecraft,* Ithaca & London: Cornell University Press, 1979.

Waterhouse, Prudence, *A Victorian Monument: The Buildings of Girton College*, Cambridge: Girton College Cambridge, 1990.

Books

Altick, Richard D, *The Common Reader: A Social History of the Mass Reading Public, 1800-1900*, Chicago: University of Chicago Press, 1957.

Beilin, Elaine V, *Redeeming Eve: Women Writers of the English Renaissance*, New Jersey: Princeton University Press, 1990.

Black, Francis Gees, *The Epistolary Novel in the Late Eighteenth Century: A Descriptive and Bibliographical Study*, Eugene: University of Oregon, 1940.

Borer, A.C, *Willingly to School*, London: Cuttersworth Press, 1975.

Bridenthal, Renate, and Claudia Koonz, *Becoming Visible: Women in European History*, Boston: Houghton Mifflin Co., 1977.

Brink, J.R, *Female Scholars: A Tradition of Learned Women before 1800*, Montréal: Eden Press, 1980.

Bristow, Edward J, *Vice and Vigilance: Purity Movements in Britain since 1700*, Dublin: Gill and Macmillan, 1977.

Brown, Alice, *The Eighteenth Century Feminist Mind*, Michigan: Wayne State University Press, 1987.

Bryant, Margaret, *The Unexpected Revolution: A Study in the History of Education of Women and Girls in the Nineteenth Century*, London: University of London Institute of Education, 1979.

Burstyn, Joan N, *Victorian Education and the Ideal of Womanhood*, London: Croom Helm, 1980.

Cressy, David, *Literature and Social Order: Reading and Writing in Tudor and Stuart England*, Cambridge: Cambridge University Press, 1980,

Day, Robert Adams, *Told in Letters: Epistolary Fiction before Richardson*, Ann Arbor: University of Michigan Press, 1966.

Delamont, Sara and Lorna Duffin, *The Nineteenth Century Woman: Her Cultural and Physical World*, London: Croom Helm, 1978.

Devlin, David, *Jane Austen and Education*, London: Macmillan, 1975,

Dyhouse, Carol, *Girls Growing up in Late Victorian and Edwardian England*, London: Routledge and Kegan Paul, 1981.

Gardiner, Dorothy, *English Girlhood at School*, London: Oxford University Press, 1929.

Henderson, Katherine and Barbara McManus, *Half Humankind: Contexts and Texts of the Controversy about Women in England, 1540-1640*, Urbana and Chicago: University of Illinois Press, 1985.

Hollis Patricia, *Women in Public 1850-1950: Documents of the Victorian Women's Movement*, London: Allen and Unwin, 1979.

Hunt, Felicity, ed. *Lessons for Life: The Schooling of Girls and Women, 1850-1950*, Oxford: Basil Blackwell, 1987.

Kamm, Josephine, *Hope Deferred*. London: Methuen, 1965.

Kelly, Joan, *Women, History and Theory*, Chicago: Chicago University Press, 1984.

Kersey, Shirley Nelson, *Classics in the Education of Girls and Women*, London: Scarecrow Press, 1981.

Killham, John, *Tennyson and 'The Princess': Reflections of an Age*, University of London: Athlone Press, 1958.

Labalme, Patricia, *Beyond their Sex: Learned Women of the European Past,* New York: New York University Press, 1980.

Lacey, Candida Ann, *Barbara Leigh Smith and the Langham Place Group,* London: Routledge and Kegan Paul, 1987.

Lagarde, André et Michard Laurent, *XVII Siècle: les grands auteurs français du programme,* Paris: Bordas, 1962.

Levine, Phillipa, *Feminist Lives in Victorian England,* Oxford: Basil Blackwell, 1990.

Maclean, Ian, *The Renaissance Notion of Women,* Cambridge: Cambridge University Press, 1980.

Mahl, Mary and Helen Koon, *The Female Spectator: English Woman Writers before 1800,* Bloomington and London: Indiana University Press, 1977.

Mc Williams Tullberg, Rita, *Women at Cambridge: A Men's University – Though of a Mixed Type,* London: Victor Gollancz, 1975.

Myres, Sylvia Harcstark, *The Bluestocking Circle,* Oxford: Clarendon, 1990.

Percival, Alicia C, *The English Miss Today and Yesterday,* London: George Harrap, 1939.

Phillips, Patricia, *The Scientific Lady: A Social History of Women's Scientific Interests, 1520-1918,* London: Weidenfeld & Nicolson, 1990.

Porter, Roy, *English Society in the Eighteenth Century,* London: Allen Lane, 1982.

Power, Eileen, *Medieval Women,* Cambridge: Cambridge University Press, 1975,

Prior, Mary, *Women in English Society, 1500-1800,* London: Methuen, 1985.

Probyn, Clive T, *English Fiction of the Eighteenth Century,* London: Longman, 1987.

Purvis, June, *A History of Women's Education in England,* Milton Keynes: Open University Press, 1991

Richards, S.A, *Feminist Writers of the Seventeenth Century,* London: David Nutt, 1914.

Rose, Mary Beth, *Women in the Middle Ages and the Renaissance,* New York: Syracuse University Press, 1986.

Simons, Judy, *Fanny Burney,* London: Macmillan, 1987.

Todd, Janet, ed. *A Wollstonecraft Anthology,* Cambridge: Polity Press, 1989,

Travitsky, Betty, *The Paradise of Women: Writings by English Women of the Renaissance,* Conneticut: Greenwood Press, 1981

Turner, Cheryl, *Living by the Pen: Women Writers in the Eighteenth Century,* London and New York: Routledge, 1992.

Uphaus, Robert W, and Gretchen M, Foster, eds., *The Other Eighteenth Century: English Women of Letters, 1660-1800,* East Lansing: Colleagues Press, 1991.

Articles

Burstyn, Joan N, 'Religious arguments against higher education for women in England, 1840-1890', *Women's Studies* 1, no. 1 (1972).

— 'Education and Sex: The Medical case against higher education for women in England, 1870-1900', *Proceedings of the American Philosophical Society* 117 (1973).

Crawford, Patricia, 'Women's Published Writings, 1600-1700'. In *Women in English Society, 1500-1800,* ed. Mary Prior, London: Methuen, 1985.

Digby, Anne, 'Women's Biological Strait-jacket'. In *Sexuality and Subordination,* eds.

Susan Mendes and Jane Rendall, London: Routledge,1989.

Dyhouse, Carol, 'Social Darwinistic ideas and the development of women's education in England, 1800-1920', *History of Education* 5, no.1 (1976).

Ellegard, Alvar, 'The Readership of the Periodical Press in Mid-Victorian Britain', *Göteborgs Universeits Årsskrift*, 33, 1957.

WORKS OF REFERENCE

Doughan, David and Denise Sanchez, *Feminist Periodicals, 1855-1984*, Brighton: Harvester, 1987.

Ferguson, Moira, ed. *First Feminists: British Women Writers, 1578-1799*, Bloomington: Indiana U.P., 1985.

Horrowitz, Janet and Myra Stark, *The Englishwoman's Review: An Index*, New York and Conn.: Garland Publishing, 1980.

Palmegiano, E.M, *A Women and British Periodicals, 1832-1867: A Bibliography*, London: Routledge, 1989.

The British Library Short-title Catalogue on CD ROM, London: British Library, 1992.

The Wellesley Index to Victorian Periodicals, 1824-1900, London: Routledge and Kegan Paul, 1824-1900,

The Waterloo Directory of Victorian Perodicals, 1824-1900, Ontario: University of Waterloo, 1976.

Todd, Janet, ed. *A Dictionary of British and American Writers, 1660-1800*, London: Methuen, 1980.

—ed. *Dictionary of British Women Writers*, London: Routledge 1991.

Wing, Donald, *Short Title Catalogue of Books Published in England, Scotland, Ireland and Wales, 1641-1700*, vols. I & II, New York: Columbia University Press, 1948.

Index